D1537869

"Opinionated. fun. and a little geeky all at the same time. Keith Schroeder's *Mad Delicious* is both a delightful read and a terrific. seriously useful compendium of cooking techniques (and accompanying explanations) and recipes. Who knew that the chef behind one of my favorite craft ice creams. High Road. had this kind of book in him?"

—ED LEVINE, founder, Seriouseats.com

Cooking Light

MAD DELICIOUS

"Every recipe in this book looks like something I'd make every day and hide from my wife so I could eat it all myself."

—J. KENJI LÓPEZ-ALT, author of The Food Lab, a column unraveling the science of home cooking

Cooking Light

MAD DELICIOUS

THE SCIENCE OF MAKING HEALTHY FOOD TASTE AMAZING!

KEITH SCHROEDER

Oxmoor House®

TABLE OF CONTENTS

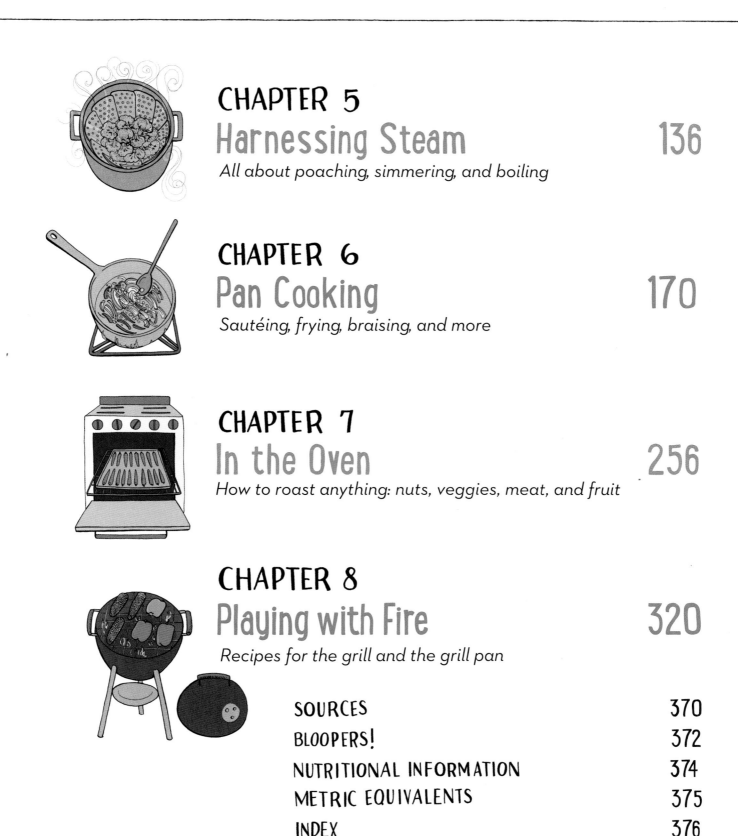

INTRODUCTION

I was a budding home cook by the age of 6. When I was growing up, eating was the only thing I did regularly that I truly, deeply enjoyed. *I guess I pretended to be interested in cooking at the onset so I could get the hottest, freshest sliver of steak off the grill or the first mushroom from the gravy.*

A LOVE AFFAIR WITH COOKING

When Thanksgiving time came and my mother needed help in the kitchen, I would pull up a step stool and make the crudité platter (we didn't call it that) with buttermilk dressing (with the packet). *I marveled at how a packet of spices and sugars and starches would morph from thin, drippy, and undesirable to thick, rich, and (admit it) addictively appetizing after an hour or so in the fridge. So began my love affair with the transformation of ingredients.*

Over time, I began to formulate opinions about what was delicious and what was not, and how to prepare food in ways that were both aesthetically pleasing and crowd-winningly tasty, but the wonder that came from tinkering with ingredients, and the satisfaction I got from being helpful, never left me. Eventually, it pushed me into professional kitchens. You'd think that was where the real cooking happened, in restaurant kitchens. What's hard for a chef to admit, though, is that cooking at home can be more satisfying than cooking in a restaurant. After all, cooking is an intimate, generous, and personal act, expressive of culture, place, community, and tradition.

Thanks to a lifetime of cooking in restaurants and hotels as well as teaching both home cooks and culinary professionals, I've had the luxury of living, working, traveling, food shopping, and eating in many places around the world. That, I suppose, qualifies me to teach you about food science, culinary technique, and the alchemy that we call cooking. What I want to share most, however, is that it's important to pay attention to what's in front of you, whether it's a tomato, a beautifully forged knife, or your third cousin coming over for dinner. And while there are elements of chemistry, biology, and physics to be explored and understood, and techniques involved, being a great cook is about more than being the best technician. *Maintaining an emotional connection with food, while developing a comfort level with the whys of cooking, will help you become more intuitive in the kitchen. My aim is to teach you to work with your head, your heart, and your hands.* I want to encourage exploration, and to equip you with the methods and mindset necessary to be a nimble and confident home cook.

HAUTE CUISINE

THREE STARS

BISTRO

MY TEACHING METHOD

I wanted to write this book because I'm a teacher at heart. I offered the team at *Cooking Light* some recipes with a format that mirrored the way I approach cooking, one that explained the purpose for using each and every ingredient in each and every recipe—in tabular format. Ingredient. Amount. Why.

It's a format I've long used when teaching people how to cook. Sometimes the why was fundamental to the recipe's success. Often-times, I offered up some science-meets-life experience reasons for tinkering with tradition. Good cooking's like that—attentive and purposeful—without being sterile or rote. I was told the format and the voice were "unique." **Pause. Look at serious editor. Whew. It was "good" unique.**

Being a first-time cookbook author and gazillion-hour veteran cook, I had to translate the techniques and the methods I use intuitively and automatically in the kitchen—my culinary autopilot—into words. What follows in this book are many, many words. Rather than being dense and academic as a book about kitchen science could be, these recipes are not only really well developed (they work—I promise), they're fun to read. You'll find yourself *being there,* whether *there* is your ready-to-rock kitchen or the village or city or home or professional kitchen from where the recipe is inspired. **The recipes "talk a lot," but with the very honest intent of making you a commanding cook. Bear with me. The results are worth it.**

THE MEANING OF MAD DELICIOUS

With the good intention of eating healthier, many home cooks cut out the sugar, salt, and fat from their favorite recipes. But in doing so, they often sacrifice flavor and texture. **You shouldn't settle for subpar meals in the name of better health. Actually, you don't have to. Good-for-you food can taste amazing.** That's where this book comes in.

Mad Delicious shares the science behind light cooking, from selecting the right ingredients and choosing the proper cooking technique to composing flavors so every bite is delicious. Not just delicious— *impressively* delicious, *stunningly* delicious, *insanely* delicious, *Mad Delicious.*

A FEW NOTES ON THE RECIPES

» The recipes may look complicated at first glance, but they're not. Promise.

» Each recipe addresses nuance: sound, feel, timing, balance. Nothing is missed.

» They talk about the "space between," so you don't have to read between the lines for a dish to turn out as it should.

» These recipes do not assume the reader (that's you) is an experienced cook.

WHAT YOU'LL LEARN

The intent of *Mad Delicious* is to make you a more purposeful cook, certainly to teach the "how," but most importantly to spotlight the critical "whys" of methods, ingredients, ingredient combinations, traditions, phenomena, et al. *I want you to understand the recipe you're cooking, not just survive the process.*

As you work your way through the lessons and recipes in the book, begin thinking of the many variables in cooking as tools. Don't make the cooking method—the application of heat—the focal point of your cooking from here forward. The cooking method is really just the final act of a recipe's production. Thus, become a "producer" of meals, giving each facet of your production, from selecting and prepping ingredients to serving the meal at your table, equal attention.

Throughout this book, I hold your hand, tell you jokes, make fun of you, and anticipate many of the slip-ups common among cooks (even experienced ones). You're getting the "light" edition of what professional cooks endure when they're ruining their first chicken stock. And the book is science-y only insofar as most things in life have an applied science element. Geography. Chemistry. Biology. Psychology. Anthropology. Science!

SPLATTERS ARE OKAY!

PAY ATTENTION AND BREAK THINGS

Great cooks are mindful. That is to say, they see cooking as a series of situations to observe and monitor (like an air traffic controller). Following a recipe instruction to the letter does not mean you'll have absolute control over the outcome. You're only an influencer. We're working with nature here. Flex, breathe, bend, engage. *Get your soul in there. And give yourself a break if you mess something up. Many great culinary breakthroughs have mistakes as their origin.* Now, let's cook!

Cheers,
Keith Schroeder

MENTAL MISE EN PLACE

Getting you and your kitchen ready to cook

Professional cooks learn the concept of *mise en place* before they're allowed to crack open their knife kits. As culinary freshmen, they stand at attention while a seasoned chef shares the simple, foundational law of the kitchen. Proper mise en place is a smart rule to follow in the home kitchen, too. If honored, it will lead to ballet-like culinary performances. At its heart it's about ritualized organization. It's as much a mindset as it is a series of activities. If ritual is ignored in a kitchen, chaos ensues. If, as an aspiring top-shelf home cook, you ignore the rituals, dinner won't be done on time, cleanup will take forever, and you'll likely not enjoy cooking.

Yes, cooking involves applying heat to foods to make them edible, but it's an act of service to others, too. It is a dance. Enjoy the process. Shop reverently. Unpack deliberately. Activate soundtrack. Strategically position your cookbook. Read the whole recipe. Gather tools. Prep your ingredients. Clean as you go. Follow directions carefully. Enjoy your meal.

Welcome to the Ritual

A good home cook is part ballet dancer, part chemist, part juggler, part anthropologist, part laborer, and part project manager. The best inherently understands the following five principles and embraces them in their kitchens and their souls.

>> Planning is the most important step. The best intentions for cooking a meal can be derailed by gradually realizing you don't have 25 percent of the ingredients suggested in a recipe. And while you'll know how to improvise quite competently after reading this book, some dishes require specific ingredients to be true to themselves. So, before you start, take the time to inventory your pantry, make a quick and easy shopping list, and be sure you have the right equipment for the job. *When you have everything you need to produce a dish, cooking can be downright euphoric.*

>> **Cook to suit your mood.** Tackle recipes with a degree of difficulty that matches your emotional tolerance level for the day—and your ability to focus at the stove. Have plans A and B in mind, with A being the "I'm ready to cook anything" mood, and B being the "I've got to get dinner on the table" mood. Make cooking easy for yourself. In professional kitchens, we speak of cross-utilization of ingredients. That means you keep a number of ingredients or preparations on hand that can be used in an array of recipes. It streamlines meal prep. This book encourages that; you'll find that many of the recipes in *Mad Delicious* respect our hurried lifestyle while offering respite from the grind.

>> **Flow matters.** For great, stress-free meals to come together, an organized work space is key. Utensils and ingredients should have a designated space in the kitchen. Frequently used items should be within arm's reach. It's okay to store whisks and spoons and salt on your countertop. Writers keep pens on their desks, artists keep paintbrushes at the ready, so it makes sense for cooks to keep the tools of their craft out within easy reach. Cooking requires you to move easily from ingredient to utensil to pan to stove to oven to sink to trash can. Remove unnecessary clutter, keep yourself organized, and build in flow.

>> **Multitasking is a myth.** Repeat after me: "It is very tricky to do more than one thing at a time." Our brains are not multiprocessors. We do things more competently when we handle one specific task at a time. You'll find that the recipes in this book are crafted differently than in most cookbooks. First, I explain the "why" of every ingredient decision, so that you don't have to wonder. Second, the tasks are segmented into single strokes, so that you don't lose your place while cooking and so that you're reminded to grab this, that, or the other well in advance of needing it.

Make a game plan for meal prep connected to the clock. It'll help. You will feel like a pro in short order. You're not doing "a thousand things at once." You're cooking, one step at a time. Commandingly.

>> **Cooking is not a chore.** You bought this book, or someone bought it for you, because *you like to cook.* (If you don't like to cook, please re-gift this. Sign my name on the title page so no one thinks it's used. I'll vouch for you.) Cooking well requires both engagement and enjoyment. *This is not your job. It's your chosen hobby, craft, or diversion.* Grab your favorite apron, choose a playlist based on your mood *du moment,* pour yourself a beverage, and get your mind on the *mise en place.*

LITERALLY "EVERYTHING IN ITS PLACE," MISE EN PLACE REFERS MORE TO AN ABSOLUTE LEVEL OF READINESS THAT ALLOWS A COOK TO STAY IN RELATIVE PHYSICAL & MENTAL "FLOW" WHEN COOKING.

Learn the Language of Food

Don't be tempted to jump right into the ingredients and dishes. Part of being a great cook is respect for the process: being more aware, more observant of history, ingredient, point of origin, or technique. Cooking is as much about understanding a dish as it is the application of heat to transform foodstuffs.

If you're encountering an ingredient for the first time, read about it. Taste it on its own. See who pairs it with what, where, and why. Then, and only then, approach the how. While you might not be able to embark on a world tour to taste the best the planet has to offer, you can find plenty of information online, in books, at specialty food markets, and by chatting with knowledgeable friends, neighbors, and co-workers. To become a really, truly competent cook, you have to learn to speak the language of food. It'll help you go wherever your chosen dish is intending to take you. Here are some suggestions for developing more complete culinary frames of reference.

>> **Bookmark newspaper food and dining sections, food magazines, blogs, and websites from around the world.** Read them often or occasionally. Even if they're in a foreign language, you'll encounter images that can prove valuable as you embark on a lifetime of serious home cooking. Plus, there are myriad instant-translation tools online to help you read recipes and techniques.

SEEMS CREDIBLE

>> **Research.** Type the name of the dish or ingredient you'll be cooking into a search engine. Toggle through image mode, standard mode, and news mode. Take it to the next level by looking for references in online book archives, or, for real geeks, in scholarly databases.

>> **Seek out online video content** pertaining to a dish, a technique, or an ingredient. Yes, you may be subject to information overload, but just start absorbing information. You'll soon figure out which sites have the best content. Seeing people make things is wonderfully helpful (even more helpful than this book).

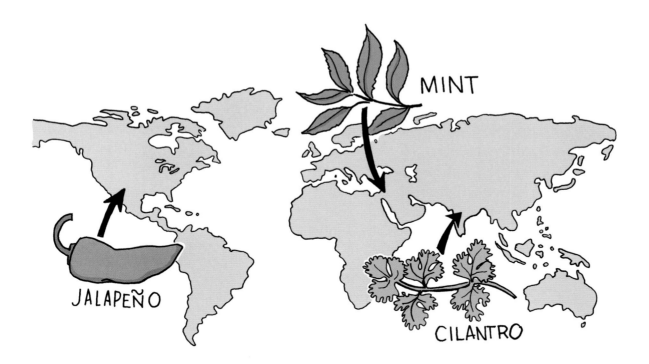

>> Be a food tourist. Some metro areas have neighborhoods or markets that are just as authentic as hopping on a plane and going "there." Whether it's a brief trip to a neighborhood Thai market or a flight to Bangkok, there's little substitute for real-world touch, smell, hear, see, taste.

>> Ask questions. Engage with the author of a book (I'll respond) or article. See what the fishmonger thinks is best today. Bring a copy of the recipe you're preparing. Strike up conversations with fellow shoppers. Food people tend to be magnetic and are all about the exchange of ideas and information.

>> Invite people who know. Encourage them to give you feedback. Cook carnitas for your sister-in-law from Michoacán, Mexico. Make grits for your cousin from Georgia. Put on a pot of feijoada (like the one on page 238) for your Brazilian neighbors. Not only will they glow from your hospitality, you will have honored our common humanity.

>> Don't dislike anything. If being a commanding cook is a goal, you'll have to be completely open-minded. *You can't make the gross face ever again. Replace it with the wow!-interesting face.* More cooks will share tricks with you.

Setting Up Your Kitchen

Finding flow as a cook is largely determined by thinking through possible ways to move around your physical space. Regardless of the size of your kitchen, keeping the majority of your tools and ingredients within a few steps helps to move a recipe along fluidly. Now, I've listed 13 distinct "stations," and if you have a kitchen that's on the smaller side, you'll not achieve this idealized organizational nirvana—and that's okay. However, you will likely employ all the *actions* that follow. What's important is that you're not all over the place. Each of these "areas" will exist at some point in the making of a dish.

>> **The cutting area.** Keep it front and center, and reasonably close to the range and oven. Make sure there's plenty of space around the cutting board, as this is often the most cluttered area. It shouldn't be.

>> **The tool area.** You can use a cylindrical utensil holder, as many cooks do, but I prefer a sheet pan lined with parchment or paper towels. Line up only the tools you'll need for preparing the recipe.

>> **The appliance area.** If you'll be using a food processor, spice grinder, blender, or other electric tool, plug it in and get it ready before beginning.

>> **The ingredient area.** Line your ingredients up at or near your cutting board, being mindful of whether you're left- or right-handed. It matters.

>> **The finished mise en place area.** See cutting area above. That's where all the cut foods typically land. Look at the ingredient quantities called for in the recipe. Make sure you clear counter space for that much.

>> **The prep area.** It's not all cutting. You'll be stirring, mixing, shaking, and tossing. You'll need a place to do that. Ideally, it's as large as your cutting area.

>> **The shelf in the fridge.** Make space to keep prepped items cold while you're doing other things.

>> **The scrap area.** It's more convenient to discard food scraps into a nearby container rather than head for the trash bin every time you need to trash something. Plus, there are cross-contamination concerns related to interacting with the garbage while you cook.

>> **The pot and pan area.** Stacked, laid out, whatever. Take pots out in advance. Bending over a thousand times to unearth one messes with your flow.

>> **The cooking area.** The place where the magic happens—where you monitor the effects of heat on the ingredients you carefully prepped. You should be able to see everything and move easily in this area.

THE SCRAP AREA

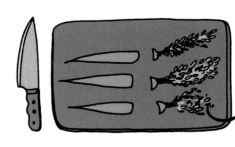

SCRAPS

>> **The plating area.** This is another oft-forgotten area that typically lands in the cutting area. Clean an area of your counter in advance, or clear everything away while the meal is cooking. Then, your entire counter can be the plating area.

>> **The sani-station.** While you work, keep a container of hot soapy water with a clean cloth consistently replenished, and have another with a gallon of room temperature water with a tablespoon of non-scented, regular ol' bleach and a clean towel. *The pros work like this. You should, too.* Use the soapy water to clean splatters, spills, bits, and germs off your work area. Follow with the bleach solution and a clean towel, which you can also use to freshen your work space between tasks.

>> **The dishwashing area.** If things start to get cluttered or messy, perform a clean sweep. Clean your surfaces and utensils, and get back on track. It's great if you empty the dishwasher before you start prepping.

The Larder

Pretend your pantry is a market. Think in "departments." If it can be shopped by a guest kitchen helper, then you're moving in the right direction. Storing food ingredients from waist level up to eye level is ideal. Here's a suggested plan-o-gram (retail industry term) for keeping your home marketplace looking sharp and feeling functional.

>> Dry bulk items such as grains, flours, starches, nuts, rice, beans, and seeds.

>> Boxed shelf-stable items.

>> Canned foods.

>> Unopened jarred things.

>> Shelf-stable bottled things: oils, vinegars, and the like.

>> Dry spices and seasonings.

>> Refrigerated meats, honoring the food-storage hierarchy. See page 22 for more information.

>> Produce, separating by durability. Allow greens and herbs plenty of airspace. See page 21 for more about properly storing fresh produce.

>> Prepped items. In clear containers, covered, labeled, and dated.

>> Condiments, organized by theme and container size. Keep sandwich-friendly relishes, mustards, and mayonnaise near one another for convenience.

>> Dairy, by usage frequency, application, and container size. *We use quite a bit of yogurt in this book. You might want to buy quarts.*

FIFO, OR FIRST IN FIRST OUT, IS A METHOD OF MOVING THROUGH INVENTORY THAT IS MINDFUL OF HOW LONG FOOD ITEMS HAVE BEEN IN STORAGE. IT'S PARTICULARLY IMPORTANT WHERE OPEN CONTAINERS & PERISHABLE FOODS ARE CONCERNED.

Equipping Your Kitchen

It's possible to spend thousands, even tens of thousands, on equipping a home kitchen, but that's certainly not necessary. However, craftsmanship is important in ensuring that you select kitchen equipment that will last decades, if not a lifetime or beyond. When it comes to small appliances, invest. Research. Read online reviews. And if it feels like a box of feathers, leave it on the shelf. These are tools. You want 'em durable. Spend maximum possible dollars (based on your budget, of course) on knives, cookware, and cutting boards. You can go leaner on almost every other kitchen gadget.

Basic (The Kit)

A solid, reliable, utilitarian collection of pots, pans, knives, and such. Very good.

>> Knives: paring, chef (8 to 10 inches), serrated, knife block or wall magnet for safe storage
>> Cutting board (ideally one large butcher block–style board and a couple small boards)
>> Hand tools: stainless steel tongs, wire whisk, wooden spoons, a medium-sized silicone spatula, a ladle or two, box grater, stainless steel solid and slotted spoons, swivel-blade vegetable peeler
>> Measuring cups and spoons
>> Can opener
>> Grill (either gas or charcoal)
>> Kitchen scale
>> Mini food processor

>> Steamer basket
>> Stockpot with lid
>> A couple saucepans with lids
>> Large skillet (10 to 12 inches)
>> Large, straight-sided skillet
>> Cast-iron skillet
>> Basic roasting pan
>> A couple baking sheets
>> A couple wire racks
>> Small ramekin or bowl for salt and black pepper
>> Pepper mill
>> A place to store spices
>> A packet of wooden skewers
>> Colander
>> Hand strainer
>> Pocket probe-style thermometer

Intermediate (The Collection)

A nimble, broad assemblage of everything a serious cook might need to pull off a meal. Excellent.

>> "The Kit" knives + cleaver, oyster knife, clam knife, bird's beak knife, pizza wheel, a meat-carving fork
>> "The Kit" hand tools + basic mortar and pestle, meat mallet, harp vegetable peeler, apple corer, various microplanes (from fine to coarse), rasp grater, rotary grater, nut cracker, lobster cracker, needle-nose pliers
>> Kitchen shears
>> Salad spinner
>> Rice mill
>> Mandoline
>> Gravy separator
>> Grill pan
>> Enameled Dutch oven
>> Pro-grade pots and pans
>> Half-sheet pan or two
>> Silpats
>> A nice spice rack
>> "Salt pig"
>> Long, flat stainless skewers
>> Soufflé ramekins
>> Stand mixer

Advanced (The Exhibit)

This category is for the serious cook who wants a very well outfitted kitchen. Extraordinary.

>> "The Kit" and "The Collection" knives + various Japanese knives, one specific for cutting fish, "Chinese cleaver" (Japanese-made), cheese knives, scimitar, cake knife, double-bladed mezzaluna
>> "The Kit" and "The Collection" hand tools + an oversized ladle, kitchen tweezers, whisks in all shapes and sizes, Chinois and China cap, top-quality mortar and pestle
>> Top-of-the-line pots and pans, including a collection of enameled cookware and French black steel skillets
>> Rondeau (a wide, shallow pot)
>> Large baker's peel
>> French mandoline
>> Professional blender
>> A fancy vegetable juicer
>> Professional-grade stand mixer
>> Professional-grade kitchen scale
>> Standing citrus juicer
>> Kettle-style porcelain smoker grill

Ingredients: Stocking Your Shelves

The best kitchens, home or professional, are shrines to ingredient handling. For one thing, it's cost effective to make sure that foods are stored properly. Untimely spoilage is avoided. Thankfully, there's a renewed consciousness regarding the sources of our food. More than ever, people care that their eggs are cage-free, for instance, and that their olive oil actually contains oil from, um, olives. Great food producers tell their stories at point-of-purchase displays, through the butcher, in store circulars, in the blogosphere, and, typically, right on their packaging. Since ingredients are at the heart of cooking, here are some tips to ritualize the care and keeping of your groceries.

Fish

» If possible, buy fish the day you cook it, particularly if you're buying fillets. If you're buying frozen (which is okay, I promise), make sure it's been flash frozen on the boat. Often, the flash frozen stuff, properly and gently thawed under refrigeration, is better than the "fresh" fish sold at the grocery store's fish counter.

» Let's create a new definition for "fresh," by the way. Fresh does not mean "never been frozen." Fresh, with fish, ideally means, "I was just extracted from the water, carefully buried in plenty of crushed ice, and then rapidly transported to your engaged, enthusiastic fishmonger." Don't buy the stuff that the supermarkets are thawing for you since there's no way to know how many times it's been thawed and refrozen. If your supermarket doesn't have a great fish selection, find a good mail-order source. It's worth it.

Meats and Poultry

» Whenever possible, get your hands on something that has been cut the same day. If you go to the market once a week or so, freeze the meats *the day* you bring them home, and thaw them under refrigeration. Not on the counter. And preferably not in the microwave.

» Try making a paste of garlic, salt, and sugar, as done in a number of recipes in the book (such as Grilled Beef Tenderloin, page 40). Rub it on the surface of whole or individual cuts, and store them in the refrigerator in a zip-top plastic bag with a sprig or two of thyme or rosemary. The salt and sugar are natural preservatives, and the garlic is antibacterial, so you'll get longer shelf life than if you left it in the butcher paper or foam tray.

Produce

» While there are super-thick industry manuals on how to care for produce, one thing is universal: Produce needs the right balance of air circulation and moisture. If possible, look at how the produce comes into the store and how it's packaged. The growers and packers know best how to care for their products.

» For leafy greens and herbs, a safe bet is to wash it, dry it, take off any of the rubber bands or twist ties (the stuff always rots where it's bunched too tightly), and put it in containers where it can "breathe." It was a growing, living thing, after all. Lightly cover it, and use it as quickly as possible.

Herbs

» These are worth growing, if possible. If not, get them out of their rubber bands or plastic packaging as quickly as possible. Lay down a clean paper towel, "fluff" your herbs to separate the sprigs (they may have started to "mulch" together in the market), discard any mushy bits, and lay the good sprigs in a pile on the paper towel. Wrap loosely, as to mimic a paper towel roll. Label the wrap with a piece of masking tape and a permanent marker. Your herbs will last. You can put the money you save toward sending your kids to college.

A Primer on Food Safety

Getting sick from food is beyond unpleasant. Thankfully, there are folks who have spent their careers helping farmers, manufacturers, food service professionals, and home cooks handle food safely. What follows is nowhere near comprehensive—you can get a PhD in food microbiology to get the full scoop, if you'd like—but it will help prevent most of the careless mistakes that often result in someone being stricken by a foodborne illness.

READY-
TO-EAT

PRODUCE

EGGS &
DAIRY

SEAFOOD

MEAT &
POULTRY

Personal Hygiene

It's important to note that it's often the cook who makes food unsafe. Three very simple principles, if adopted, will help keep you from spoiling the meal.

First, wash your hands. Frequently. The professional standard for washing your hands is to get them wet under very warm water, then soap and lather them quite well while singing "Happy Birthday" to yourself—twice. *(Go ahead and belt it out loud. People will want to know why you're singing to yourself when it's not your birthday. You will have encouraged both a silly and important habit.)* Rinse quite thoroughly under water that's as hot as you can handle. Then, turn the knob off with a clean paper towel. What's the sense in washing your hands deeply if only to touch the raw chicken-y hot water knob immediately after? And make sure that you have plenty of paper towels or kitchen towels with which to dry your hands. If you're using a kitchen towel, use it only to dry your hands, not to wipe the kitchen surfaces, too.

Second, don't cook when you're sick if you can help it. Lastly, wear clean clothes or a fresh apron when you're cooking. *As much as we all love our pets, it's best not to get all huggy with your schnauzer who is a little slobbery, and then hit the kitchen.*

Food-Storage Hierarchy

A clean and organized refrigerator is also important. It's always disappointing to find wilted or damaged food that wanted to be used fresh. If you find that happens in your fridge often, then shop for less, more frequently. You'll save money.

Allow space around your foods and store them in this order, top to bottom: ready-to-eat (and any home-prepared/cooked) foods on top > then produce (unfortunately bins are often on the bottom) > then dairy products > then eggs > then raw seafood > then whole cuts or portions of meat > then ground meats > then raw poultry. No one likes raw chicken drippings on the arugula.

If you don't have eight levels to your fridge (I don't), then do your best to keep things from touching by using airtight containers. Respect the hierarchy and get sick less.

Cross-Contamination

This one is so simple to avoid but is the most common mistake. Simply stated, cross-contamination is the touching of things that shouldn't touch. Cut veggies and raw meats on separate cutting boards with separate knives, and clean with separate towels and washed hands. Work with all your raw meat, poultry, eggs, and other potentially hazardous ingredients first, if possible; store them in sealed containers in the refrigerator, and clean your surfaces as to start anew before moving onto making the salad or sliced fruit platter.

Time and Temperature

Keep cold food cold and hot food hot. Your refrigerator should store foods well below 40°. Hold hot foods over 140°, covered, and on your lowest range setting or in a warm oven. Don't keep stuff on the counter. If you discover that something's been out of temperature for a couple of hours (meaning two hours, not nine), throw it away.

THOUGH REGULATORS LIKE TO JOCKEY WITH THE SO-CALLED **TEMPERATURE DANGER ZONE** FROM TIME TO TIME, JUST ADHERE TO THE OLD-SCHOOL 40°-140° AND YOU'RE SAFE & SOUND.

Potentially Hazardous Foods

Here's an acronym to remember: FAT TOM. The National Restaurant Association and ServSafe use it in the food industry to teach the pros about food safety. Use it at home, too. Each of the letters stands for a word that refers to a condition that helps food pathogens grow like, well, pathogens. Control these conditions to keep your dining companions safe and happy.

>> **Food:** There's some kind of nutrient, usually protein, that helps pathogens grow.

>> **Acidity:** Pathogens grow in slightly acidic to ever-so-slightly alkaline foods. Chicken juice, raw eggs, standing water, stuff like that. Look at it this way: If it's not packed in vinegar or boiled in baking soda solution, it's probably hazardous.

>> **Time:** We talked about this above.

>> **Temperature:** This too.

>> **Oxygen:** This is the scary one. Some of the creepiest foodborne pathogens and toxins come from seemingly innocuous situations, like the few cloves of garlic and sprig of garden rosemary in that bottle of oil you bought at the country fair. Yep, it can be dangerous. Throw it out. A baked potato that's been sitting in a barely-too-cool, semi-warm situation. Yep. Dangerous. Don't make potato salad with it. The rice you left in the rice-cooker overnight? That too. Trash.

>> **Moisture:** Pathogens generally prefer moist environments.

Where You Buy Your Food

This is easy. Buy refrigerated foods cold and make sure freezers are holding things frozen deep. Make sure dry goods shelves are tidy. Cans are not dented, bulging, or dusty. It's not "adventurous" to buy questionable foods from questionable sources. Places with good reputations earn them and work hard to keep them.

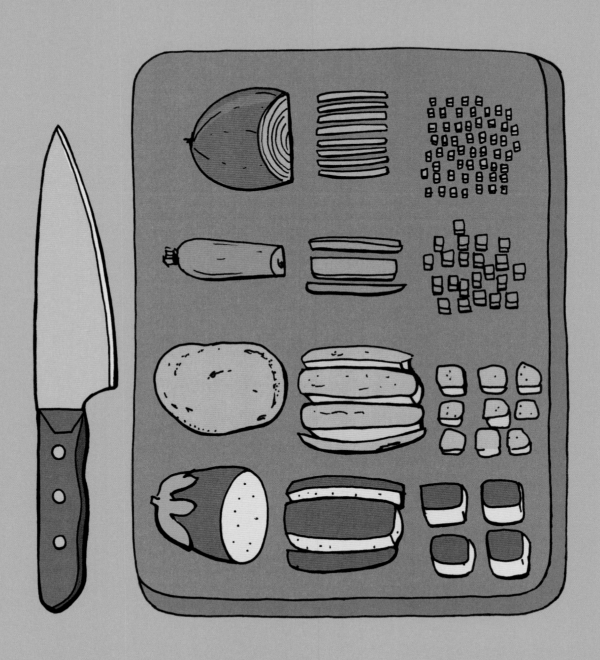

HANDS-ON

Developing manual
dexterity in the kitchen

Being a good cook does not require techno-gizmos, immersion circulators, and things that make a whole bunch of froth. Instead, in this book, we use everyday knives, pots and pans, and fire. This chapter is the first step in an immersive-style culinary course. It's essentially a dissection of a traditional knife skills class.

Knives. Invest in good ones. You'll use them frequently. In the creation of a recipe, you're not just cutting to make things look pretty. The decision to have a particular ingredient julienned instead of diced is made deliberately—with concern for mouthfeel, flavor, and cook time, among other variables. In this chapter, your knives will get a good workout, and you'll engage in some repetitive tasks that'll build competence and confidence in the kitchen. You'll make a couple of foundational items, preparations that will be used multiple times throughout the book. If there's one recipe you should prepare, it's the Culinary School Chicken (page 37). It will throw you right into a handful of cooking techniques that we'll explore more deeply, chapter by chapter, lesson by lesson.

Bits and Pieces

Classically, knife cuts are taught in terms of geometric precision, which is, well, super-silly. What follows are more sensible product- and texture-conscious knife moves that should cover most of the skills you'll need to work your way around the book and in general. Lessons on cutting meat and poultry will take place later, and are tied to recipes.

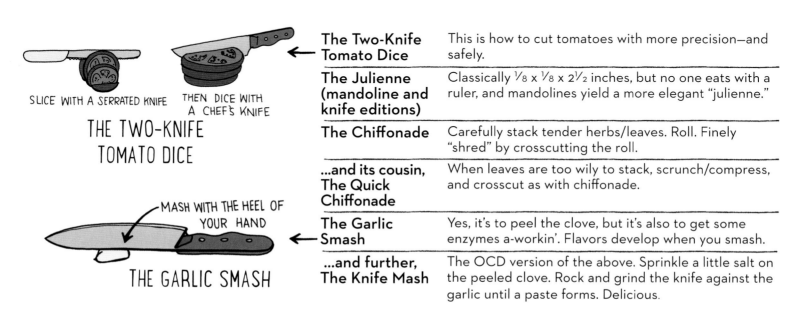

SLICE WITH A SERRATED KNIFE · THEN DICE WITH A CHEF'S KNIFE

THE TWO-KNIFE TOMATO DICE

MASH WITH THE HEEL OF YOUR HAND

THE GARLIC SMASH

The Two-Knife Tomato Dice	This is how to cut tomatoes with more precision—and safely.
The Julienne (mandoline and knife editions)	Classically $\frac{1}{8}$ x $\frac{1}{8}$ x $2\frac{1}{2}$ inches, but no one eats with a ruler, and mandolines yield a more elegant "julienne."
The Chiffonade	Carefully stack tender herbs/leaves. Roll. Finely "shred" by crosscutting the roll.
...and its cousin, The Quick Chiffonade	When leaves are too wily to stack, scrunch/compress, and crosscut as with chiffonade.
The Garlic Smash	Yes, it's to peel the clove, but it's also to get some enzymes a-workin'. Flavors develop when you smash.
...and further, The Knife Mash	The OCD version of the above. Sprinkle a little salt on the peeled clove. Rock and grind the knife against the garlic until a paste forms. Delicious.

The Herb Chop	Rock your very sharp knife through the herbs. Don't do that hammering, noise-making, herb-bruising thing. It makes your herbs ugly.	
The Citrus Seviche-Style Fillet	Cut off exterior "fillets." I learned this from a Peruvian chef-friend. You'll yield more juice, and it's easier to squeeze.	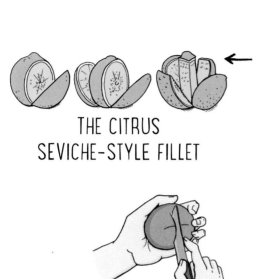
The Pepper and Fresh Chile Fillet	Depending upon roundness, shape, and the taper of the pepper, you're looking for flat "panels" of pepper. Cut to desired shape from there.	

THE CITRUS SEVICHE-STYLE FILLET

The Rough Chop	This does not refer to how you will use your knife. You're looking for rustic-looking, semi-uniform pieces. Don't hurt your food.	
...and its manic cousin, The Mince	Again, don't do the rock/hammer-thing with your knife. Make sure you glide the knife through the pile. Repeatedly. Deliberately.	
The Pestle Pound	There's nothing wrong with a little tamp and grind. Repeat until you get the desired texture.	
The "X" for Peeling	This gives you somewhere to start pulling away the peel with your fingers. Not every peel slips off daintily, though, so forgive yourself now.	

THE "X" FOR PEELING

The Sexy Peel	Think of every beautiful photo of chef-prepared carrots. You're sculpting the fruits and vegetables for grace and evenness.
...and its just-can't-stop cousin, The Ribbon	Here, you apply firmer pressure, using broad strokes to get tagliatelle-like (or broader) ribbons. Zucchini. Carrots. Cucumbers.
The Dice (small, medium, and large)	Food is cut into perfect 1/4-inch (small), 1/2-inch (medium), or 3/4-inch (large) cubes.
The Onion Dice	Forget the weird, old-school horizontal cut. Nature already designed that into the onion. Vertical cut toward the root. Crosscut for "dice."

THE SEXY PEEL

THE ONION DICE

CUT TOWARDS THE ROOT

THEN CUT ACROSS THE RINGS

THIS SALSA IS BEST SERVED THE DAY YOU MAKE IT. BEYOND THAT, IT'LL TASTE A LITTLE LESS VIBRANT & THE TEXTURE WON'T BE THE SAME.

FIRST-CUT SALSA FRESCA

HANDS-ON: 8 MIN. **TOTAL:** 23 MIN.

Why salsa first? You'll use many of the knife cuts just taught: Chiffonade. Onion Dice. Citrus Seviche-Style Fillet. To get this recipe right, have a sharp serrated knife and chef's knife ready for action. You'll learn to move deftly among your knives the more you practice. Just don't get too finessed with this one. Rustic is beautiful.

Food

Food	How Much	Why
ripe tomato, best of the season *(heirloom, ugly, or vine-ripe preferred)*	1 cup (about ½ pound)	The tomato simply has to be ripe. This recipe is made or broken by the quality and handling of your tomatoes.
jalapeño or serrano chile, ribs and seeds removed	2 tablespoons	The level of heat is really up to your preference. Remove the seeds, because, well, they just look ugly in this salsa, but feel free to leave some of the ribs on the chile based on your pain tolerance.
fresh cilantro	¼ cup quick chiffonade	Vibrant herbs show up in almost all salsas around the globe. Cilantro is found frequently from Mexico to Thailand and places in-between. Don't fear the tender stem, as its texture is pleasant.
lime	1, cut "seviche-style"	Lime is classic. Its floral notes and bracing acidity are perfect for this salsa. Lemon is fine, too.
red onion	⅓ cup finely diced	Honestly, red onion is just a preference. Bright white onion would take a close second place here.
kosher salt	¼ teaspoon	Salt, in addition to elevating flavor, helps draw moisture out of your carefully cut ingredients.

Follow These Steps:

>> Ready a stainless steel bowl.

>> Wash the tomatoes and the chiles. Let dry on a clean kitchen towel.

>> Wash the cilantro in a large bowl containing at least 1 quart of very cold water. Handle it somewhere between vigorously and gingerly in the water, separating and agitating all the while. Drain in a colander. Repeat the process. Spin in a salad spinner for optimal effect (after both washings).

>> Cut the lime for juicing. Set aside.

>> Using a small serrated knife, cut the tomatoes into ¼-inch slabs. Then crosscut them into a proper dice with your chef's knife.

>> Cut the tops off the chiles, split them lengthwise, and then quarter them lengthwise. You're quartering them so you have relatively flat surfaces to work with. Now, julienne and finely dice them. *Nice work!*

>> Dice the onions. Brag about your increasing knife skills confidence. *Now, look at your fingers. Still there!*

>> Chiffonade the cilantro.

>> Combine all of your knife work in the stainless steel bowl.

>> Squeeze the lime over the mixture. You want about 1 tablespoon of juice.

>> Put the salt in your hand and sprinkle over the salsa with a sense of fanfare and exuberance. *It doesn't matter if no one is watching. You know what you did!*

>> Let the mixture sit at room temperature for anywhere from 15 minutes (good) to 1 hour (glorious) before serving.

SERVES 4 (SERVING SIZE: ¼ CUP)
CALORIES 15; **FAT** 0.1G (SAT 0G, MONO 0G, POLY 0.1G); **PROTEIN** 1G;
CARB 4G; **FIBER** 1G; **CHOL** 0MG; **IRON** 0MG; **SODIUM** 144MG; **CALC** 9MG

CHARRED TOMATO PASSATA

HANDS-ON: 10 MIN. **TOTAL:** 1 HR. 40 MIN.

Chefs survive on a group of foundational recipes, such as stocks, mother sauces, and mirepoix. This is one of those. When you can get your hands on wonderfully ripe roma tomatoes, make this passata and use it liberally. It freezes well and can be used in recipes in place of canned tomato sauce. Because of the incredible char achieved, we bypass the food mill (commonly used for passata) and make a more rustic edition using a food processor.

Food	How Much	Why
roma tomatoes	24 (about 3 pounds), stem end trimmed	Romas have a consistent ratio of flesh to "gel," making them a solid choice for a foundational recipe. However, feel free to experiment with other tomato varieties.
olive oil	2 tablespoons	A classic pairing with tomatoes.
kosher salt	1 teaspoon	The taste of salt against the sweet acidity of tomatoes? It's a reason for living.
fresh basil leaves	12	Fresh leaves provide a lingering perfume and brightness that dried basil simply cannot. Don't be a fresh herb snob, though, as there's a time and place for good quality dried herbs.

LIKE, WHEN YOU DON'T WANT LINGERING PERFUME & BRIGHTNESS, BUT EARTHINESS & PUNGENCY.

Follow These Steps:

≫ Preheat your oven to 450°.

≫ Wash the tomatoes, then remove the stem end, and, using a paring knife, score an "X" into the pointed end of the tomato. Place the tomatoes in a mixing bowl.

≫ Drizzle the olive oil over the tomatoes.

≫ Using a tossing motion, coat the tomatoes with the olive oil.

≫ Sprinkle the salt over the tomatoes. *Now, toss them again, showing off your Mad Skills.*

≫ Place the seasoned tomatoes on a baking sheet in an even layer, with an inch or so separation between the tomatoes.

≫ Bake the tomatoes at 450° for 1 hour and 20 minutes, stirring every 20 minutes. They'll be blistered, super-soft, and markedly wilted.

≫ Remove the tomatoes from the oven and let cool at room temperature for about 10 minutes.

≫ Peel the tomatoes, if desired. You can leave as much or as little of the charred skin as you desire.

≫ Using a food processor or a blender, blend until nearly smooth.

≫ In your hands, crush the basil leaves. Throw the crushed leaves into the passata. *Now, bring your hands to your nose as if to pray. Open your hands toward your nose. Enjoy.*

≫ Now, stir the passata, or process the passata again to blend in the basil. It's better when the leaves are just wilted-in whole.

≫ Reserve in a refrigerator-friendly container until ready to use. Yes, you can freeze it.

SERVES 8 (SERVING SIZE: ½ CUP)
CALORIES 61; **FAT** 3.8G (SAT 0.6G, MONO 2.6G, POLY 0.6G); **PROTEIN** 2G; **CARB** 7G; **FIBER** 2G; **CHOL** 0MG; **IRON** 1MG; **SODIUM** 249MG; **CALC** 18MG

E, YOU'RE LEARNING VARIATIONS
A CLASSIC CONCASSÉ, OR
USH." THE TERM IS TYPICALLY
D IN REFERENCE TO TOMATOES,
WE'LL USE IT FOR ANYTHING
CAN BE "HEAT PEELED" AND
SHED — LIKE A STONE FRUIT.

CHARRED PEACH PASSATA

HANDS-ON: 15 MIN.   **TOTAL:** 40 MIN.

We can thank Escoffier and Carême for organizing culinary technique as it is commonly taught in the Western world today, but one of the luxuries of being a cook in America is our inherent willingness to take creative license with techniques. This is one of those recipes you can experiment with. If the fruit or vegetable can ripen, has tender, juicy flesh, and can be peeled, it's a candidate for becoming a passata. Serve this one on crostini, biscuits, toast, anything.

AUGUSTE ESCOFFIER

MARIE-ANTOINE CARÊME

Food	How Much	Why
peaches	8 (about 3 pounds)	Peaches are so gently sweet, they lend themselves to savory applications. Be sure to select super-ripe peaches. And don't be that person who leaves fingerprint-shaped bruises on all the peaches in the bin. Make passata, not war.
extra-virgin olive oil	1 tablespoon	Flavor-forward extra-virgin olive oil draws out the savory characteristics of foods—even sweet ones.
kosher salt	½ teaspoon	To punch the peaches in a savory direction.
sugar	½ teaspoon	To facilitate charring, not to add sweetness.
fresh thyme leaves	½ tablespoon chopped	Thyme is the super-herb. A veritable culinary power-house. It deserves its own book.

Follow These Steps:

≫ Set your broiler to high.

≫ Wash the peaches and, using a paring knife, score an "X" into the pointed end of the peach. Place them in a stainless steel bowl.

≫ Drizzle the olive oil over the peaches. Gently toss the peaches with the oil.

≫ Sprinkle the salt and sugar over the peaches. Now, toss them again.

≫ Place the seasoned peaches on a broiler pan in an even layer, with good separation between the peaches—about an inch if possible. The skins will blister and "shrink" away from the peach if they're not touching. You want this.

≫ Sprinkle the thyme leaves across the peaches. Broil the peaches until the skins char and split, about 15 minutes, turning the peaches during cooking, trying to char evenly all around.

≫ Remove the peaches from the broiler and let cool at room temperature for about 10 minutes.

≫ Peel the peaches. *Don't stress if there are a few stray bits of skin stuck to the peaches.* You'll be processing them further.

≫ Using a food mill (preferably), blender (acceptable), or food processor (also okay), pass the slightly warm peaches and surrounding drippings through the mill. *The food mill makes you look fancy, is a conversation piece, and creates textural magic.*

≫ Reserve in a refrigerator-friendly container to use as a sauce for grilled chicken or pork, or for Chicken-Pecan Meatballs (page 247). Yes, you can freeze it.

SERVES 8 (SERVING SIZE: ½ CUP)
CALORIES 75; **FAT** 2.1G (SAT 0.3G, MONO 1.4G, POLY 0.4G); **PROTEIN** 1G; **CARB** 15G; **FIBER** 2G; **CHOL** 0MG; **IRON** 1MG; **SODIUM** 120MG; **CALC** 11MG

THIS CHIMICHURRI GETS A TOUCH OF HEAT FROM
THE RED PEPPER FLAKES THANKS TO THE
CAPSAICIN, A COMPOUND FOUND IN ALL HOT CHILES.
IT DOES INDEED CREATE A BURNING SENSATION,
AS IT IS AN IRRITANT.

SMOKY CHIMICHURRI

HANDS-ON: 10 MIN. **TOTAL:** 50 MIN.

Arguments often ensue about the definition behind and authenticity of this recipe—important for historical perspective, but often not for flavor integrity. This chimichurri, a relish of herbs, garlic, acid, and oil common in Argentine steakhouses and homes, is a hybrid of classic red and green varieties. It brings the best of earthy, bright, smoky, grassy, and pungent all together into one amazing workhorse sauce for grilled meats.

Food

Food	How Much	Why
fresh flat-leaf parsley	½ cup coarsely chopped	Flat-leaf parsley is more flavorful than curly parsley and, when pounded and bruised, has an almost basil-like oiliness that curly does not.
shallot	3 tablespoons minced	More elegant than onion in this application. Understated. A harmonizer.
garlic cloves	2, minced	It's a prominent flavor in this sauce, so make sure it's fresh.
dried oregano	1 teaspoon	Earthy and concentrated, it's quite a punctuation mark.
kosher salt	¼ teaspoon	The coarseness of kosher is helpful in a mortar and pestle application.
freshly ground black pepper	⅛ teaspoon	Black pepper tastes wonderful against most anything, but is particularly magical against cooked red meat juices.
smoked paprika	⅛ teaspoon	Powerful, distinct, and, well, smoky.
red pepper flakes	⅛ teaspoon	The capsaicin in red pepper flakes helps you "feel" what you're eating. It's also adds a distinct layer of sweetness.
extra-virgin olive oil	1 tablespoon	For mouthfeel and as a carrier of ingredients that come alive in oil—oregano, pepper, garlic.
sherry vinegar	3 tablespoons	Sherry vinegar is more subtly acidic and has a more complex flavor than most common vinegars.
fresh lemon juice	1 teaspoon	To brighten.

Follow These Steps:

>> Combine all but the liquid ingredients in a mortar and pestle or a durable mixing bowl (you can use the blunt end of a rolling pin if you don't have a mortar and pestle).

>> Pound the mixture firmly, *marveling as you bruise perfectly beautiful herbs with the shallots and garlic (which you minced with your great knife work).*

>> When the mixture looks appropriately shaggy and the juices of the shallot seem to have moistened the mass, stir in the olive oil, continually pounding and vigorously mixing for another minute.

>> Let it rest for 10 minutes or so to weep and wilt further.

>> Stir in the vinegar and the lemon juice using a spoon.

>> Either in the refrigerator or at room temperature, let rest for about a half hour before spooning over grilled meats.

SERVES 4 (SERVING SIZE: ABOUT 2 TABLESPOONS)
CALORIES 50; **FAT** 3.6G (SAT 0.5G, MONO 2.5G, POLY 0.5G); **PROTEIN** 1G;
CARB 6G; **FIBER** 1G; **CHOL** 0MG; **IRON** 2MG; **SODIUM** 130MG; **CALC** 24MG

CULINARY SCHOOL CHICKEN

HANDS-ON: 30 MIN. **TOTAL:** 1 HR. 45 MIN.

This recipe is the course prerequisite. Meaning, it's probably not prudent to proceed with further cooking until you absolutely master this one. Learning the art of cutting a chicken is liberating, and you'll save money by buying the thing whole. You'll also experience the magic of mirepoix and see a no-fuss pan sauce emerge before your eyes. Cut. Cook. Repeat.

Food	How Much	Why
roasting chicken	1 (5-pound) chicken, rinsed and dried well	Because knowing how to break down a chicken is vital to being a cook.
cooking spray		
kosher salt	½ teaspoon	Because salt "steers" flavor.
sugar	½ teaspoon	In recipes where browning is encouraged, a blend of Maillard reaction and bona fide caramelization contributes to much of what we experience as "delicious."
black pepper	½ teaspoon	It does magical things when cooked.
fresh thyme leaves	1½ tablespoons chopped	The super-herb. It's less neutral than it is perfect for most savory foods. It's the vanilla bean of savory cooking.
celery	about 5 stalks (2 cups diced)	One of the trio that makes up mirepoix.
onion	1 large (2 cups diced)	This is the workhorse of mirepoix. When gently cooked, then caramelized, it provides tremendous aromatic depth.
carrots	6 medium (2½ cups peeled and diced)	The "meat" of mirepoix, providing depth of texture and significant sugars to caramelize.
lemon	1	Acidity and brightness are important characteristics to consider in cooking. Lemon is both acidic and bright.
olive oil	2 tablespoons	It works, flavor-wise.
fresh thyme leaves	1½ tablespoons chopped	We're hammering home the utility of thyme in this chapter.
bay leaves	2, preferably fresh	Warmth. Undertones of happiness.
sherry vinegar	2 tablespoons	Sherry vinegar provides a contrasting earthiness, plus a more complex acidity than the citric acid present in the lemon. Playing with the balance between acid sources can make a dish more engaging and satisfying than using one acid alone.
butter	1 tablespoon	To "enrich" and round out the sauce.

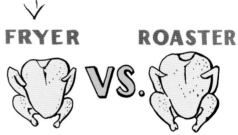

FRYER   VS.   ROASTER

AGE: 6-8 WEEKS   **AGE:** >8 MONTHS
WEIGHT: 2.5-3.5 LB   **WEIGHT:** 3.5-5 LB

GO FOR A ROASTING CHICKEN—
IT CAN TAKE LONGER COOKING
TIMES AND GIVE YOU BIGGER
PIECES THAN A FRYER.

CONTINUED

CULINARY SCHOOL CHICKEN

1 (5-pound)
roasting chicken,
rinsed and dried well

cooking spray

½ tsp. kosher salt

½ tsp. sugar

½ tsp. black pepper

1½ Tbsp. chopped fresh
thyme leaves

5 celery stalks

1 large onion

6 medium carrots

1 lemon

2 Tbsp. olive oil

1½ Tbsp. chopped fresh
thyme leaves

2 fresh bay leaves

2 Tbsp. sherry vinegar

1 Tbsp. butter

Follow These Steps:

›› Preheat your oven to 425°.

›› Find your heaviest-bottomed roasting pan or shallowest oven-friendly dish. You'll also need a large skillet.

PREP THE CHICKEN

›› Rinse your chicken under cold running water. *Allow to air dry or pat it dry with good quality paper towels. Use the cheap ones and eat paper.*

›› Prep the chicken following the step-by-step photos on page 39.

›› Place the chicken in a bowl. Lightly spray the chicken with cooking spray; toss with the salt, sugar, pepper, and thyme leaves. Put it in the refrigerator until it's time to cook.

›› Clean up after yourself. Cross-contamination is a very bad thing indeed.

CHOP YOUR VEGGIES

›› Set up a vegetable scrap container for the imperfect work you're about to do. You can compost the scraps or discard them. Grab a medium bowl for the prepped veggies, too.

›› It's time to apply the knife skills lesson you learned on page 26. Start with dicing the celery. It's the easiest.

›› Now, dice the onion.

›› *Great! Now that your confidence is up, finish with the most challenging of the three veggies to dice nicely—the carrots.*

›› Thinly slice the lemon. Keep the sliced lemon separate from the diced veggies.

BROWN THE BIRD

›› Heat a large skillet over medium-high heat. Add 1 tablespoon of oil and swirl. *If the oil smokes, you've gone too far. It happens.* Back off the heat and lift the pan from the cooking area to let the smoke subside. Return to calm.

›› Add half the chicken to the pan, skin side down. Cook for 4 minutes until the chicken skin looks like the best, crustiest bread you've ever seen. Turn and cook 3 minutes more.

›› Remove from pan. Repeat procedure with remaining oil and chicken.

›› Drain oil from pan. It's exhausted.

›› Add the celery, onion, carrots, and thyme; cook 4 minutes or until lightly browned, scraping pan to remove brown bits. As the vegetables collapse and release their liquid, they're deglazing the pan, and that spells delicious.

EVERYTHING INTO THE OVEN!

›› On the roasting pan, make a uniform bed of the cooked vegetables, and lay all of the chicken pieces on top neatly. Like an artist, tuck the lemon slices and the bay leaves into the pockets between the chicken pieces. Nearly bury the bay leaves. You want those to fall into the juices as the chicken roasts.

›› Roast the chicken at 425° for just over an hour, checking after 30 minutes, until the internal temperature (at the bone) of the thickest piece of chicken is 155°. *This is the point where many think the juices should run fully clear. Not yet. We have to account for carry-over cooking.* Remove the chicken from the oven.

CARRY-OVER COOKING IS REALLY JUST HEAT TRANSFER. THE EXTERIOR OF WHAT YOU'VE COOKED IN THE OVEN IS ALWAYS HOTTER THAN THE INTERIOR. THE EXTERIOR IS "COOKING" THE INTERIOR.

MAKE A PAN SAUCE

>> After 10 minutes, grab your smallest saucepan and carefully tilt the roasting pan to drain off the juices. Add the sherry vinegar to the pan; bring it to a boil over medium heat. Let it reduce until nearly syrupy, about 6 minutes or until reduced to ½ cup. *Turn off the heat and swirl in the butter as you walk away with the pot in your hand, looking like a pro.*

>> Grab a platter, tongs, a serving spoon, and a large soup spoon. Move the chicken out of the way of the vegetables for a moment so you can mound your mirepoix on the platter—front and center. *We want everyone to know about your Mad Skills.*

>> Now, place the chicken pieces on and around the veggies. Don't be precise; be deliberate. There's a difference. The layout should look natural, comforting, and casual.

>> Pour your beautifully rustic sauce over the top and all around.

SERVES 5 (SERVING SIZE: 2 PIECES OF CHICKEN, 2 TABLESPOONS SAUCE, ¼ CUP VEGETABLES)
CALORIES 484; FAT 15.6G (SAT 4.4G, MONO 7.2G, POLY 2.4G); PROTEIN 68G; CARB 16G; FIBER 4G;
CHOL 186MG; IRON 3MG; SODIUM 451MG; CALC 89MG

STEP BY STEP: Breaking Down a Whole Chicken

1) Cut through the skin between the leg and body. Twist the leg down until the joint pops out of the socket.

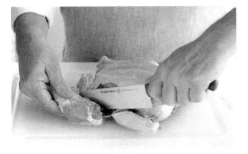

2) Use your chef's knife to remove the leg by cutting through the exposed joint. Repeat on other side.

3) Remove the wings.

4) Cut each wing crosswise into two pieces.

5) Hold the chicken vertically with the tail end up. Cut through the skin and cartilage to remove the backbone.

6) To split the breast, cut through both sides of the breastbone until you hit the sternum. Cut through the bone.

GRILLED BEEF TENDERLOIN

HANDS-ON: 18 MIN. **TOTAL:** 28 MIN.

You're about to pick up some cool butchering skills. Not only will you feel a sense of satisfaction from learning how to peel a beef tenderloin (see the in-depth step-by-step on page 43), this technique is transferable to pork and lamb as well. It's easier, albeit more expensive, to learn on a beef tenderloin. You'll see the garlic paste method outlined below used various times throughout the book, and you can use it in your own improvisational cooking. The real win in this lesson, though, is learning how to masterfully "temp" (measure the doneness of) an individual cut of meat, so you can cook "to order" for your family and friends.

WELL DONE — AS HIGH AS YOU LIKE
MEDIUM-WELL — 140°F
MEDIUM — 130°F
MEDIUM-RARE — 120°F
RARE — 110°F

Food	How Much	Why
beef tenderloin steaks	4 (4-ounce) steaks, trimmed	Four-ounce medallions "eat well;" that is to say, the ratio of the cooked exterior to buttery less-cooked interior is ideal.
garlic cloves	2	Provides aroma and flavor depth, and makes the charred flavor slightly more complex. A touch of burnt garlic isn't a bad thing.
sugar	1 teaspoon	Wait until you see those grill marks.
kosher salt	½ teaspoon	A must for meat.
cooking spray		Let the beef speak for itself and allow the fat from the chimichurri to highlight the steak. Butter's not required here.
Smoky Chimichurri *(page 35)*	½ cup	Beef tenderloin is mellow, and the chimichurri enlivens the cut. Sure, beef enthusiasts prefer cuts such as rib eye and New York strip for flavor, but the textural pleasantness of beef tenderloin is undeniable.

GRILLED BEEF TENDERLOIN

4 (4-ounce) beef tenderloin steaks, trimmed

2 garlic cloves

1 tsp. sugar

1/2 tsp. kosher salt

cooking spray

1/2 cup Smoky Chimichurri (page 35)

Follow These Steps:

>> Preheat your grill, hibachi, grill pan, or wood-fired device to medium-high heat. To test this, hover your hand, palm side down, about 4 inches above the grate and count how long you can hold it there comfortably. Three to four seconds is the sign it's reached medium-high heat (350° to 400°).

>> If you're trimming and cutting the tenderloin medallions yourself, follow the instructions on page 43. If you're not adept at this process yet, you might want to do this before preheating your grill.

>> Peel the garlic cloves. Snip the woody tips off the cloves.

>> Place the garlic cloves on a cutting board (preferably wooden) and pour the sugar and salt over the cloves. Roughly chop the garlic/sugar/salt mixture until pieces are about the size of grains of rice. Then, using the side of your knife, pull the blade across the chopped mixture to mash it to a paste. Repeat the process until there is a uniform paste.

>> Rub the paste evenly on the cut sides of the tenderloin filets.

>> Grill on a grill rack coated with cooking spray for about 2 1/2 minutes on each side for medium-rare, 4 minutes on each side (no more than 8 minutes total) for medium. *Cooking any further really does detract from the quality of this cut, all snobbery aside.*

>> Place the finished tenderloin medallions on a plate and allow them to rest for 10 minutes before "flashing" on the grill or grill pan.

AFTER THE MEAT RESTS & THE EXTERIOR HAS COOLED SIGNIFICANTLY, A QUICK FLASH IN THE PAN WILL REHEAT THE SURFACE WITHOUT HAVING A MARKED EFFECT ON THE INTERIOR TEMPERATURE.

>> Serve with Smoky Chimichurri.

SERVES 4 (SERVING SIZE: 1 STEAK AND 2 TABLESPOONS SMOKY CHIMICHURRI)
CALORIES 241; FAT 12.2G (SAT 3.5G, MONO 6.1G, POLY 0.9G); PROTEIN 25G; CARB 2G; FIBER 0G; CHOL 75MG; IRON 2MG; SODIUM 305MG; CALC 35MG

STEP BY STEP:
Peeling a Beef Tenderloin

1) Unwrap and pat dry.

2) ID Sections: chain, head, tenderloin.

3) Isolate chain.

4) Remove membrane.

5) Cut off the chain.

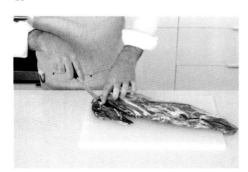

6) Detach the head.

7) With a knife, thread out the silverskin, angling the knife up and away.

8) Trim excess fat, membrane, and silverskin.

9) Flip and trim off rib fat.

10) Cut into tips, medallions, or center-cut filets.

11) Trim the head and cut as a roast or as two filet portions.

SWEET GARLIC SLAW

HANDS-ON: 12 MIN. **TOTAL:** 1 HR. 12 MIN.

This is a lighter, brighter slaw, worthy of piling high against grilled and roasted meats or poultry. Patience pays off with this slaw: The longer it steeps, the better it eats. Sharpen your knives and your skills. That's really why this recipe was designed.

Food	How Much	Why
savoy cabbage	2 cups chiffonade	In stark contrast to traditional white or red cabbage, savoy is more tender and a tad less funky, and most important to this recipe, wilts more quickly when combined with the dressing.
shallot	¼ cup thinly sliced (about 1 large)	Shallot is subtler and more sophisticated than the onion found in many slaws.
flat-leaf parsley	2 tablespoons quick chiffonade	Bright and grassy, it'll make the slaw more versatile.
garlic cloves	2	It's in the title and thus is the focal point of the recipe.
sugar	1 teaspoon	It sweetens, but it's also hygroscopic—it'll draw moisture from the vegetables to help with the "sauce."
kosher salt	¼ teaspoon	Also hygroscopic. Essential for balance and flavor development.
apple cider vinegar	2 tablespoons	Go for the unfiltered kind; it seems to retain the perfume of fresh apples and has the right kind of acid for a cabbage dish.
buttermilk	2 tablespoons	This dish is intended to be paired with roasted meats and/or poultry, so buttermilk helps with mouthfeel without the extra fat that mayonnaise would lend.
freshly ground black pepper	¼ teaspoon	Garlic, salt, sugar, and pepper work in masterful harmony. Look at blended spice mixtures in the supermarket. They're in there.

Follow These Steps:

➤➤ Chiffonade the cabbage. Place in a medium bowl.

➤➤ Peel and thinly slice the shallot. Throw it on top of the cabbage.

➤➤ Quick-chiffonade the parsley. Throw it on top of the cabbage and shallot.

➤➤ Peel the garlic cloves (or use peeled). Snip the woody tips off the cloves.

➤➤ Place the garlic cloves on a cutting board (preferably wooden), and pour the sugar and salt over the cloves. Roughly chop the garlic/sugar/salt mixture until pieces are about the size of grains of rice. Then, using the side of your knife, pull the blade across the chopped mixture to mash it to a paste. Repeat the process until there is a uniform paste.

➤➤ In a small bowl, combine the vinegar, buttermilk, pepper, and garlic paste. Combine well.

➤➤ Pour the buttermilk mixture over the undressed slaw. Toss well.

➤➤ Then, in the bowl, hand-crush the slaw. You should repeatedly make firm fists full of slaw and release. *This isn't weird. This helps crush the cellular structure of the cabbage so that when it sits it can absorb the full glory of your buttermilk-garlic dressing.*

➤➤ For ideal results, let the slaw sit, covered with plastic wrap, at room temperature for an hour. Serve chilled or at room temperature.

➤➤ Serve it with your Culinary School Chicken (page 37), grilled and/or roasted meats, or as a sandwich side.

SERVES 4 (SERVING SIZE: 1 CUP)
CALORIES 32; **FAT** 0.2G (SAT 0.1G, MONO 0.1G, POLY 0G); **PROTEIN** 1G; **CARB** 7G; **FIBER** 1G; **CHOL** 1MG; **IRON** 0MG; **SODIUM** 164MG; **CALC** 33MG

SAUCES & DRESSINGS

The skinny on lighter
dressings and sauces

Cooking is as much about the manipulation of texture as flavor. Silky, smooth, and creamy foods—particularly in the form of sauces—are almost universally celebrated for adding a touch of finesse to a meal. Indeed, from the food scientist who's formulating a better shelf-stable dressing to the home cook who's experimenting with his or her own twists on traditional techniques (like, say, for making a lighter *beurre blanc*), tinkering with sauces and emulsification is pretty fun business. This chapter will equip you with just enough science for an evening of table talk, along with a repertoire of deceptively light and flexible formulas for making sauces and dressings.

Who's Your Momma?

In the Western world, cooks are largely taught the art and science of sauce-making via the five so-called mother sauces:

>> **Béchamel:** a milk-based sauce thickened with roux

>> **Velouté:** a light-colored stock thickened with a similarly light (in color) roux

>> **Espagnole:** the roasty-toasty brown sauce edition of the prior

>> **Tomate:** a salt-porky, mirepoix-bodied, starch-thickened tomato puree

>> **Hollandaise:** the odd-bird of mother sauces, a delicately cooked emulsion of eggs and melted butter, with the slight tang of acid (classically vinegar), and a pinch of pepper.

All sauces are delightful, for sure, but can one really build all that is saucy from the aforementioned? No. One can't. It seemed imprudent to continue the old-school Francocentric manner of teaching sauce-making (though the French shall forevermore be given props for informing modern cuisine). Indeed, tackling the idea of codifying everything that can moisten finished foods and make them taste better seemed...daunting...infinite. However, the question "What am I trying to accomplish?" is a great way to inform the construction of a meal, a dish, a sauce. With nothing but that question as inspiration, I sought to create a framework for building a sauce, with form and function as the parents of a new taxonomy of sauce-making.

THANKS, FRANCE!

THE SAUCES FAMILY

TO GIVE YOU AN IDEA OF HOW VAST AND VARIED THIS CATEGORY OF FOOD IS, YOU'LL FIND A MONSTROUS FAMILY TREE OF SAUCES ON THE NEXT PAGE. THE CHART IS INTENDED TO BE POKED & PRODDED & ADDED TO AS YOU MAKE NEW SAUCY DISCOVERIES. WRITE ON IT. GO AHEAD. IT WON'T BE COMPLETE. EVER.

FLIP THE PAGE TO MEET THE FAMILY.

THE SAUCES

CONDIMENTS, PRESERVES, & THE SHELF-STABLE

- RELISHES
- QUICK-PICKLES
- CHUTNEY
- JAMS
- KETCHUPY
- MUSTARDY
- BARBEQUE
- HOT SAUCES
- DIPPING SAUCES

MOSTARDA!

IN THE INTEREST OF PEACE, NO RULES WILL BE DISCUSSED, THOUGH *NEUTRAL QUE* WILL GET YOU STARTED PG.57

MAD FRESH SRIRACHA PG.58 & MAD SPICY HARISSA PG.60

REDUCTIONS
- DEMI-GLACE
- STOCK-BASED
- CREAM-BASED

BROTHY
- STOCK-BASED
- BROTH-BASED
- VEGETABLE-BASED

VEGETABLE STOCK
VEGETABLE JUICE

CARROT-GINGER CONSOMMÉ PG.75

SUGAR-BASED & DESSERT SAUCES

CULTURED
- YOGURT-BASED
- CRÈME FRAÎCHE-BASED
- BUTTERMILK-BASED
- SOUR CREAM-BASED

RANCH!

THESE ARE TYPICALLY SIMPLE MIXTURES—SOMETHING MIXED INTO THE BASE.

THE ACIDIC

PURÉE MEETS VINAIGRETTE IN WARM TOMATO VINAIGRETTE PG.85

- VINAIGRETTES
- MIGNONETTE-LIKE
- THINGS STEEPED IN VINEGAR
- VINEGAR REDUCTION

HABANERO-ORANGE MIGNONETTE PG.65

THINK SOUTHERN-STYLE PEPPER VINEGAR

TYPICALLY, YOU'D WANT THE VINEGAR TO HAVE SOME RESIDUAL SUGAR, LIKE A BANYULS OR BALSAMIC

SANS OIL

VINEGAR-BASED

AIOLI GETS DOCTORED WITH LEMON JUICE FOR A RIFF ON *CAESAR DRESSING*, ON PG.89

BRUSHED, SQUEEZED, OR SPLASHED

- LEMON JUICE
- LIME JUICE
- BLENDS
- CITRUS-BASED VINAIGRETTES

SUGAR OR SYRUP + VINEGAR

GASTRIQUE

CITRUS-BASED

FRUIT & VEGETABLE-BASED
- JUICE-BASED
- PUREES
- SALSAS

GARLIC CREAM PG.60

SALSA FRESCA PG.29 MINT & SUMAC "SALSA" PG.76 & MARIA'S CILANTRO CEBOLLAS PG.79

FAMILY

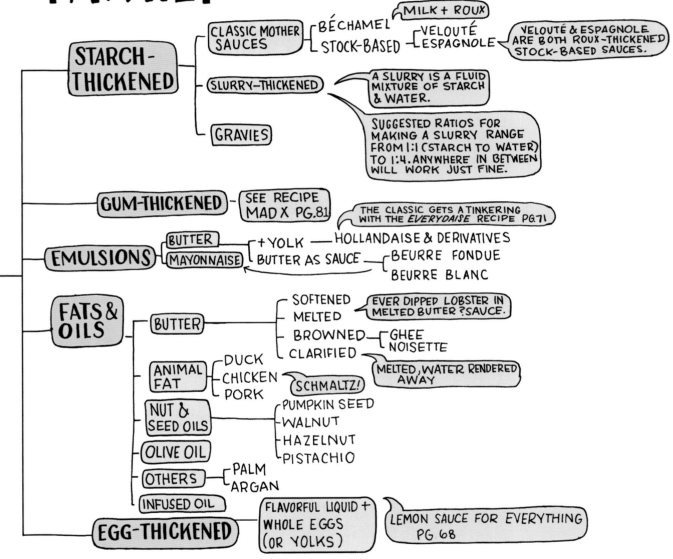

STARCH-THICKENED

CLASSIC MOTHER SAUCES
- BÉCHAMEL — MILK + ROUX
- STOCK-BASED
  - VELOUTÉ
  - ESPAGNOLE

> VELOUTÉ & ESPAGNOLE ARE BOTH ROUX-THICKENED STOCK-BASED SAUCES.

SLURRY-THICKENED

> A SLURRY IS A FLUID MIXTURE OF STARCH & WATER.

GRAVIES

> SUGGESTED RATIOS FOR MAKING A SLURRY RANGE FROM 1:1 (STARCH TO WATER) TO 1:4. ANYWHERE IN BETWEEN WILL WORK JUST FINE.

GUM-THICKENED

> SEE RECIPE MAD X PG. 81

> THE CLASSIC GETS A TINKERING WITH THE *EVERYDAISE* RECIPE PG. 71

EMULSIONS
- BUTTER
- MAYONNAISE
  - +YOLK — HOLLANDAISE & DERIVATIVES
  - BUTTER AS SAUCE
    - BEURRE FONDUE
    - BEURRE BLANC

FATS & OILS
- BUTTER
  - SOFTENED
  - MELTED
  - BROWNED
    - GHEE
    - NOISETTE
  - CLARIFIED

> EVER DIPPED LOBSTER IN MELTED BUTTER? SAUCE.

> MELTED, WATER RENDERED AWAY

- ANIMAL FAT
  - DUCK
  - CHICKEN
  - PORK

> SCHMALTZ!

- NUT & SEED OILS
  - PUMPKIN SEED
  - WALNUT
  - HAZELNUT
  - PISTACHIO
- OLIVE OIL
- OTHERS
  - PALM
  - ARGAN
- INFUSED OIL

EGG-THICKENED

> FLAVORFUL LIQUID + WHOLE EGGS (OR YOLKS)

> LEMON SAUCE FOR EVERYTHING PG. 68

Emulsions: The Basics

In exploring sauces, let's get back to the basics for a moment and talk about what lies at the base of many of them: emulsions. We'll keep this straightforward, because an afternoon of Googling "emulsification" can twist your brain into its own brand of mayonnaise.

》 Emulsification: It's the process of mixing a (typically liquid) fat into a water-based liquid—or vice-versa—that often involves some form of emulsifier (more on that term in a moment).

》 Emulsion: The resultant blend of the ingredients put through the aforementioned process. In food, the resulting texture typically ranges anywhere from a pourable creamy texture to a thick and clingy mayonnaise-like mixture.

There are essentially two types of emulsions in the food world:

》 Fat dispersed in water: The everyday kitchen emulsifications are historically made of some kind of fat dispersed in water. Think about hollandaise sauce, one of Western cuisine's so-called mother sauces, where warm clarified butter (the liquid fat) is slowly and steadily whisked into a blend (mostly water by volume) of egg yolks, water, and lemon juice (over a simmering water bath). Or mayonnaise, hollandaise's cold-kitchen cousin.

》 Water dispersed in fat: Far fewer culinary examples exist of water-in-fat emulsions, though butter is a clear standout in the category. Peanut butter qualifies as well.

The other important thing to note about emulsions is that while the fat and water seem like they've become "one," they're actually retaining their stand-alone characteristics. Oil is still oil. Water is still water. So what's bringing them together in delicious union? Most of these emulsions are made possible through the presence of a third ingredient: a surfactant, or in kitchen terminology, an emulsifier. Common culinary emulsifiers are mustard (both powdered and prepared) and egg yolks.

To keep things light, we've got to reimagine emulsification. By playing with the ratios of ingredients, or replacing them, recipes become hybrids of old-school emulsions and starch- or gel-thickened water-based foundations. If you look at a bottle of any light or fat-free dressing, the manufacturers have done just that—with results that leave an odd filmy feeling in your mouth. To make things worse, they often use an absurd amount of sugar to tinker with the viscosity, making the results unpleasantly sweet. Any chance for a dressing with the perfect balance of salt and acid is lost. What's exciting, however, is that in the home kitchen, we can think of flavor first.

EMULSIFIERS ARE AMPHIPHILIC—THAT MEANS THAT PART OF THE EMULSIFIER MOLECULE WANTS TO LATCH ONTO WATER, THE HYDROPHILIC PART (MMM, WATER), AND THE OTHER WANTS TO LATCH ONTO FAT (MMM, OLIVE OIL).

Common Emulsified Foods

MAYONNAISE &
MAYO-BASED SAUCES SUCH AS AIOLI

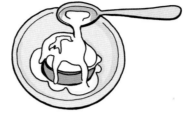

COOKED EGG YOLK- BASED SAUCES

VINAIGRETTES & SALAD DRESSINGS

BUTTER SAUCES

HOMOGENIZED MILK & CREAM

CHOCOLATE

NUT BUTTERS

BUTTER & MARGARINE

SMOOTH-TEXTURED SAUSAGES
SUCH AS FRANKFURTERS & KNOCKWURST

COMMERCIAL BAKED GOODS

EMULSIFY WITH ANY OF THESE:

GRANDMA'S MASON JAR: 89¢
(BONUS: YOU GET TO
HANG OUT WITH GRANDMA!)

 FORK: $2.50

 WHISK: $8

 EGG BEATER: $20

 IMMERSION BLENDER: $40

 MINI FOOD PROCESSOR: $40

BLENDER: $50

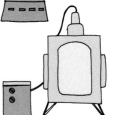 ULTRASONIC
EMULSIFIER: $4,500

Ways to Mix

»» Whisking: This is the first technique all the culinary kids learn. You often see folks feverishy whisking. That's unnecessary. A successful emulsion, using the whisking technique, is achieved by steadily and evenly whisking while gently streaming in oil or other liquid fat (typically). Thankfully, we're emulsifying on the lighter side, so you're unlikely to force in so much oil that your emulsion breaks.

»» Shaking: This will, in most cases, yield a relatively unstable (temporary) emulsion. However, it's a perfect method for a quick vinaigrette, in which some "breaking" (separation of the oil from the vinegar) is often welcome.

»» Blending: using an immersion blender or other tools.

»» Homogenization: What we think of as a natural, everyday product—milk—is actually subject to some intense mechanical energy. To create innumerable tiny droplets of suspended milkfat, the liquid is forced, under intense pressure, through very tiny holes (after being pounded against a medieval-looking stake). The emulsion is so stable that the cream never separates as it will in non-homogenized milk overnight. Buy a jug of non-homogenized milk, shake, drink some, and find your "creamline" all over again in the morning.

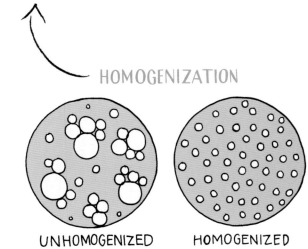

HOMOGENIZATION

UNHOMOGENIZED   HOMOGENIZED

Controlling Fat Content in Sauces and Dressings

To create your own sauces that are lighter in calories but still rich in flavor and texture, use these tips as your starting point:

» Use something (think overripe fruit, soft cooked vegetables) that can be pureed smooth without an added fat as a base for your sauce or dressing. That something can be slow-cooked onions, fruit purees, or mashed sweet potatoes, for instance.

» Incorporate starch or Mad X-style thickened liquids (see page 81) into sauces and dressings. These will allow you to emulsify with just a touch of fat added for richness and mouthfeel, rather than requiring fat as the foundation of a recipe.

» Learn how to work with cooked eggs, water, and acids, as in our Lemon Sauce for Everything on page 68. You can get Mad Creative from there.

» Learn and apply the Mad Vinaigrette Method to gain freedom from constraints and create a light dressing that's better than anything you can buy in a bottle. See page 82 to get started.

MAD VINAIGRETTE METHOD

BASE + ACID + GUEST STAR +
SALT SOURCE + SWEET SOURCE (IF ANY)
+ FINISHING OIL

What You'll Learn

In this chapter, we'll explore:

» **Building body with plant-based purees.** In one recipe in this chapter (Brown-Buttered Mango Coulis on page 72), we'll use mango, but feel free to experiment with other smooth-pulped fruits or slow-cooked vegetables.

» **Natural gums.** Be not afraid. Thickeners such as xanthan gum can be indispensable tools in the light kitchen (like in Mad X on page 81). While it's used sparingly in this book, it's a wonderfully flexible ingredient that allows the cook to explore a full range of viscosities. And it's soluble in cold or hot water, making it a cinch to use.

» **Classic methods.** Not everything in the chapter is a full-on, science-textbook emulsion either, but that's not the point. The recipes ahead are crafted to be flavor-forward (arguably more nuanced, complex, and satisfying) iterations of sauces from eras long before iPads and immersion blenders.

"NEUTRALQUE"

HANDS-ON: 3 MIN. **TOTAL:** 1 HR. 10 MIN.

There's no easier way to bring yourself to the verge of an anxiety attack than to read the contentious comment threads attached to anything online about barbecue—wait, BBQ, no, barbeque. The word is an evolution of the Spanish barbacoa. No? Maybe not? Okay, then it's a mash-up of the French barbe and queue—suggestive of snout-to-tail cooking—and therefore, nothing is really barbecue unless it involves the whole pig. People, please. I propose a new definition: Barbecue is the universal word for togetherness. This recipe is as neutral as it gets and can be used in any way you'd normally use barbecue sauce. You have to build on top of it to make it yours, your town's, your state's (take it away, Montana!). Feel free to tinker with ratios. Now, stop arguing and cue up.

Food	How Much	Why
white vinegar	2 cups	It's tangy. And straight-forward.
brown sugar	2 cups packed	It's sweet. And adds a little depth that works beautifully against fire-cooked things.
onions	2 cups rough chopped	Adds a savoriness that, I think, stretches the application of this base well beyond meats.
kosher salt	1 teaspoon	To balance. Sweet. Salty. Tangy. These are your flavors to harmonize before you start layering.

Follow These Steps:

>> Combine all ingredients in a medium saucepan.

>> Bring to a boil.

>> Cover and simmer gently for 10 minutes, covered.

>> Carefully remove the lid, and blend with an immersion blender (or put the mixture into a blender with the center lid removed; cover opening with a towel). Puree until as smooth or as chunky as you like. ***This formula is a building block, and it's time to play.***

>> Add a splash or two of water if needed.

>> Return the mixture to the pan, and, over low heat, simmer until the sauce is the texture you desire. Again, you can reduce tightly to a syrupy consistency, or not at all. It can take as long as an hour if you prefer sticky-sweet-syrupy sauces.

>> Now, look at the sauces chart (page 50), look in your cupboard and your fridge, and start playing with herbs, spices, spirits, condiments, what have you.

SERVES 22 (SERVING SIZE: 2 TABLESPOONS)
CALORIES 82; **FAT** 0G (SAT 0G, MONO 0G, POLY 0G); **PROTEIN** 0G; **CARB** 21G; **FIBER** 0G; **CHOL** 0MG; **IRON** 0MG; **SODIUM** 113MG; **CALC** 20MG

MAD FRESH SRIRACHA

HANDS-ON: 5 MIN. **TOTAL:** 40 MIN.

Admittedly, this is not an iteration of the original Sriraja, a sweet, barely viscous chili sauce from the coastal town of Si Racha, Thailand. That sauce is properly pronounced "SEE - RAH - JAH," and, well, this isn't that. This is a knockoff of the knockoff from California. And one wonders why the California company borrowed the term Sriracha, as it's a dramatically different condiment, with a much more Punk Rock flavor profile. This Cooking Light interpretation isn't elegant, smooth, or nuanced either. It's an in-your-face culinary compound that begs to be played until the strings snap. Use it in soups, pasta, burgers, pizzas, wherever you like to add some spice.

Food

Food	How Much	Why
red chiles: Fresno, serrano, and/or jalapeño, in any ratio	2 cups, seeded and split	It's a chile sauce.
garlic cloves	½ cup (about 10 peeled)	We're nodding to both iterations of Sriracha, and they both have garlic. Without the garlic, it's just another hot sauce.
sugar	3 tablespoons	The sweetness is a signature of both Srirachas. Oddly, the U.S. version is actually less sugar-forward.
salt	¾ teaspoon	To balance. This is a sauce for savories.
white vinegar	¼ cup	The acid is what ties all of these flavors together. White vinegar provides straightforward, mid-tone, neutral acid. We want to highlight the chiles. This does that.
hot water	¼ cup	Because a half cup of vinegar would make the sauce too strong.
xanthan gum	⅛ teaspoon	Just enough to keep the sauce from separating in the fridge.

Follow These Steps:

>> In a small saucepan, combine the chiles, garlic cloves, sugar, salt, and white vinegar. Cover and heat gently, as if to steep, on very low heat for 30 minutes.

>> Combine ¼ cup hot water and the xanthan gum in a small bowl, stirring with a whisk. Add the xanthan mixture to the chile mixture. Return to the heat and bring to a boil over high heat, stirring frequently. Boil 1 minute.

>> Transfer the mixture to a blender (removing the center piece of the lid, and covering the opening with a towel—so you don't injure yourself or those anywhere near you) or food processor (using a towel to cover the opening is also likely a wise idea) and blend until silky smooth, adding a touch more hot water if necessary.

>> Store in an airtight container, chilled. It rarely lasts longer than a few days in my fridge, but it will stay fresh-tasting for a week to 10 days as long as you keep it sealed well.

SERVES 8 (SERVING SIZE: 2 TABLESPOONS)
CALORIES 21; **FAT** 0.1G (SAT 0G, MONO 0G, POLY 0.1G); **PROTEIN** 1G; **CARB** 5G; **FIBER** 0G; **CHOL** 0MG; **IRON** 0MG; **SODIUM** 101MG; **CALC** 9MG

VARY THE AMOUNTS OF EACH
TYPE OF CHILE YOU USE TO
CUSTOMIZE THE FLAVOR TO
YOUR LIKING.

MAD SPICY HARISSA

HANDS-ON: 35 MIN. **TOTAL:** 45 MIN.

While this condiment has its origins in Tunisian cuisine, I first discovered harissa when a French chef I worked for pulled a tin tube of it out of his pocket and added it to a saffron mayonnaise that we slathered on charred toasts for bouillabaisse. In those days, chefs still had secrets, so I didn't dare ask. But I did my research, and noted that harissa could be found all over North Africa, where it's used liberally and flexibly. This version is fantastic on everything from grocery-store roasted chicken to some simply grilled steaks. Stir it into stews. Use it as a base for a vinaigrette. This is another versatile condiment in your repertoire. Put it next to your Sriracha in the fridge.

THIS IS A CHILE PASTE MADE OF POUNDED OR CHOPPED FRESH RED CAYENNE CHILES FLAVORED WITH SALT, A LITTLE SUGAR, AND VINEGAR. IT DOESN'T CONTAIN GARLIC OR SPICES, SO ITS TASTE IS PURE HOT CHILE ESSENCE.

Food	How Much	Why
red Fresno chiles	8	There is a very harmonious blend of herbs and spices that follow. Anything bolder than a Fresno would overpower.
red bell pepper	1	This provides body and sweetness.
onion	2 (½-inch) slices	This is a departure from super-authentic recipes. The charred onion adds some welcome smokiness and makes the finished dish less like a paste—and more like a relish.
olive oil	½ cup, divided	When in North Africa...
garlic cloves	12 to 24	24 may seem like a lot, but you'll be pan-toasting the garlic to sweet perfection. Use it all.
cumin seeds	1 tablespoon	Commonly used in harissa.
coriander seeds	½ tablespoon	The "lead" spice in Tunisian cuisine, with a majority role in the Tunisian spice blend, tabil.
kosher salt	½ teaspoon	Salt has this way of tying flavors together. Even though you're likely to add it to salted foods, this recipe needs the salt.
fresh mint	6 leaves	Fresh mint adds a welcome, almost sweet perfume.
sambal oelek (ground fresh chile paste)	1 tablespoon	This is a quick and easy way to regulate the spiciness of the harissa. Use the California-made stuff, as it's chile-forward. There's also some vinegar in there.
fresh lemon juice	1 tablespoon	It's the Mediterranean. Where there's olive oil, lemon usually follows.

MAD SPICY HARISSA

8 red Fresno chiles

1 red bell pepper

2 (½-inch) slices onion

½ cup olive oil, divided

12 to 24 garlic cloves

1 Tbsp. cumin seeds

½ Tbsp. coriander seeds

½ tsp. kosher salt

6 fresh mint leaves

1 Tbsp. sambal oelek
(ground fresh chile paste)

1 Tbsp. fresh lemon juice

Follow These Steps:

➤➤ Set up a kitchen blender. Grab a small sauté pan.

➤➤ Ready a grill pan or grill. *The final product will be even more incredible if you cook outdoors and use good quality charcoal.* Preheat to medium.

CHAR YOUR PEPPERS

➤➤ In a medium bowl, toss the chiles, the red bell pepper, and the onion slices in 2 tablespoons of olive oil. Coat evenly.

➤➤ Grill the chiles, the bell pepper, and the onions over medium heat. We're not fully charring here, as you would for roasted peppers, but evenly, deliberately wilting. The pepper and the onions should have desirable char, of course, but should look "ready to eat" when they're cooked tender. Cook the Fresno chiles and onions 10 minutes, turning occasionally. Grill the bell pepper 15 minutes, turning occasionally.

➤➤ Set the grilled items aside to cool on a platter.

TOSS YOUR AROMATICS

➤➤ Now, fire up the sauté pan to just past medium-low. The pan should be too hot to touch, but not raging.

➤➤ Add 1 tablespoon of olive oil. Swirl. Add the garlic cloves. Toss.

➤➤ Gently cook the garlic cloves, stirring from time to time, until they are tender to the tooth, about 15 minutes. *If you are a garlic aficionado, use the full 24 cloves in the recipe, as you'll find yourself snacking.*

➤➤ When the garlic is tender, set aside in a small bowl.

➤➤ Now, in the same pan used to cook the garlic, add the cumin and the coriander. Toast over medium heat until the aroma of the spices fills the room, about 2 minutes.

➤➤ Your chiles and bell pepper should be sufficiently cooled by now. Using a paring knife, remove their tops. Seed the bell pepper according to the how-to photos on page 63, but not the chiles.

GET YOUR BLENDER READY

➤➤ Throw the chiles and pepper into the blender. Don't turn it on yet. The garlic, too.

➤➤ Now add the spice mixture, salt, mint, sambal oelek, and lemon juice to the blender.

➤➤ Cover the blender, and progressively increase the speed to high.

➤➤ If the ingredients don't liquefy fully, add a splash or two of water to help the process along.

FINISH WITH SOME OLIVE OIL

>> When the ingredients are fully liquefied, and with the blade speed of the blender reduced to moderate, remove the lid of the blender, and slowly drizzle in 5 table-spoons of olive oil. *The sauce will emulsify, becoming almost creamy, but not quite.*

>> Store in an airtight container, refrigerated. This version is pretty perishable, so use it within a week.

SERVES 32 (SERVING SIZE: 1 TABLESPOON)
CALORIES 40; **FAT** 3.5G (SAT 0.5G, MONO 2.5G, POLY 0.4G); **PROTEIN** 0G; **CARB** 2G; **FIBER** 0G; **CHOL** 0MG; **IRON** 0MG; **SODIUM** 41MG; **CALC** 7MG

STEP BY STEP: Peeling and Seeding Bell Peppers

1) Using a paring knife, cut around the stem of the pepper.

2) Remove the stem. Most of the seeds should come with it.

3) Cut off the bottom of the pepper, and then cut the pepper in half.

4) Remove the membranes and any seeds that still remain.

5) Carefully remove the skins.

HABANERO-ORANGE MIGNONETTE

HANDS-ON: 10 MIN. **TOTAL:** 30 MIN.

History connects Sauce Mignonette firmly to the peppercorn. Mignonette pepper, broadly speaking, is the good stuff, typically a blend of (ground, cracked, or otherwise) peppercorn varieties. Relative to peppercorns, though, mignonette is an archaic term. If you're talking oysters, though, the word has come to mean "thin, clear, acidic liquid, to which is added little bits of something that pickles quickly, and something spicy." It's usually a very, very simple sauce of (typically) shallot, just-beyond-cracked pepper, and some kind of vinegar. Here, we take creative license, inspired by flavors of the Yucatán.

Food	How Much	Why
fresh orange juice	½ cup	In the Yucatán, they use a native Sour Orange. Don't use the bottled stuff, either. Buy an orange or two...
white vinegar	½ cup	...and add this.
kosher salt	⅛ teaspoon	Acid + salt + the rich-tasting recipient of this sauce = delicious.
dried oregano	⅛ teaspoon	We'd find this in our Mexican pantry.
freshly ground black pepper	¼ teaspoon	To honor the origins of the sauce.
red onion	¼ cup finely diced	Shallot is typically used in mignonette sauce. Red onion is a little more assertive here.
habanero chile	1½ tablespoons seeded and minced	Found in the Yucatán, and marries beautifully with orange.

Follow These Steps:

≫ In a small bowl, combine the orange juice, the white vinegar, the salt, the dried oregano (rubbed finely with the heel of one hand into the palm of the other), and the black pepper.

≫ Add the red onion and let steep.

≫ Put your smallest sauté pan on the stove. Crank it to high. Let it get hot for about a minute. Now, turn it off.

≫ Have a soup spoon handy, and then put the chile into the pan. *Keep your face away. Even this small amount can take your breath away.*

≫ Let the chile wilt for 1 minute while stirring. *You might get some char. That's good.*

≫ Spoon the chile into the vinegar mixture. Stir, and let macerate at room temperature for 15 minutes before serving.

SERVES 12 (SERVING SIZE: 2 TABLESPOONS)
CALORIES 7; **FAT** 0G (SAT 0G, MONO 0G, POLY 0G); **PROTEIN** 0G;
CARB 2G; **FIBER** 0G; **CHOL** 0MG; **IRON** 0MG; **SODIUM** 25MG; **CALC** 3MG

GARLIC CREAM

HANDS-ON: 5 MIN. **TOTAL:** 35 MIN.

Purees have earned their place in professional kitchens for a number of reasons. First, if made well, they add a silken luxuriousness to a dish. Secondly, purees are malleable; they can be used to highlight the simple elegance of a chosen ingredient—or, conversely, they can be folded into things as a finish of sorts. There's something about a well-made puree that suggests you're the type of cook to revere an ingredient enough to painstakingly transform it into something that can be experienced with every bite of a composed dish. That's respect.

Food	How Much	Why
garlic cloves	1 cup (about 20 cloves, peeled)	Garlic lends itself to almost all savory applications, softens beautifully, and mellows when cooked.
kosher salt	½ teaspoon	
white pepper	⅛ teaspoon	Playing old-school. Trying not to interfere with the color of your three-Michelin-star puree.
chicken broth	1½ cups	It's neutral enough so that you can use this with everything from fish to venison.
half and half	½ cup	Softens and mellows the flavor. Contributes to silken texture.

Follow These Steps:

>> Combine all ingredients in a small saucepan and simmer over medium heat for about 30 minutes, or until the liquid level is reduced to ½ cup (meeting the level of the garlic cloves).

>> Allow to cool slightly. Drain and reserve poaching liquid.

>> In a mini food processor, add the garlic cloves and pulse until smooth. *Slowly drizzle in the reserved poaching liquid while the blade is running until the mixture resembles homemade mayonnaise.*

>> Serve warm under something like Port-Stained Beef Medallions (page 156 or any simply pan-roasted meat using the illustrations below as inspiration.

SERVES 4 (SERVING SIZE: 3 TABLESPOONS)
CALORIES 48; **FAT** 1.8G (SAT 1.1G, MONO 0.5G, POLY 0.1G); **PROTEIN** 2G; **CARB** 7G; **FIBER** 0G; **CHOL** 6MG; **IRON** 0MG; **SODIUM** 236MG; **CALC** 47MG

A SPOON DRAG

THE BRUSH STROKE

THE DRAW-WITH-THE-SQUEEZEBOTTLE LOOK

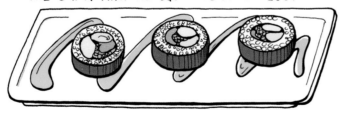

THE UNDERLINER

LEMON SAUCE FOR EVERYTHING

HANDS-ON: 20 MIN. **TOTAL:** 20 MIN.

Okay, it's true: This is essentially the classic Greek lemon-egg soup, avgolemono. Every time I encountered a bowl of this creamy, rich, perfectly balanced soup, I thought to myself, "This is a sauce." And then I remembered my very first culinary instructor telling us that the only difference between a sauce and a soup was presentation. I agree, and this is a sauce. Put it on everything.

Food	How Much	Why
unsalted chicken stock	2 cups	Stock picks up natural gelatin from the bones of the chicken and provides a tad more body than broth.
large eggs	3	Whole eggs are essential to the viscosity of the sauce.
lemon zest	2 tablespoons grated	Aroma.
fresh lemon juice	2½ tablespoons	Acidity and brightness.
kosher salt	½ teaspoon	Requirement, particularly against acid.
olive oil	1 tablespoon	To enrich and provide a silkier mouth feel.

Follow These Steps:

❯❯ Heat the chicken stock over medium-high heat in a heavy, medium saucepan to 180° or until tiny bubbles form around the edge. Do not boil.

❯❯ Combine the eggs, lemon zest, lemon juice, and salt in a medium bowl. Whisk until the eggs are frothy and lighter in color. (Alternatively, you can use a blender.)

❯❯ Ladle about a cup of the hot chicken stock into the egg mixture ¼ cup at a time, while stirring constantly (but not too vigorously) with a whisk.

❯❯ Lower the heat on the remaining chicken stock to as low as possible. Wait for 2 minutes, and then add the egg, lemon, and stock mixture back to the pot, stirring to combine.

❯❯ Warm the sauce gently, until it reaches 180° and coats a spoon. Turn off the heat.

❯❯ Whisk in the olive oil to finish.

❯❯ Serve warm.

SERVES 10 (SERVING SIZE: ¼ CUP)
CALORIES 39; **FAT** 2.8G (SAT 0.7G, MONO 1.5G, POLY 0.4G); **PROTEIN** 3G; **CARB** 1G; **FIBER** 0G; **CHOL** 56MG; **IRON** 0MG; **SODIUM** 169MG; **CALC** 10MG

EVERYDAISE

HANDS ON: 20 MIN. **TOTAL:** 20 MIN.

Hollandaise is glorious. The classic version's volume of fat and suggested holding temperature, however, make it questionable for our everyday eating. Here, we've rearranged proportions while maintaining the essence of the original: Eggy. Buttery. Slightly acidic. Slight tinge of heat. Perfect salt balance. And this version's way more stable than the original. It can be saved and reheated, too. Bonus.

Food	How Much	Why
butter	3 tablespoons	This provides the round richness indicative of a hollandaise-type sauce.
large eggs	3	This serves as the structure.
fresh lemon juice	3 tablespoons	Where there is fat, there should be acid. Counter-balance. Brightness.
kosher salt	½ teaspoon	To complete the triumvi-rate of key flavor ingredi-ents, making this a truly glorious sauce.
hot water	¾ cup	Lightens up the egg froth.
ground red pepper	⅛ teaspoon	For a little tickling heat.

Follow These Steps:

➤ Melt the butter however you find most convenient. Hold it warm.

➤ Fill a small saucepan ¾ full with water. Bring to a steady simmer.

➤ In a stainless steel bowl, whisk the eggs together with the lemon juice and salt.

➤ Place the bowl over the simmering water (the bowl shouldn't touch the water) to make a double boiler, and *whisk constantly, adding ¾ cup of hot water a few tablespoons at a time, until the eggs have thickened into a ribbony, lemon-yellow, creamy, uniform mixture.*

➤ Turn off the heat and slowly whisk in the butter, adding it a tablespoonful at a time.

➤ Add the red pepper.

➤ Serve warm.

SERVES 18 (SERVING SIZE: 2 TABLESPOONS)
CALORIES 44; **FAT** 4.1G (SAT 2.2G, MONO 1.2G, POLY 0.4G); **PROTEIN** 2G; **CARB** 0G; **FIBER** 0G; **CHOL** 54MG; **IRON** 0MG; **SODIUM** 123MG; **CALC** 8MG

BROWN-BUTTERED MANGO COULIS

HANDS-ON: 6 MIN. **TOTAL:** 6 MIN.

This is a technique more than it is a recipe. Brown butter pairs gloriously with the bright-sweet tang of a fresh mango. If you're using fresh fruit, try not to use super-fibrous, stringy mangoes, as they'll adversely affect the outcome. Frozen pulp from Latin American markets (often sold in plastic pouches) is typically outstanding and affordable. This coulis is good with all things grilled.

Food	How Much	Why
fresh or frozen mango pulp	1¼ cups	Mangoes have incredible body and fine texture, making them an ideal choice for a puree-based sauce.
fresh lemon juice	2 tablespoons	To brighten, particularly if the mangoes are quite sweet and ripe.
kosher salt	⅛ teaspoon	To offset the sweetness and tilt the sauce toward the savory.
parsley sprigs	2 sprigs	To add a grassy note and to "warm" the color a bit.
butter	1 tablespoon	For richness, an intro to the Maillard reaction and "nuttiness" from the browned butter solids.

A HEAT-INDUCED BROWNING. IT'S IMPORTANT TO NOTE THAT IT'S NOT CARAMELIZATION, THOUGH BOTH ARE A FORM OF SO-CALLED "NON-ENZYMATIC BROWNING."

Follow These Steps:

» Set up your blender or mini food processor.

» Fire up a small sauté pan. Medium heat.

» Add the mango pulp to the blender.

» Throw in the lemon juice, the salt, and the parsley.

» Blend on high speed until the mixture is fully liquefied. Add a tablespoon or two of water if the mango pulp is resistant to being liquefied. *Water always wins against pulp. Every time.*

» Turn off the blender for a moment. *Say, "Please hold."*

» Slip the butter into the sauté pan. Swirl it around until the solids begin to brown. You'll smell it before you see it, so be careful not to burn. And remember, the pan is not glued to the burner. You can pull the pan off the heat to slow the cooking, too.

» Now, go back to the covered blender and fire it up progressively to high speed. You can now safely remove the lid, and slowly drizzle the butter into the coulis while the blade is running. *You'll see an almost mayonnaise-y sheen to the sauce. It's emulsified. Delicious. And done.*

SERVES 5 (SERVING SIZE: ABOUT 3 TABLESPOONS)
CALORIES 47; FAT 2.5G (SAT 1.5G, MONO 0.7G, POLY 0.1G); PROTEIN 0G; CARB 7G; FIBER 1G; CHOL 6MG; IRON 0MG; SODIUM 79MG; CALC 6MG

CARROT-GINGER CONSOMMÉ

HANDS-ON: 15 MIN. **TOTAL:** 55 MIN.

*Yes, it's true. Consommé is a soup. It's also a broth, which can be used as a sauce.
And I want you to think of light, flavorful broths as sauces, particularly where you're
working with moist-heat cooking techniques like steaming. Allowing yourself to think
beyond standard terms and expectations liberates you from "the rules." This recipe
is an encouragement to deeply watch the pot. It does boil. And clarify. And inspire.*

Food	How Much	Why
fresh carrot juice	3 cups	It separates when boiled, breaking into vibrant orange solids and a muted orange, almost clear broth.
chicken stock	2 cups	Because carrot alone would be cloying.
rice vinegar	2 tablespoons	For contrast against the sweetness of carrots.
fresh gingerroot	2 tablespoons very fine julienne	Ginger decided that it loved carrots long ago. It's not right to keep them apart.
27-Hour Chicken Legs (page 298) **or rotisserie chicken**	1½ cups shredded meat	Shredding is not necessary, just an option. Warm larger pieces through for 5 minutes longer than instructed if you don't shred.
Thai chile	2, minced	Where there is sweet and sour, hot is welcome.
enoki mushrooms	1 (3.5-ounce) package	They're meaty. They're cute.
fresh chives	2 tablespoons snipped as thinly as possible	Makes the dish decidedly savory. When used as a finish, the perfume of chives is on the front end of the olfactory experience. It says, "I am a meal—here to satisfy your soul."

Follow These Steps:

» Bring carrot juice to a boil in a medium saucepan over high heat. Boil 3 minutes. *The carrot solids will "break" away from the clearer liquid during boiling.*

» Turn off the heat and let stand 5 minutes, allowing the carrot solids to settle to the bottom of the pot. Ladle off the clear liquid. Strain through a double layer of cheesecloth. Discard the solids.

» Return the strained carrot juice to the pan. Add the stock, the rice vinegar, and the ginger.

» Bring to a simmer over medium-high heat; reduce the heat and simmer for 30 minutes.

» Add the chicken and the chile. Reduce the heat to low and steep for 5 minutes more.

» Serve, garnished with enoki mushrooms and chives.

SERVES 6 (SERVING SIZE: ¾ CUP)
CALORIES 152; **FAT** 2.9G (SAT 0.7G, MONO 1G, POLY 0.7G); **PROTEIN** 14G; **CARB** 18G; **FIBER** 2G; **CHOL** 37MG; **IRON** 1MG; **SODIUM** 275MG; **CALC** 42MG

MINT AND SUMAC "SALSA"
(FOR KEBABS AND SUCH)

HANDS-ON: 10 MIN. **TOTAL:** 10 MIN.

It was late. A group of fellow chefs and I had just finished celebrating after a barbecue cook-off in Austin, Texas. Walking back to my hotel, I stumbled across a kebab truck in a parking lot. And they had the most incredible Adana-style kebabs. This is a conjuring-up of what topped those kebabs, courtesy of my olfactory and gustatory cortices. You have those, too. Pack your life with culinary reference points, and you'll be able to recreate and re-interpret life's great-tasting moments.

Food	How Much	Why
fresh flat-leaf parsley	¼ cup quick chiffonade	First, parsley is quite common in Turkish fare. It provides the textural backbone of this salsa—as it is in the Italian salsa verde.
fresh mint	2 tablespoons quick chiffonade	A must. It was in there, and it was fresh. When testing, we really refined the proportion of mint and parsley to balance.
ground sumac	½ teaspoon	It's tangy while being earthy. There's nothing quite like it. If you can't find it, use about a tablespoon of freshly squeezed lemon juice, though it won't be comparable.
marash pepper	¼ teaspoon	With mellow heat and an almost raisin-y sweetness, this is the right choice against tangy sumac.
olive oil	¼ cup	Ground meat kebabs have a somewhat matte exterior finish. The olive oil slicks the surface. That's satisfying.
raisin vinegar	1 tablespoon	Gentle acidity. A hint of fruit. Alternatively, mimic this by warming some cider vinegar with an equal volume of raisins in the microwave. Mash the raisins with a fork. Strain. Use the vinegar.
kosher salt	1/16 teaspoon	To bite back against any sweetness.

Follow These Steps:

❯❯ Combine the parsley, the mint, the sumac, and the marash pepper in a small bowl with the olive oil. Toss.

❯❯ Just prior to serving, add the raisin vinegar and fold. *If you add it too early, it will discolor the herbs and make the sumac look muddy.*

❯❯ Season with salt, and serve with Adana-Inspired Turkey-Lamb Kebabs (page 327) or simply grilled anything.

SERVES 4 (SERVING SIZE: 1½ TABLESPOONS)
CALORIES 123; **FAT** 13.5G (SAT 1.9G, MONO 9.9G, POLY 1.4G); **PROTEIN** 0G; **CARB** 1G; **FIBER** 0G; **CHOL** 0MG; **IRON** 0MG; **SODIUM** 40MG; **CALC** 8MG

SUMAC CAN BE FOUND AT MOST
MIDDLE EASTERN OR PERSIAN
FOOD MARKETS.

MARIA'S CILANTRO CEBOLLAS

HANDS-ON: 15 MIN. **TOTAL:** 25 MIN.

These onions were a mainstay of family meals at a little catering company I worked at in New York. It was the best little catering company a young chef could ever find: uncompromising owners, an open-minded clientele, and a hyper-diverse staff—nurtured by Maria. Every day, we'd all eat lunch together, and most days, Maria would make these onions. Liquid? No. "Saucy?" Yes. To enliven virtually anything off the grill, put these on the table.

Food	How Much	Why
sweet onion	1 large (about a 1 pound), thinly sliced	If you have a v-slicer, use it. Slice along, not against, the grain, as the onions will hold up a little crisper.
kosher salt	⅛ teaspoon	Just enough to assist the wilting and to sense its presence.
fresh Key (or Mexican) lime juice	4 tablespoons (about 2 limes)	There's a boldness to those little limes, and a perfume that the big Persian limes just don't offer.
fresh cilantro	2 tablespoons chopped	While there is a camp of those who dislike cilantro, none of them works with Maria.

Follow These Steps:

>> Shave the onion very thinly, following the curvature of the onion and preserving the integrity of the onion's cell wall structure. It matters.

>> *Throw in the salt. Toss. Toss again. One more time. Good.*

>> Now, add the lime juice. Tumble the onion a couple of times.

>> Let the onion mixture sit for 10 minutes at room temperature.

>> Right before serving, add the cilantro. Not a second sooner.

>> Serve atop Cocoa-Crusted New York Strip (page 188), grilled meats, hearty roasts, or...pretty much anything in the universe. *Thank Maria. She'll feel good inside.*

SERVES 8 (SERVING SIZE: ABOUT ⅓ CUP)
CALORIES 9; **FAT** 0 (SAT 0G, MONO 0G, POLY 0G); **PROTEIN** 0G; **CARB** 2G; **FIBER** 0G; **CHOL** 0MG; **IRON** 0MG; **SODIUM** 37MG; **CALC** 5MG

CILANTRO IS A POLARIZING HERB. MOST LIKE IT, BUT SOME LOATHE IT. THAT'S LIKELY BECAUSE OF SO-CALLED "SOAPY" FLAVORS FROM AN UNSATURATED ALDEHYDE CALLED TRANS-2-DECENAL.

THE AMOUNT OF XANTHAN GUM CAN BE ALTERED. TYPICALLY, YOU WOULDN'T PUT MUCH MORE THAN 0.5% BY WEIGHT IN ANY RECIPE—SO NO MORE THAN ABOUT 3/4 TEASPOON IN THE AMOUNT OF LIQUID.

MAD X

HANDS-ON: 10 MIN. **TOTAL:** 10 MIN.

Xanthan gum was discovered by Allene Rosalind Jeanes, an influential (WWII-era) U.S. government chemist. It's a polysaccharide that forms as a by-product of bacterial fermentation of sugars. It's not nearly as "chemical-y" as it sounds, however, and can be found in non-GMO form at natural foods markets. While it has become a star in the molecular gastronomy movement and is a key ingredient in gluten-free baked goods, there's little modern about it at all. It's been in our food chain since the late sixties and is found in everything from ice cream to bottled salad dressings—we'll use it in dressings, too. Break out your bell-bottoms.

Food	How Much	Why
fat-free, lower-sodium chicken broth or vegetable broth	2 cups	So your slurry will carry some flavor. Feel free, however, to use all water.
xanthan gum or cornstarch	¼ teaspoon	To thicken the liquid.
very warm water (120° to 130°)	¼ cup	To pre-hydrate the gum. Once you get the hang of using xanthan, however, you can just whisk it directly into liquids, so long as you sprinkle lightly and slowly.

Follow These Steps:

›› Put the broth in a small saucepan. Heat on medium-high and bring to a full, though not out-of-control, boil.

›› Combine the xanthan gum and warm water (or cornstarch and warm water). *Be particularly mindful when using the xanthan; use a fork and keep the water moving vigorously while slowly sprinkling in the gum.*

›› Pour the gum mixture into the boiling liquid. Reduce heat to medium and cook for 1 minute. Pour into a heatproof container; cover and reserve for use in various emulsified preparations throughout the book. It'll last for a few days, well refrigerated.

SERVES 9 (SERVING SIZE: ¼ CUP)
CALORIES 3; **FAT** 0.1G (SAT 0G, MONO 0G, POLY 0G); **PROTEIN** 0G; **CARB** 0G; **FIBER** 0G; **CHOL** 1MG; **IRON** 0MG; **SODIUM** 213MG; **CALC** 0MG

MAD DELICIOUS VINAIGRETTE

HANDS-ON: 6 MIN. **TOTAL:** 6 MIN.

Backing off on the oil not only helps control calories, it takes some of the oily "weight" off tender salad greens. Once you get the gist of this recipe, you can modify and iterate like mad. Don't just use this on salads, though. This vinaigrette can be warmed lightly and served with fish or over grilled chicken. Wherever you need a sauce on the fly, reach for this method.

Food	How Much	Why
Mad X (*page 81*)	½ cup	This is a viscous liquid, allowing us to use far less oil than in a classic vinaigrette.
red wine vinegar	½ cup	Old-school red wine vinegar is bright and just neutral enough to allow herbs and mustards to pop. Know when to use the "good" stuff.
fresh thyme leaves	1 teaspoon	It's an addiction, really. Thyme is to savory dishes as 1999 is to New Year's Eve playlists. Continue.
Dijon mustard	1 teaspoon	Mustard is an incredible emulsifier. Plus, it's delicious.
sugar	½ teaspoon	For balance.
kosher salt	⅛ teaspoon	Elevates and accentuates.
garlic cloves	2, grated	Raw garlic provides glorious pungency and character.
walnut oil	2 tablespoons	The aroma is downright intoxicating. The flavor: euphoric.

Follow These Steps:

≫ In a chilled mixing bowl, combine Mad X and red wine vinegar. Whisk to incorporate into a uniform liquid.

≫ Add the thyme leaves, the Dijon mustard, the sugar, the salt, and the garlic. Whisk.

≫ *Slowly drizzle the walnut oil into the vinaigrette while steadily (but not madly) whisking.*

≫ Chill, covered, until ready for use. It'll hold up for at least a week in an airtight container, but the garlic's intensity will taper with time.

SERVES 18 (SERVING SIZE: ABOUT 1 TABLESPOON)
CALORIES 16; **FAT** 1.5 (SAT 0.1G, MONO 0.3G, POLY 1G); **PROTEIN** 0G; **CARB** 0G; **FIBER** 0G; **CHOL** 0MG; **IRON** 0MG; **SODIUM** 44MG; **CALC** 1MG

SPLURGE ON A GOOD OIL (LIKE THE WALNUT OIL HERE) WITH GREENS. LET THE OIL BRING THE FLAVOR & FINISH WITH SALT.

SPLURGE ON A GOOD VINEGAR WHEN THE VINAIGRETTE IS THE FOCAL POINT OF THE DISH—SAY, AS A SAUCE FOR ROAST CHICKEN.

SERVE WITH GRILLED SNAPPER,
SAUTÉED SHRIMP, OR SLOW-
ROASTED LAMB.

WARM TOMATO VINAIGRETTE

HANDS-ON: 5 MIN. **TOTAL:** 20 MIN.

Chefs didn't embrace vegetable puree–based sauces simply because they're light, but because they're quick, easy, and malleable. Cooked purees like carrot, garlic, onion, fennel, and parsnip can be taken in myriad directions by changing up fat and acid choices, and by finishing with various accents. For instance, carrot puree pairs with walnut oil, sherry vinegar, and tarragon as it does with rice vinegar, ginger, and a grapeseed/sesame oil blend. The point of this recipe is to help you understand the functional building blocks of this vinaigrette: Oil means virtually any culinary oil. For vinegar, any pleasantly acidic liquid will do. For the puree, just make sure it's not fibrous or overly "seedy," and you're good to play. Here, we build on the Charred Tomato Passata recipe you learned in Chapter 2.

Food	How Much	Why
garlic cloves	6	These vinaigrettes aren't really designed to dress salads and greens as they are meant to be bona fide sauces for center-of-the-plate items. Garlic gives body and creaminess when cooked—helping to keep the emulsion semi-stable.
water	¾ cup	For boiling the garlic.
kosher salt	½ teaspoon	Salt + fresh tomatoes = culinary bliss.
freshly ground black pepper	¼ teaspoon	To keep this simple and straightforward.
Charred Tomato Passata *(page 30)*	1 cup	You'll have it on hand.
sherry vinegar	¼ cup	It's the all-purpose vinegar of finer kitchens.
olive oil	3 tablespoons	Olive oil is no stranger to tomatoes. Feel free to go bold here.

Follow These Steps:

》 Place the garlic and ¾ cup water in a small saucepan. Cover and bring to a boil.

》 Reduce the heat to medium-low and simmer until the garlic is tender, about 15 minutes. Keep the lid around, as *you don't want to evaporate off all of the water. You're looking to boil the garlic until it's fork-tender.*

》 Combine the garlic, the water, and the next 4 ingredients in a blender. Remove center piece of blender lid (to allow steam to escape); secure blender lid on blender. Keep a clean towel over opening in blender lid while firing it up.

》 Once it's running, remove the towel, and slowly drizzle in the olive oil, allowing it to emulsify into the vinaigrette.

》 Serving ideas: Grilled snapper (add one roasted jalapeño, a squeeze of lime, and a handful of cilantro), sautéed shrimp (exchange a tablespoon of olive oil with one of melted butter and throw in a dozen or so leaves of basil), slow-roasted lamb (add juice of half a lemon and ½ teaspoon dry-pan-toasted cumin).

SERVES 10 (SERVING SIZE: 2 TABLESPOONS)
CALORIES 55; **FAT** 4.8G (SAT 0.7G, MONO 3.5G, POLY 0.4G); **PROTEIN** 0G; **CARB** 4G; **FIBER** 0G; **CHOL** 0MG; **IRON** 1MG; **SODIUM** 150MG; **CALC** 7MG

MAD DELICIOUS AIOLI

HANDS-ON: 12 MIN. **TOTAL:** 12 MIN.

Aioli, a garlic mayonnaise found in various iterations and spellings from Provence to Catalonia to California and beyond, is typically packed with olive oil and often built on a paste of egg yolks and mashed garlic. While no doubt delicious, it can be downright heavy. Here, it's built on a foundation of mashed avocado, which ends up surprisingly neutral when layered with blanched garlic (you can use raw if you like it punchy) and a bold olive oil. The absence of egg yolks gives this version a more elegant, sleek presence. You'll likely find yourself addicted to this recipe, so feel free to double the volume. It scales well.

Food	How Much	Why
water	2 cups plus 3 tablespoons, divided	To blanch the garlic and to thin the viscosity of the avocado a bit.
garlic cloves	5, peeled	It's a garlic mayonnaise. Omit it and then call it something else.
Mad X (page 81)	⅓ cup	So you can stabilize the emulsion. It'll keep for up to a week in the fridge.
ripe peeled avocado	½	It has to be ripe. This is the body of the sauce. If it's the slightest bit firm, the whole thing won't work. I promise.
kosher salt	¼ teaspoon	So you can eat it from the spoon.
olive oil, a strong one	¼ cup	To strong-arm the avocado and provide the necessary flavor profile for the sauce.

Follow These Steps:

›› Bring 2 cups water to a boil in a small saucepan. Add garlic; cook 1 minute. Remove garlic; cool. Discard cooking liquid. *Blanching the garlic takes out some of the bite, and allows for a much more versatile sauce. It'll be more even in texture, too.*

›› In a mini food processor (a must have, or you'll need to scale up the recipe to fit your device), combine the 3 tablespoons water, garlic, Mad X, avocado, and salt.

›› Process on high speed, scraping down the sides periodically, until the mixture is uniform and smooth.

›› Before adding the olive oil, be sure that the mixture is scraped down fully and that the mixture is sufficiently mounded near the center of the blade to catch.

›› While the blade is running, drizzle in the olive oil until the mixture is fully uniform, with no oil pockets visible.

›› Transfer to a small plastic or glass container, cover, and refrigerate until ready to use.

SERVES 8 (SERVING SIZE: 2 TABLESPOONS)
CALORIES 83; **FAT** 8.9G (SAT 1.3G, MONO 6.2G, POLY 1.2G); **PROTEIN** 0G; **CARB** 2G; **FIBER** 1G; **CHOL** 0MG; **IRON** 0MG; **SODIUM** 109MG; **CALC** 5MG

IF YOU PREFER RAW GARLIC, SKIP STEP 1 & GRATE THE GARLIC TO A FINE PASTE USING A RASP GRATER.

MAD GARLICKY CAESAR DRESSING

HANDS-ON: 5 MIN. **TOTAL:** 5 MIN.

*The elegant, almost slippery texture of the Mad Delicious Aioli becomes romaine-friendly
perfection with more garlic and fresh lemon. It's gentler on greens, too, so now you can
take your cravings for Caesar to more tender greens, like Bibb or baby arugula,
without wilting them to mulch. And don't restrain this edition. Smear a tablespoon on
a plate under sliced grilled meats, and then revel in the cheers of a meal well made.*

Food	How Much	Why
Mad Delicious Aioli *(page 86)*	½ cup	Caesar is garlicky. And creamy. So is this aioli. Build on that.
fresh Parmesan	2 tablespoons grated (¼ ounce)	To add nuttiness, sharpness, and a bit of saltiness.
warm water (100° to 110°)	2 tablespoons	To thin the mixture a bit, so it's not mayonnaise-y.
garlic cloves	2, finely grated	A must. Pungency and bite against slightly bitter greens is sensory perfection.
fresh lemon juice	about 1 tablespoon	To brighten and enliven all flavors. There's enough lemon in there for it to stand out, too.
freshly ground black pepper	¼ teaspoon	Freshly ground offers an oily, spiced perfume.
kosher salt	⅛ teaspoon	To punch up the sodium content to a perfect point.

Follow These Steps:

≫ In a chilled mixing bowl, combine the aioli, the Parmesan, 2
tablespoons of warm water, and the garlic, using a rubber spatula
or favorite wooden spoon. It's Caesar. Go old school.

≫ Add the lemon juice progressively, not all at once. (Depending
on the source and the season, lemons not only differ in size and
the amount of juice inside, but also intensity.) Taste progressively,
too. *When you have a perfect balance of nutty Parmesan, pungent garlic, acid, and an almost-there salt level, it's right. And,
it's up to you. Trust yourself.*

≫ Season with pepper and salt. Stir.

≫ Chill, covered, until ready to serve.

SERVES 6 (SERVING SIZE: 2 TABLESPOONS)
CALORIES 65; **FAT** 6.4G (SAT 1G, MONO 4.3G, POLY 0.9G); **PROTEIN** 1G;
CARB 2G; **FIBER** 1G; **CHOL** 2MG; **IRON** 0MG; **SODIUM** 138MG; **CALC** 24MG

HOT LIQUIDS

Steeping, poaching, simmering, and boiling

First, let's uncomplicate this chapter. We're talking about water. Regardless of the cooking liquid employed, water dominates the composition of many of the ingredients in this chapter (and in much of what we eat as well). Carrots: 87% water. Celery: 94% water. Onions: nearly 90% water. Beer: well, you get the point. In this chapter, we delve into some everyday "water-based" culinary techniques and explore how to build a pleasantly complex dish by looking at what I call the Four Fs.

Form

Okay, so we're leveraging a cooking liquid—something like chicken broth, milk, wine, or water—to gently cook a variety of foods. But what's the *form* of the finished dish? This chapter explores four forms:

>> **Something softened.** That is to say, we're going to apply constant heat to soften the structure of a food, like, say, a tomato. Then we'll blend it (carefully) to create a puree.

>> **Something hydrated,** such as rice, polenta, or pasta, where hot liquid makes starches swell and gelatinize.

>> **Something exchanged.** A broth (as in the Mad Basic Chicken Soup on page 94), where things such as onion and celery retain some of their natural flavor but also "melt" into the parent liquid, making the broth as delicious as the solid morsels within.

>> **Something removed.** These are things you eat without the cooking liquid, like the Spice-Simmered Pork "Bánh-Mì-Style" Salad (page 107) or the Red Curry Boiled Peanuts (page 125). You can be either a) pretty playful, where you make the cooking liquid something crazy-intense (where you wouldn't want to consume the liquid on its own), or b) pretty straightforward, like salted water. The liquid is there primarily, though, to act as a conductor of heat, and you, with your fancy wooden spoon, bring convection into the mix, by stirring and helping the heat distribute more evenly.

REMEMBER, THEY'RE MOSTLY WATER, & SOME OF THE SUGARS & MINERALS FIND THEIR WAY INTO THE BROTH (WHETHER THEY'RE TEMPORARILY SUSPENDED – OR FULLY DISSOLVED), & THESE THINGS IMPACT FLAVOR.

Foundation

Now, on to the foundation of the recipe, or, more simply, the cooking liquid, which is usually water, vegetable and fruit juices, milk, stock, broth, or a combination. We play with acid and heat to "crack" milk into curds and whey with the handcrafted Buttermilk Ricotta (page 114). That's about as complicated as we'll get.

Otherwise, we need only be mindful of heat intensity. There's a spectrum, from steeping on the very gentle end to a raging boil on the high end. (At the very gentle end, chefs often employ a cooking method called *sous vide*. Food is sealed in airtight bags and held at a very constant low heat to cook delicate things quite evenly. It's neat stuff. Steeping low and slow mimics the approach—without the bags or pricey equipment. The Matcha-Steeped Salmon on page 104 rocks.) At the raging end, the exciting thing about boiling water is that it is water in the midst of a phase change, so once it starts boiling, it remains at or near 212°. After many minutes of boiling, even in a pot against a raging flame, the water is still 212°. (The water, of course, will eventually evaporate.) That's a very helpful phenomenon for, say, cooking multiple batches of broccoli rabe.

Flavor

From herbs and spices to aromatic vegetables to acidic things, such as lemon, vinegar, and buttermilk, conscious development of flavor matters. Browning is largely avoided in this chapter's batch of recipes; working with water is a relatively elegant and restrained approach. We'll get more aggressive later when we crank up the oven and play with fire. For now, think mixology.

Finish

The finish should serve to either a) tie the ingredients together or b) punch the flavor forward. Often the finish is a fat—a drizzle of heavy cream or a pat of butter—that enriches the dish, provides depth, and creates an alluring mouthfeel. Acids work, too. While they can get muddied during the cooking process, a splash of vinegar, a few spoonfuls of buttermilk, or a squeeze of lemon juice work at the final moment to heighten flavors. Herbs, too, are great finishers, best sprinkled on top of a dish just as it's being served.

You'll put the Four Fs to work in the recipes that follow. Vodka-spiked yogurt finishes the Full-Bodied Borscht (page 116). The 19th Century–Style Potage (page 99) transforms root veggies into a rich soup topped with crème fraîche and chives. And after making the Congee (page 133), you won't look at rice the same again. Promise.

SPECTRUM OF COOKING LIQUID INTENSITY

STEEP

POACH

SIMMER

BOIL

RAGING BOIL

MAD BASIC CHICKEN SOUP

HANDS-ON: 35 MIN. **TOTAL:** 2 HR. 40 MIN.

The process is called sweating because just enough heat is applied to soften and subsequently extract the moisture from the thing(s) being cooked. In this case, it's the vegetables. Sweating is a celebrated culinary technique for layering flavor into stews, soups, sauces, and braised dishes. Layering the chicken on top is an exercise in culinary discipline. The thighs are a timer of sorts: When they're cooked through, the vegetables are sweated to perfection.

MIREPOIX
=
2 PARTS ONION +
1 PART CARROT +
1 PART CELERY
=
THE "STICKIEST"
IDEA IN SAVORY
CULINARY HISTORY

Food	How Much	Why
onion	1½ cups diced	In practically all cuisines, the onion serves as both an aromatic and a textural foundation. Its flavor is as malleable as its texture. In this case, it's presented as part of a classic mirepoix.
carrot	⅔ cup diced	Adds a certain "meatiness" to the aromatic base.
celery	⅔ cup diced	Adds perfume and brightness to the mirepoix.
chayote	⅔ cup diced	It's delightfully neutral and provides sweetness and a silken quality to broths.
fennel bulb	¼ cup diced	When sweated, fennel is like luxury celery. Its anise-like flavor just makes life more interesting.
olive oil	2 tablespoons	Choose one with some oomph to it, as little droplets of flavored oil will enrich this soup far better than a neutral oil. Think of it as liquid black pepper.
sugar	1 teaspoon	As the vegetables sweat, the sugar helps facilitate the gentlest of "syrups" to enrich the soup without thickening.
garlic cloves	5, sliced	Because this soup would be boring without it.
bone-in chicken thighs	8, trimmed of excess fat	Chicken. Soup.
water	2½ cups	While you can use all broth, the water lightens up the dish a bit and allows the flavors of the vegetables to be more prominent.
unsalted chicken stock	2½ cups	To make it more chicken-y.
kosher salt	1¼ teaspoons	What follows is the balancing act of the dish. Start with an essential: salt.
lemon zest	1 teaspoon grated	Punch forward the aroma.
fresh lemon juice	2 tablespoons	Lift and separate with lemon juice.
Angostura bitters	1 teaspoon	Highlight with bitters. It works.

CONTINUED →

1½ cups diced onion

⅔ cup diced carrot

⅔ cup diced celery

⅔ cup diced chayote

¼ cup diced fennel bulb

2 Tbsp. olive oil

1 tsp. sugar

5 garlic cloves, sliced

8 bone-in chicken thighs, trimmed of excess fat

2½ cups water

2½ cups unsalted chicken stock

1¼ tsp. kosher salt

1 tsp. grated lemon zest

2 Tbsp. fresh lemon juice

1 tsp. Angostura bitters

Follow These Steps:

>> In a large stainless steel bowl, combine all of the vegetables, the olive oil, the sugar, and the garlic. Toss to combine.

>> Place a heavy-bottomed soup pot over very low heat.

START SWEATING

>> Lay the vegetables in an even layer in the pot. Evenly layer the chicken thighs over the vegetables, overlapping slightly if necessary.

>> Cover with a parchment lid (see photos at right) and sweat for about an hour. Parchment lids help to retain just enough moisture in foods you're sweating or stove-top quick-braising. Plus, *making one in front of guests serves as a cool party trick.*

>> The vegetables should be tender and almost translucent. If you've done this perfectly, some liquid will have rendered into the pan, and you'll have a juicy base on which to build the soup.

SIMMER SOME MORE

>> Add the water and stock, and simmer for another hour.

>> Using tongs, remove the chicken thighs to a cutting board and let them cool until you can safely handle. Remove and discard the bones, shred the meat by hand, and return the chicken to the pot.

DON'T JUST INDISCRIMINATELY PULL THE MEAT APART. BE GENTLE & BE MINDFUL. GET TO KNOW THOSE THIGHS, THE WAY THE FIBERS COOKED, AND WHERE (AND HOW) THEY NATURALLY SEPARATE.

>> Finish with salt, lemon zest, lemon juice, and bitters. *This soup base is perfect for freezing and subsequent "doctoring."*

SERVES 6 (SERVING SIZE: 1⅓ CUPS)
CALORIES 261; **FAT** 10.3G (SAT 1.8G, MONO 4.6G, POLY 2.7G); **PROTEIN** 29G; **CARB** 12G; **FIBER** 3G; **CHOL** 115MG; **IRON** 2MG; **SODIUM** 554MG; **CALC** 56MG

MEXICAN VARIATION:

>> In a bowl, stir together 1 cup ripe, charred, and coarsely chopped tomato, ¼ cup chopped cilantro, 1 charred and minced jalapeño, the juice and zest of 1 lime, and 1 diced avocado. Dollop this into bowls of the soup.
CALORIES 257; **FAT** 13.2G (SAT 2.3G); **SODIUM** 569MG

BASQUE-INSPIRED VARIATION:

>> Add a generous pinch of saffron to the soup while it simmers. Finish with 1 cup peeled, diced, ripe tomato and 2 tablespoons coarsely chopped fresh flat-leaf parsley.
CALORIES 202; **FAT** 8.3G (SAT 1.6G); **SODIUM** 567MG

STEP BY STEP: Making a Parchment Lid

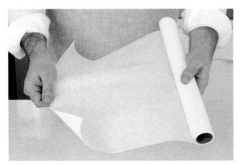

1) Pull out a sheet of parchment paper a little wider than the container you're "lidding."

2) Fold the paper in half...

3) ...and again.

4) Fold across as to mock a paper airplane, being mindful to align the folded edges.

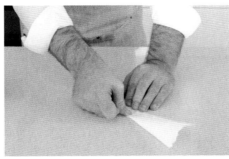

5) Fold the parchment over and over, until it becomes diffcult to create a seam.

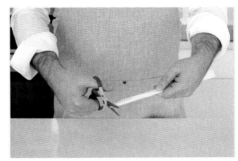

6) Snip off the tip. This creates a little steam hole so the lid won't blow off a simmering pot.

7) Place the tip of the lid at the center point of the pot, then trim the far end so the lid will fit the pot exactly.

8) Unfold your lid. You'll know you folded it the wrong way if it ends up as two halves.

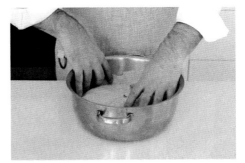

9) Place the lid in contact with the food you're cooking.

IN MODERN KITCHENS, THE WORD "POTAGE" IS USED TO REFER TO A SOUP THAT IS FAIRLY THICK.

19TH CENTURY-STYLE POTAGE
OF CELERIAC, GARLIC, AND SWEET ONION

HANDS-ON: 20 MIN. **TOTAL:** 1 HR. 20 MIN.

Old-school French chefs are serious about sweating vegetables for soups. Farm-fresh vegetables at their peak, slowly sweated in the right fat, can become a glorious soup, with nothing but water to adjust viscosity. We take sweating a touch further here, rounding out the almost citrusy aroma of celery root with chicken broth and fresh thyme. (This makes a heck of a vegetable puree if you use 2 cups of broth. Think of it as an alternative to mashed potatoes.) Serve with slightly charred rustic—preferably multi-grain—bread rubbed with garlic and spritzed with olive oil.

Food	How Much	Why
butter	1 tablespoon	Potages need beurre.
celery root	4 cups peeled and cut into 2-inch dice (1 pound)	It has the subtle perfume of celery, the typical sweetness of a root vegetable, and an almost lemony tinge. Buy the small ones—they're more tender.
sweet or Vidalia onion	3 cups vertically sliced (1 pound)	When cooked, they collapse and render to a silken puree.
garlic cloves	8, peeled, tipped, split, and germ removed	Slowly cooked, transforms into an almost dairy-like cream. It's textural magic.
fresh thyme leaves	2 tablespoons	An important herb in French cuisine, its flavor absolutely bursts when warmed with butter and/or oil.
lower-sodium chicken broth	2 quarts	For comfort. Water could be substituted, but then I'd recommend browning the onion mixture slightly.
kosher salt	1/8 teaspoon	Because it needs a bit to finish.
lemon zest	1 (2-inch) strip	Works well against the celery root and perfumes the soup.
French bread, stale or oven-dried	1 (1-ounce) slice, cubed (about 1/2 cup)	This is your thickening agent. Flavors of yeast and toast are wonderful against sweet onions.
buttermilk	1/4 cup	The lactic acid from buttermilk perks up flavors.
crème fraîche	2 tablespoons	The luxe finish. It's both rich and bright at the same time.
fresh chives	2 tablespoons sliced	This is a dish where most of the flavors are deep and rich. Chives provide a fresh, grassy finish.

GARLIC GERM

THE GERM CAN TASTE SOMEWHAT PUNGENT, PARTICULARLY IF THE GARLIC HAS BEEN IN YOUR FRIDGE FOR A WHILE. I THINK THE FLAVOR OF GARLIC IS SOFTER WITHOUT THE GERM & IT WORKS BETTER SANS-GERM IN THIS RECIPE.

CONTINUED

19TH CENTURY-STYLE POTAGE

1 Tbsp. butter

4 cups peeled and diced celery root

3 cups vertically sliced sweet onion

8 garlic cloves, peeled, tipped, split, and germ removed

2 Tbsp. fresh thyme leaves

2 qt. lower-sodium chicken broth

1/8 tsp. kosher salt

1 (2-inch) strip lemon zest

About 1/2 cup cubed French bread

1/4 cup buttermilk

2 Tbsp. crème fraîche

2 Tbsp. sliced fresh chives

Follow These Steps:

>> In a large Dutch oven, melt the butter over low heat.

SOFTEN THE VEGETABLES
>> Add the celery root, the onion, garlic, and thyme to the melted butter. Tumble. Cover and raise the heat to medium-low.

>> Sweat the vegetables for 25 minutes.

>> Remove the lid, and add the chicken broth, salt, and the lemon zest.

>> Bring the soup to a steady simmer, reduce heat, and cook, covered, for at least 20 minutes, until all the vegetables are quite soft.

>> Remove the lid and carefully pull out the lemon zest with a pair of tongs.

THICKEN AND BLEND A SMOOTH SOUP
>> Ready a blender or, preferably, an immersion blender.

>> Add the bread to the soup. Stir with a wooden spoon. *It's the 19th century, remember?*

>> In mere seconds, the bread will have broken down into the soup. Now, being extremely careful, blend the soup until silky smooth: Use an immersion blender right in the pot or place about a quarter of the mixture in a blender. Remove the center piece of blender lid (to allow steam to escape); secure blender lid on blender. Drape a clean towel over opening in blender lid (to avoid splatters). Blend in small batches until smooth, pouring into a large bowl.

>> Repeat procedure until all of the soup is well blended. If you've used a traditional blender, return the soup to the pot.

>> Stir in the buttermilk and heat the soup over medium-high heat until very hot.

>> Ladle the hot soup into bowls and garnish with crème fraîche and chives.

SERVES 8 (SERVING SIZE: 1½ CUPS)
CALORIES 112; **FAT** 3.9G (SAT 2.5G, MONO 0.8G, POLY 0.2G); **PROTEIN** 6G; **CARB** 14G; **FIBER** 2G; **CHOL** 15MG; **IRON** 1MG; **SODIUM** 278MG; **CALC** 55MG

BLACK BEAN SOUP
WITH HABANERO CREMA

HANDS-ON: 15 MIN. **TOTAL:** 45 MIN.

Sofrito. It's a method, really. It falls somewhere between sweating and sautéing. Take ingredients such as onion, garlic, bell pepper, and chile, and apply heat sufficient to soften. At that point, you can tweak the fire, add dry spice, and brown it to your liking. Play with it. Build things on top of it.

Food	How Much	Why
light sour cream	¼ cup	This provides an acid contrast against the savory bean soup.
fat-free milk	2 tablespoons	Thins out the sour cream.
habanero chile	1 teaspoon, seeded and minced	The pleasant "ouch" factor. And the habanero has an almost citrus-y perfume.
extra-virgin olive oil	1 tablespoon	It offers some "spice" to the sofrito.
yellow onion	1 cup finely diced	Part one of your sofrito.
green bell pepper	½ cup finely diced	Delightfully vegetal against the beans, this pepper's flavor "cuts" through the beans.
mild green chile	¼ cup finely diced	To harmonize the green bell pepper.
ground cumin	½ teaspoon	A restrained amount adds to the aromatic depth of the soup.
dry oregano	½ teaspoon	Dry has a more pointed flavor than fresh, and is great in many-ingredient dishes like this.
black pepper	¼ teaspoon	Supports the savory nature of the dish.
garlic cloves	8, minced	It's downright meaty when browned and cooked down.
unsalted chicken stock	3 cups	Soup.
unsalted black beans	2 (14-ounce) cans, drained and rinsed	You're in a hurry. That's why. Keep some cans around.
kosher salt	½ teaspoon	
cider vinegar	1 teaspoon	Cider vinegar is glorious against habanero.

Follow These Steps:

>> Make the crema. Combine the sour cream, the milk, and the habanero in a small bowl. Cover and chill until about 15 minutes before serving—*it's best not to put super-cold crema into your hot soup.*

>> Fire up a medium-sized saucepan over medium-high heat.

>> Add the olive oil and swirl.

>> Add the onion, bell pepper, green chile, cumin, oregano, black pepper, and garlic. Stir and cook for 4 minutes, until the vegetables have softened slightly.

>> Add the stock and beans, bring to a simmer, and cook 20 minutes.

>> Add the salt and stir.

>> Ready a tabletop blender. Fill the blender pitcher halfway with the soup. Remove center piece of blender lid (to allow steam to escape); secure blender lid on blender. Place a clean towel over opening in blender lid (to avoid splatters). Blend the first batch until super-smooth. Pour into a large bowl.

>> Blend the next batch a bit coarsely. If there's any remaining, don't blend it. Some textural variation is welcome here. (That said, if you like it silken, then blend it all.) Pour the super-smooth batch and the coarse batch back into the saucepan.

>> Stir and return to a simmer for 3 minutes. Stir in the vinegar.

>> Serve the soup in shallow bowls, drizzled with the crema.

SERVES 7 (SERVING SIZE: ¾ CUP)
CALORIES 114; **FAT** 3G (SAT 0.9G, MONO 1.7G, POLY 0.3G); **PROTEIN** 7G; **CARB** 19G; **FIBER** 6G; **CHOL** 3MG; **IRON** 2MG; **SODIUM** 446MG; **CALC** 66MG

MATCHA-STEEPED SALMON
WITH GINGER-TOASTED PANKO

HANDS-ON: 32 MIN. **TOTAL:** 32 MIN.

Matcha is a powder-fine green tea, quite intense in flavor, with tannins dominating the mouth-feel (think red wine). It's rendered glorious with a splash of cream, and its boldness is a striking companion to salmon's richness. The trick in this recipe is to cook as gently as possible. If you can get your hands on truly fresh wild salmon, feel free to undercook this dish to your liking.

Food

Food	How Much	Why
water	4 cups	Your steeping liquid.
matcha (green tea) powder	3 tablespoons	Matcha is worth the money. Its flavor is unparalleled, and it dissolves quite well.
salt	1¼ teaspoons, divided	As a foil to the fatty nature of salmon.
heavy cream	2 tablespoons	To soften the tannins of the matcha.
salmon fillets	4 (6-ounce) fillets	The size of the fillet dictates the steeping time.
grapeseed oil	1 tablespoon	It's neutral. Matcha needs the starring role here.
fresh gingerroot	1 tablespoon grated	Provides some liveliness against the tea.
panko breadcrumbs	¼ cup	They're crunchy!
lime zest	½ teaspoon grated	Loves ginger.
canola mayonnaise	1 tablespoon	This adheres the crumbs and adds some richness.
fresh chives	1 tablespoon minced	Its onion-y flavor pops the savoriness of the dish.
lime wedges	4	Without it, the dish would fall flat. Always balance fat-forward things with acid.

Follow These Steps:

>> In a large high-sided skillet, add the water and bring to a simmer.

>> Gradually whisk in the matcha powder, followed by 1 teaspoon salt, followed by the cream. Reduce the heat to low and let the temperature of the liquid sink below 180°.

>> Slide in the salmon fillets, skin sides up. Turn off the heat. Depending on the thickness, let the fillets poach for 10 minutes.

>> *Sacrifice the perfection of one of the fillets.* Using a spoon, try to make a clean break at one of the flakes. If the salmon still has a tint of translucency in its flake, it's done.

>> Transfer to a plate. *(That tester is your piece, by the way.)* Put the fillets somewhere warm, like in a oven with a pilot light, or on the plate over the warm liquid (providing the plate's diameter is wide enough).

>> In a small skillet, add the grapeseed oil. Turn the heat to medium. Add the ginger. Yes, now.

>> As the grapeseed oil warms, *you'll start to smell the sweet essence of cooked ginger.* Stir constantly.

>> Now, add the crumbs, and raise the heat to medium-high.

>> Tumble the crumbs while shaking the pan, popcorn-style, until well toasted. Remove the pan from the heat and stir in the lime zest.

>> Arrange the fillets on plates or a platter, skin sides down; sprinkle with ¼ teaspoon salt.

>> Now, lightly brush the salmon fillets with the mayonnaise, and sprinkle the toasted crumbs in an even blanket on top of the fillets.

>> Garnish with chives. Serve with lime wedges.

SERVES 4 (SERVING SIZE: 1 SALMON FILLET)
CALORIES 409; **FAT** 23.2G (SAT 5.4G, MONO 8.5G, POLY 6.4G); **PROTEIN** 39G; **CARB** 9G; **FIBER** 1G; **CHOL** 98MG; **IRON** 2MG; **SODIUM** 504MG; **CALC** 27MG

SPICE-SIMMERED PORK "BÁNH-MÌ-STYLE" SALAD

HANDS-ON: 1 HR. 7 MIN. **TOTAL:** 1 HR. 17 MIN.

Food	How Much	Why
baguette	1 (4-ounce) unsliced baguette	Buy one that's airy and crisp. You need the light texture.
yellow onion	1 medium, peeled and halved crosswise	This provides depth to the broth. You'll have fun burning it. On purpose.
fresh gingerroot	1 (2-inch) piece, cut into 4 (½-inch) slices	For perfuming the broth.
pork tenderloin	1 pound, trimmed	When cooked gently, it's textural magic tossed in this dish's dressing.
lower-sodium beef broth	4 cups	To evoke to the flavors of pho.
sugar	2 teaspoons	See above.
kosher salt	1 teaspoon	To keep the flavors straightforward.
cinnamon stick	1	Adds depth to the mild-flavored pork.
star anise	1 pod	Creates a "browned" flavor similar to the effects of a dry-heat method. Cool.
radishes	8 ounces, thinly sliced	Use the slicer. Cut these paper-thin.
carrots	2, peeled and thinly sliced	Try to get the longest, thinnest strips possible. This is the body of the salad.
English cucumber	1, cut into 3-inch sections, sliced thinly	Slice, as for the carrots above, but a tad thicker.
red onion	1, thinly sliced	For some pungency and textural contrast.
ripe tomato	1 large, sliced	Glorious against chiles and onions.
canola mayonnaise	¼ cup	The bulk of the dressing. If you can find a Japanese-made mayo, use it.
fresh lime juice	¼ cup (2 limes)	The acid for your dressing.
serrano chiles	2, minced	Provide the perfect heat level.
water	1 tablespoon	To thin the mayo a bit.
fresh cilantro	1 bunch, stems trimmed	These are your "greens." Include the stems; they're tender and delicious.
green onions	4, split lengthwise and cut into 1-inch pieces	The other half of your "greens."

If you haven't invested in a razor-sharp Japanese-style mandoline or German V-style slicer, do it now. Ribbon-thin vegetable cuts are essential to this dish. In technique, it's a mash-up of the Lebanese bread salad, fattoush, with some components of a classic Vietnamese bánh-mì sandwich. The cooking broth is a nod to pho, the meaty noodle soup that's omnipresent in Vietnamese-American neighborhoods. This is killer with a squeeze of Mad Fresh Sriracha (page 58).

IF USED IN CONJUNCTION WITH A DRY-HEAT METHOD, IT COMPOUNDS THE MEATY FLAVOR.

CONTINUED

SPICE-SIMMERED PORK "BÁNH-MÌ-STYLE" SALAD

1 (4-oz.) baguette

1 yellow onion, peeled and halved crosswise

4 (½-inch) slices fresh ginger

1 lb. pork tenderloin, trimmed

4 cups lower-sodium beef broth

2 tsp. sugar

1 tsp. kosher salt

1 cinnamon stick

1 star anise pod

8 oz. radishes, thinly sliced

2 carrots, peeled and thinly sliced

1 English cucumber cut into 3-inch sections, sliced thinly

1 red onion, thinly sliced

1 large ripe tomato, sliced

¼ cup canola mayonnaise

¼ cup fresh lime juice

2 serrano chiles, minced

1 Tbsp. water

1 bunch fresh cilantro, stems trimmed

4 green onions, split lengthwise and cut into 1-inch pieces

Follow These Steps:

>> Tear the baguette into bite-sized chunks. *Be deliberately inconsistent.*

>> Heat a large cast-iron or heavy-bottomed skillet over high heat. Add the bread a few chunks at a time, and toast 1½ minutes or to the point of being slightly charred, stirring frequently.

>> Do this in 2 batches. Set the toasted bread aside in a single layer for now.

CHAR THE VEGETABLES

>> In the pan you cooked the bread in, add the yellow onion, cut sides down, and cook 2 minutes to char the surface. Remove the onion and set it aside.

>> Go back to the pan you charred the onion in. Heat to high again. Slightly char the ginger, about 1 minute.

SIMMER THE PORK

>> In a 3-quart saucepan, add the pork tenderloin and the beef broth, along with the sugar and salt. Add the cinnamon stick, the star anise, and the charred yellow onion and ginger. Bring to a slight simmer, so slight that the pot bubbles every four or five seconds.

>> Simmer the pork for about 20 minutes, very gently.

>> Remove the pork from the liquid and place it on a plate to rest for a moment. *Leave the broth in the pan on the stove. You'll need it in a few.*

>> While the pork simmers, prep all of your vegetables for the salad.

MAKE THE SALAD

>> In a large mixing bowl, combine the radishes, the carrots, the cucumber, the red onion, and the tomatoes. Add the mayonnaise, the lime juice, the serrano chiles, and 1 tablespoon of water. Toss the vegetables to evenly coat.

>> Let this mixture marinate at room temperature for about 15 minutes.

NOW, THE FINISHING TOUCHES

>> Now, return to the pork tenderloin. Using your hands, hand-pull into long strands. Use a fork to assist the process if necessary.

>> Toss the pork with the marinated vegetable mixture. Add a few spoonfuls of the simmering broth. Toss again.

>> At service time, add the cilantro and the green onions. *Those are your "greens."*

>> At the last moment, add the charred bread. Toss and plate or platter.

>> Serve with side bowls of the hot broth for dipping the bread. Serve with Mad Fresh Sriracha (page 58).

SERVES 6 (SERVING SIZE: ABOUT 1 CUP SALAD)
CALORIES 249; FAT 9.1G (SAT 1.2G, MONO 4.6G, POLY 2.4G); PROTEIN 19G; CARB 23G; FIBER 4G; CHOL 50MG; IRON 2MG; SODIUM 569MG; CALC 55MG

POT AU FEU

HANDS-ON: 20 MIN. **TOTAL:** 5 HR. 30 MIN.

This is not a classic pot au feu, in that we're limiting the meat to one cut, but the purpose here is to learn how to control heat in order to convert the collagen to gelatin. The result makes for the most tender and unctuous of one-pot meals. Much has been written about all things low and slow, but the key is to maintain a temperature just below boiling, which makes for a magically textured result.

Food	How Much	Why
cold water	4 cups	It's part of the cooking liquid, and makes the dish humbler, less muddy, and less rich. However...
unsalted beef stock	4 cups	...stock helps to enrich and supplement the broth that's built as the beef simmers. Water alone could work, but the finished liquid would be too flaccid.
boneless beef chuck roast	2 pounds	Chuck is one of the most collagen-rich cuts of beef, and because we're cooking very gently over a prolonged time period, we need the abundance of collagen to convert to sticky, unctuous gelatin.
kosher salt	1 teaspoon, divided	The truth here is that the salt simply contributes to the salt-forward flavor we expect from our savory dishes. It has little to no functional impact.
garlic cloves	4, peeled	Adds depth to the stock. The long cooking makes it as soft as mashed potato and neutralizes allicin, the compound responsible for raw garlic's pungency.
black peppercorns	12	Perfume and pungency.
thyme sprigs	5	The boldest herb of the classic bouquet garni.
whole cloves	3	Sweet spice pairs beautifully with richer-flavored beef cuts such as chuck.
fresh bay leaves	2	Quite honestly, you can 100% omit them, but research suggests they'll help keep the pathogen count under control with your leftovers.
celery root	1 pound, peeled and cut into sections	It's properly called celeriac, but since that sounds a bit like a medical condition, we've taken literary license. This is added for mouthfeel and substance.
whole yellow or sweet onions	1 pound, peeled and quartered	This dish is French in origin, so mirepoix returns. The classic ratio, again, is 2 parts onion, 1 part carrot, 1 part celery.
carrots	½ pound, peeled and trimmed	Large, rustic cuts are ideal for long cooking times.
celery	½ pound, peeled and cut into 3-inch sections	Same as above. Celery has a fair amount of pectin, so it becomes delightfully jammy when cooked for prolonged periods.

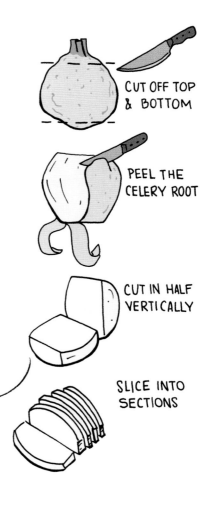

CUT OFF TOP & BOTTOM

PEEL THE CELERY ROOT

CUT IN HALF VERTICALLY

SLICE INTO SECTIONS

CONTINUED

4 cups cold water

4 cups unsalted beef stock

2 lb. boneless beef chuck roast

1 tsp. kosher salt, divided

4 garlic cloves

12 black peppercorns

5 thyme sprigs

3 whole cloves

2 fresh bay leaves

1 lb. celery root, peeled and cut into sections

1 lb. whole yellow or sweet onions, peeled and quartered

½ lb. carrots, peeled and trimmed

½ lb. celery, peeled and cut into 3-inch sections

Follow These Steps:

❯❯ Ready an enameled cast-iron Dutch oven. This is certainly the time to break out your best one. *And, by the way, if you're attempting this recipe, you're a serious cook, so the enameled stuff is supposed to be showcased on your range. Now you know.*

BUILD A TASTY FOUNDATION FOR THE CHUCK

❯❯ Fill the Dutch oven with 4 cups of cold water. If you'd drink it from your tap, then use tap. Otherwise, use filtered. Add the beef stock, too.

❯❯ Rinse the beef under cold running water. Pat it dry with paper towels.

❯❯ Rub ½ teaspoon of salt into the chuck. Think deep tissue massage.

❯❯ Place the salted chuck into the Dutch oven.

❯❯ Smash the peeled garlic cloves with the side of a chef's knife. *Please make sure the blade edge is pointing away from your smashing self.* Toss them in the pot.

❯❯ Add the black peppercorns, the thyme, the cloves, and the bay leaves.

COOK THE BEEF—SLOWLY

❯❯ Bring the temperature of the liquid up to about 200°. Whatever you can do to keep the temperature constant, do it. If you choose to put a lid on, skew it so you can clearly see inside the pot (see the illustration at right).

❯❯ Now, do something else. For a while. Like 2 hours.

❯❯ When you return to the pot, assuming you've been able to control the temperature well, the chuck will still look fairly gray and firm, though promising. *Be. Patient.*

❯❯ There will be some gray froth floating on the surface of the liquid. Skim it off and discard it. *You'll have the opportunity to nurture the pot a few times during cooking, so keep the skimming spoon and a small bowl at the ready for your purification ritual.*

❯❯ Do more of something else—for another 2 hours.

ADD VEGETABLES (MORE FLAVOR) TO THE POT

❯❯ Get a clean cutting board ready, and prepare all the vegetables as outlined in the ingredient list.

❯❯ Gently add all of the vegetables to the pot. This is a good time to grab a pair of tongs and marvel at the slow, steady transformation of the chuck.

❯❯ Continue to cook the Pot au Feu, holding the temperature at 200° for another hour or so. The dish is done when both the meat and the vegetables are fork-tender.

SERVE YOUR POT AU FEU

» Transfer the meat from the pot to a decent-sized cutting board. Let it rest for about 10 minutes. Either slice against the grain in ½-inch slabs, or gently break into portions using a pair of kitchen tongs.

» Remove the vegetables from the pot using a slotted spoon. *Arrange naturally on a big platter. Don't be fussy. This is peasant food.*

» Transfer the meat to the platter as well. Make sure to keep it rustic.

» Ladle a small amount of broth on top and go celebrate with your guests. *Wine? Yes.*

SERVES 6 (SERVING SIZE: 4 OUNCES MEAT AND 1 CUP VEGETABLES)
CALORIES 290; **FAT** 7.9G (SAT 3G, MONO 3.3G, POLY 0.4G); **PROTEIN** 34G; **CARB** 20G; **FIBER** 4G;
CHOL 96MG; **IRON** 4MG; **SODIUM** 579MG; **CALC** 91MG

GUAJILLO CHILE BEEF VARIATION:

» Omit celery root. Double the garlic. Drop in 6 seeded Guajillo chiles. Add juice of 1 lime. Add 1 tablespoon favorite Mexican hot sauce.

» Ladle off half the liquid and blend with softened chiles. Return to pot. Fold to incorporate.

» Serve with lime wedges, chopped raw onion, and cilantro.
CALORIES 297; **FAT** 7.9G (SAT 2.9G); **SODIUM** 620MG

VIETNAMESE PHO-STYLE VARIATION:

» Add the cinnamon stick, and double the cloves. Add a star anise pod and 2 teaspoons fennel seeds.

» The charred onion becomes a must. Add a 1-inch piece of ginger, sliced lengthwise. Char that, too. Add to the pot.

» To finish: Squeeze in the juice of 2 limes. Use 1 tablespoon fish sauce in lieu of salt.
CALORIES 311; **FAT** 8G (SAT 3G); **SODIUM** 545MG

ITALIAN-STYLE VARIATION:

» Replace the water with canned crushed tomatoes, and use oregano instead of thyme. Omit the clove. Omit the celery root. Double the garlic.

» Finish with a handful of fresh basil and some red pepper flakes.
CALORIES 332; **FAT** 8.2G (SAT 3G); **SODIUM** 667MG

YOU CAN USE ONE OF TWO METHODS TO KEEP A CONSTANT TEMP INSIDE A POT. IT'S YOUR CHOICE:

PEEK

LOW-TECH: PEEK
ONCE YOU'RE AT 200°, SET THE BURNER ON ONE TEMP & LEAVE IT THERE. PEEK IN THE POT NOW & THEN TO MAKE SURE IT'S NOT BOILING—YOU WANT JUST A FEW SLOW BUBBLES.

HIGH-TECH: USE A THERMOMETER
SET A PROBE THERMOMETER SO THAT THE PROBE TIP STAYS IN THE CENTER OF THE POT.

BUTTERMILK RICOTTA

HANDS-ON: 30 MIN. **TOTAL:** 50 MIN.

I grew up in New York, where excellent ricotta was readily available. I've always found the part-skim variety to be too lean, almost chalky. When I moved to the South, I embraced buttermilk, which creates a superbly zingy ricotta that mimics the rich mouthfeel of the full-fat version. It's marvelous served warm alongside crusty bread. Try folding in some grated raw garlic, lemon zest, and parsley.

Food	How Much	Why
whole milk, non-homogenized, super-fresh	1 gallon	Non-homogenized milk will allow for a slightly firmer (though not firm) curd and a richer tasting cheese. It's super-fresh if it's straight from the farm, but if you're in a market, make sure you're on the earlier end of the best-by date.
citric acid powder	2 teaspoons	Citric acid powder helps shape up the perfect curd, though lemon juice can be used as well. You'll need up to ¼ cup of lemon juice, though, to "crack" the hot milk into curds and whey.
hot water	¾ cup	To moisten the cheese to your liking.
buttermilk	¼ cup	The reasons are twofold: first, to add silken texture while keeping the cheese lean, and second, to punctuate with the tangy, cultured flavor.
heavy cream	1 tablespoon	It's just enough fat to enrich, and it adds a bright dairy note.
kosher salt	½ teaspoon	This helps the cheese keep a bit longer. Feel free to taper the quantity if you're using the ricotta immediately or as an ingredient in sweets.

YOU CAN FIND THIS IN GROCERY STORES NEAR THE CANNING SUPPLIES.

MAKE CURDS & WHEY

1. POUR THE MILK INTO A HEAVY-BOTTOMED DUTCH OVEN.
2. OVER MEDIUM-HIGH HEAT, RAISE THE TEMPERATURE TO 190°.
3. TURN THE HEAT TO LOW & ADD THE ACID POWDER. STIR GENTLY.
4. KEEP STIRRING. WATCH CLOSELY. <u>LOOK</u> AT <u>THAT</u>! YOU'RE MAKING CHEESE. THE CURDS ARE SEPARATING FROM THE WHEY.
5. TURN OFF THE HEAT.
6. USING A WOODEN SPOON, LIGHTLY AGITATE THE CURDS IN THE WARM LIQUID, ENCOURAGING THE FORMATION OF A "RAFT" OF CURDS.

STRAIN THE CURDS & FINISH THE RICOTTA

7. LINE A FINE-MESH STRAINER WITH CHEESECLOTH. PLACE THAT STRAINER OVER A VESSEL THAT CAN HOLD THE STRAINER WITHOUT YOUR ASSISTANCE AND KEEP THE DRAINED WHEY OUT OF CONTACT WITH THE DRAINING CHEESE.
8. STRAIN THIS MIXTURE FOR ABOUT 20 MINUTES AT ROOM TEMPERATURE.
9. AFTER STRAINING, TRANSFER THE RICOTTA TO A MIXING BOWL.
10. ADD SOME OF THE HOT WATER, FOLDING WITH A RUBBER SPATULA. IT'S NOT NECESSARY TO ADD ALL OF THE WATER — THE MORE YOU ADD, THE MOISTER THE FINAL CHEESE.
11. NOW DRIZZLE THE BUTTERMILK & THE HEAVY CREAM INTO THE CHEESE. SPRINKLE IN THE SALT. FOLD GENTLY WITH A RUBBER SPATULA.
12. TRANSFER TO A SMALL CONTAINER & REFRIGERATE, COVERED, UNTIL READY FOR USE. USE THE RICOTTA WITHIN A WEEK.

SERVES 26 (SERVING SIZE: 2 TABLESPOONS)
CALORIES 58; **FAT** 4.7G (SAT 2.8G, MONO 1.1G, POLY 0.3G); **PROTEIN** 4G;
CARB 0G; **FIBER** 0G; **CHOL** 16MG; **IRON** 0MG; **SODIUM** 32MG; **CALC** 108MG

FULL-BODIED BORSCHT

HANDS-ON: 50 MIN. **TOTAL:** 3 HR. 15 MIN.

*This recipe—the ultimate homage to beets—is a lesson in individualized cooking processes.
You'll use the packet-steaming method (page 119) for the beets, carrots, potatoes, garlic, and onions.
You'll brown beef. You'll wilt cabbage. The broth simply brings it all together, slowly and gently.
Keep this in mind when it's time to build a soup or stew on the fly with odds, ends, and leftovers.*

BORSCHT, WITH ITS MYRIAD PHONETIC VARIATIONS, HAS ITS ORIGINS IN UKRAINE & BECAME THE DE FACTO "NATIONAL" DISH OF THE (NOW DEFUNCT) SOVIET UNION. INTERPRETATIONS ARE FOUND ALL OVER EASTERN EUROPE. NON-JEWS WOULD USE PORK FAT TO SWEAT THEIR VEGGIES. JEWISH VERSIONS LEVERAGE SIMMER-FRIENDLY BEEF CUTS. THE DRINK: VODKA.

Food	How Much	Why
plain Greek yogurt	½ cup	Beets are deeply earthy. Some lactic tang is ideal against all things earth.
vodka	2 tablespoons	A cultural must, plus the bite of alcohol provides a peppery kick.
prepared horseradish	1 tablespoon	Pungent against earthy works.
kosher salt	1 teaspoon, divided	
red beets	5 (3-inch) beets	The foundation.
carrots	2 cups diced	To pull the sweetness in multiple directions. Beet sweet alone would be cloying.
Yukon Gold potato	1½ cups diced	For body.
onion	2 cups sliced	Along with the garlic, onion provides the savory undertone of the dish.
garlic cloves	¼ cup sliced (about 8 cloves)	See above.
canola oil	1½ tablespoons, divided	Used for its high smoke point to allow us to get a deep brown on the beef.
red cabbage	2 cups finely sliced	Can white be used? Sure, but this adds to the depth of color in the dish and is slightly higher in natural sugars.
red wine vinegar	¼ cup	Holds the color of the cabbage and is the acid component to the broth. Without it, the meal would taste too similar to garden soil.
sugar	2 tablespoons	To facilitate the wilting of the cabbage and to add sweetness.
beef chuck roast	1 pound, cut into ½-inch cubes	Makes this a meal.
ground white pepper	1 teaspoon	Ground white pepper is distinctly funky, and in this dish, is actually quite pleasant.
lower-sodium beef broth	6 cups	The medium.
fresh dill	1 tablespoon chopped	Dill's delicate aroma seems to "soften" the entire dish.

CONTINUED ⟶

FULL-BODIED BORSCHT

½ cup plain Greek yogurt

2 Tbsp. vodka

1 Tbsp. horseradish

1 tsp. kosher salt, divided

5 (3-inch) red beets

2 cups diced carrots

1½ cups diced Yukon Gold potato

2 cups sliced onion

¼ cup sliced garlic cloves

1½ Tbsp. canola oil, divided

2 cups finely sliced red cabbage

¼ cup red wine vinegar

2 Tbsp. sugar

1 lb. beef chuck roast, cut into ½-inch cubes

1 tsp. ground white pepper

6 cups lower-sodium beef broth

1 Tbsp. chopped fresh dill

Follow These Steps:

>> Preheat your oven to 400°.

>> Combine the yogurt, the vodka, and the prepared horseradish. *Steal a pinch of the salt. Add it and stir.* Set aside.

PACKET-STEAM THE VEGETABLES

>> Ready 4 sheets of aluminum foil, about 1 foot in length.

>> Prepare the beets and make a "pillow" of beets as directed on page 119.

>> Now wrap the carrots and potatoes: Combine them on a foil sheet and seal it "en papillote" style (see page 141).

>> Repeat the same process with the onions and garlic: Place them on a foil sheet, drizzle with ½ tablespoon oil, and make a packet.

>> Place all of the packets on baking sheets. Roast the onions for about 20 minutes, the carrots and potatoes for about 30 minutes, and the beets for about an hour, until tender.

>> Remove the vegetables from the oven as they're done. Open the packets and pour the garlic, onion, carrot, and potato into a bowl.

SHRED THE BEETS, QUICK-PICKLE THE CABBAGE

>> Take the beets out of the packet and rub the skins off. (Follow the tips on page 119.) Trim the edges and shred on a box grater. Set aside with the other vegetables.

>> In a stainless steel bowl, combine the cabbage, the red wine vinegar, and the sugar. Toss together. Let rest at room temperature for a few moments.

BROWN THE MEAT AND FINISH THE BORSCHT

>> Place a Dutch oven on the stove over medium heat. Add 1 tablespoon oil. Swirl to coat the pan. Add the beef when the pan approaches the smoking point.

>> Stir to brown the meat. Add the cabbage mixture, the remaining salt, and the white pepper. Stir and allow the cabbage to wilt. About 3 minutes or so.

>> Add the beef broth. Bring to a boil, then reduce the heat and let it simmer for 30 minutes.

>> Add all of the other vegetables to the pot. *Stir to combine, but don't be aggressive. Fold.*

>> Simmer for an hour and a half. (Bubbles should percolate constantly, but not rapidly.)

>> Spoon the hot borscht into soup bowls; allow the veggies to mound near the center. Top with a generous tablespoon of the yogurt mixture and a sprinkling of dill.

SERVES 8 (SERVING SIZE: 1⅓ CUPS SOUP AND 1 TABLESPOON YOGURT MIXTURE)
CALORIES 281; FAT 11.3G (SAT 2.6G, MONO 5.6G, POLY 2.4G); PROTEIN 14G; CARB 29G;
FIBER 6G; CHOL 21MG; IRON 2MG; SODIUM 444MG; CALC 80MG

STEP BY STEP: Readying Beets

1) Trim the beets, leaving the root and an inch of the stem.

2) Lay the beets on a foil sheet.

3) Top with another foil sheet, and fold the edges together to make a "pillow" of beets.

4) Pull the packet from the oven. Open carefully, and rub off the skins with gloved hands (to prevent stains) and/or a spoon or by scraping with a paring knife.

5) Trim the top end...

6) ...and the root end.

CIOPPINO

HANDS-ON: 40 MIN. **TOTAL:** 40 MIN.

As language morphs through time and locale, so does food. Yes, this fish stew has roots in Italy, but it is a distinctly San Franciscan treat. Chefs, restaurateurs, and history transformed the dish as well, from a humble soup of fish scraps and tomato-tinged broth to a carefully orchestrated celebration of the sea. Strict attention to the schedule of events in this recipe will yield glorious results.

SAN FRANCISCO

Food	How Much	Why
lemon zest	1 teaspoon grated	The perfume of lemon against tomato begs for the addition of seafood.
fresh lemon juice	1 tablespoon	Contrasts with the almost mushroom-y depth of the mussels.
saffron	1 pinch	For intoxicating aroma.
olive oil	2 tablespoons	To sauté the vegetables.
fennel bulb	1 cup sliced	The anise-like flavor pairs perfectly with saffron.
onion	½ cup sliced	Provides body and sweetness.
garlic cloves	4, divided	With fennel and onions, garlic is a must.
fresh thyme	2 teaspoons chopped	This is your foundational herb in this stew.
fresh oregano	2 teaspoons chopped	This is a punctuation mark, adding boldness. If you'd like a subtler stew, omit it.
crushed red pepper	1 teaspoon	Don't omit this. It adds a subtle piquancy.
kosher salt	¼ teaspoon	A requirement.
dry white wine	1 cup	Without this, it would be too tomato-y.
Charred Tomato Passata *(page 30)*	2 cups	Far superior to canned for this dish. Your passata will taste fresher.
water	1 cup	Again, to taper jamminess.
skinless halibut fillets	1½ pounds, cut into 1-inch pieces	Because you like the good stuff.
littleneck clams	16, scrubbed	Large clams would be too cumbersome.
mussels	16 (about ¾ pound), scrubbed and debearded	Friends of littlenecks.
large sea scallops	8, cut in half horizontally	Absolutely glorious against the tomato-wine broth. The butter of the sea.
lump crabmeat	8 ounces	Who doesn't like a big chunk of crab on their spoon?
fresh flat-leaf parsley	2 tablespoons chopped	With everything else being steeped together, this brightens at the last minute.
sourdough bread	8 (1-ounce) slices	Because sopping up deliciousness with bread is what makes us human.

CONTINUED →

CIOPPINO

1 tsp. grated lemon zest

1 Tbsp. fresh lemon juice

1 pinch saffron

2 Tbsp. olive oil

1 cup sliced fennel bulb

½ cup sliced onion

4 garlic cloves, divided

2 tsp. chopped fresh thyme

2 tsp. chopped fresh oregano

1 tsp. crushed red pepper

¼ tsp. kosher salt

1 cup dry white wine

2 cups Charred Tomato Passata (page 30)

1 cup water

1½ lb. skinless halibut fillets, cut into 1-inch pieces

16 littleneck clams, scrubbed

16 mussels, scrubbed and debearded

8 large sea scallops, cut in half horizontally

8 oz. lump crabmeat

2 Tbsp. chopped fresh flat-leaf parsley

8 (1-oz.) slices sourdough bread

Follow These Steps:

›› Combine the lemon zest, lemon juice, and saffron. This blooms the saffron, releasing maximum color and flavor.

CREATE A TASTY BASE

›› Heat a large saucepan or Dutch oven over medium-high heat.

›› Add the olive oil. Swirl.

›› Add the fennel and onion. Cook for 5 minutes, stirring frequently.

›› Smash 2 cloves of garlic.

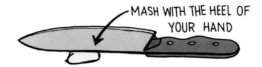

MASH WITH THE HEEL OF YOUR HAND

›› Add the smashed garlic, thyme, oregano, crushed red pepper, and salt. Stir half a minute.

›› Add the wine. Bring to a boil and stir for 2 minutes.

›› Add the passata and 1 cup water. Stir.

ADD SEAFOOD

›› Bring to a steady simmer. Add the halibut, the clams, and the mussels. Cover and cook for 6 minutes, or until the shells begin to sneak open.

›› Turn the heat to as low as possible. Add the scallops. Cook for 5 minutes, and turn the heat off.

›› Add the bloomed saffron mixture, the crabmeat, and the parsley, and gently fold to combine. The crab will simply warm through.

TOAST AND SEASON THE BREAD

>> Cut 2 garlic cloves in half. On a grill pan or under a broiler, slightly char/toast the bread for 1½ minutes, turning once. Rub the toast with the cut side of the garlic cloves.

>> Serve the Cioppino in shallow bowls with the charred bread. You'll need it to sop up all the tasty broth.

SERVES 8 (SERVING SIZE: 1½ CUPS SOUP AND 1 BREAD SLICE)
CALORIES 347; **FAT** 8.5G (SAT 1.3G, MONO 4.4G, POLY 1.6G); **PROTEIN** 38G;
CARB 26G; **FIBER** 3G; **CHOL** 91MG; **IRON** 8MG; **SODIUM** 657MG; **CALC** 90MG

STEP BY STEP:
Scrubbing and Debearding Mussels

 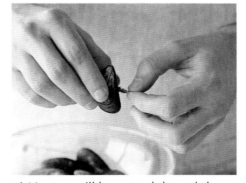

1) You'll need to scrub each mussel to remove any dirt or sand that got left behind on the shell. Use a stiff-bristled brush to give them a good cleaning.

2) Next, you'll have to debeard them. You're removing the byssal threads (the "beard"), which connect the mussel to rocks or pilings in the sea. Grab the fibers with your fingers, and pull them out, tugging toward the hinged point of the shell.

RED CURRY BOILED PEANUTS

HANDS-ON: 10 MIN.   **TOTAL:** 2 HR. 10 MIN.

Warm, soft peanuts. Say it again. Warm. Soft. Peanuts. On rural routes through the South, it's not uncommon to find salt-crusted, simmering kettles of fresh green peanuts. To temper the salt and add some depth, these fresh peanuts are given a Thai-inspired treatment of red curry paste and fish sauce. You can get your hands on fresh peanuts at farmers' markets throughout the Southeastern U.S. Online, look for raw peanuts in the shell from Georgia, Alabama, and Virginia.

Food	How Much	Why
water	1 quart, or enough to cover peanuts	You're going to boil the heck out of the peanuts. You need plenty of water.
coconut water	2 cups	Adds some residual sugar, but contributes a mineral-y quality to the boiling liquid.
kosher salt	1 tablespoon	Just enough to taste.
raw peanuts (sometimes known as green peanuts)	2 pounds	Your snack.
red curry paste	4 tablespoons	It's intensely flavored, quite complex, and just right for peanuts, boiled or otherwise.
fish sauce	1 teaspoon	Depth of aroma. A little more salt.
lime zest	1 teaspoon grated	To contrast the (good) funky aroma of fish sauce.
fresh lime juice	2 tablespoons	So far, we're pretty salt-forward. The acid treatment makes them quite irresistible.

Follow These Steps:

≫ In a 4-quart Dutch oven (or similarly sized pot), add the water, the coconut water, and the salt. Have the lid handy.

≫ Add the peanuts to the pot and bring the liquid to a full rolling boil. Reduce to a steady, but not violent boil. Cover the pot.

≫ Cook for about an hour.

≫ Meanwhile, combine the red curry paste, the fish sauce, and the lime zest in a small bowl. Mix it well.

≫ Remove the lid, and stir in the red curry mixture. Stir, turning the peanuts and incorporating the curry mixture fully.

≫ Replace the lid, and boil for another hour.

≫ *Now, it's time to taste the peanuts. The texture is a matter of taste. If you like them softer, cook them longer.*

≫ Strain the warm peanuts from the liquid, give 'em a shake, and toss with the lime juice to finish.

≫ These are an incredible snack, or can liven up the Green Beans (from the Mad Array of Vegetables on page 148) if patiently shelled.

SERVES 12 (SERVING SIZE: ABOUT ¼ CUP UNSHELLED PEANUTS)
CALORIES 240; **FAT** 16.8G (SAT 2.2G, MONO 8.2G, POLY 5.2G); **PROTEIN** 11G; **CARB** 16G; **FIBER** 7G; **CHOL** 0MG; **IRON** 1MG; **SODIUM** 30MG; **CALC** 36MG

SPICY BROCCOLI RABE

HANDS-ON: 16 MIN. **TOTAL:** 16 MIN.

Broccoli rabe's bitterness is often tempered by fatty sausages. Here, a "red peppered" and salted boiling water treatment brings the vegetable, also known as rapini, to a nearly perfect, pale-ale bitter, where olive oil can enrich without masking. Bay brings essences of clove, eucalyptus, and evergreen to add warmth and fullness to the dish. This vegetable holds well for a day or two in the fridge; just make sure you squeeze out the excess water before storing.

Food	How Much	Why
water	2 quarts	This *is* the hot liquids chapter.
ground red pepper	1 teaspoon	Broccoli rabe is often finished with red pepper flakes or some kind of chile. This method seems to pepper the rabe from the inside out. Nifty.
fresh bay leaf	1	May make the water slightly alkaline, helping to tenderize the rabe, but more importantly, it makes the vegetable taste "fuller," more savory even.
broccoli rabe (rapini)	1 pound, trimmed	The star.
olive oil	1 tablespoon	To coat and enrich, and to adhere the seasonings.
garlic	1 teaspoon grated	Raw is where it's at here. Its pungency is welcome against the subtle bitterness of cooked rapini.
fresh lemon juice	1 tablespoon	Something bitter + olive oil + garlic + lemon. It just works. Every time.
kosher salt	¼ teaspoon	Salt tames bitter. For real. It's not clear exactly why, but it does. Well.
Parmigiano-Reggiano cheese	½ ounce, shaved (about 2 tablespoons)	Adds further saltiness, a contrasting acidity to the lemon, and brings it home with some nuttiness. Despite the dish's simplicity of preparation, the flavor combination is downright harmony.

Follow These Steps:

>> Combine the 2 quarts of water, the ground red pepper, and the bay leaf in a 4-quart Dutch oven (or similarly sized pot). Bring to a full rolling boil.

>> Set a colander in the sink. Get some tongs ready, too.

>> Put half the trimmed broccoli rabe into the boiling water. Cook for 2½ minutes or until crisp-tender. *You'll have to taste it; you can't "see" tender in broccoli rabe.*

>> Take the pot and the tongs to the sink, but don't pour out the liquid. Grab all of the rabe and place it in the colander.

>> Bring the pot back to the stove. Boil again.

>> Add the rest of the broccoli rabe. Cook for 2½ minutes or until crisp-tender. Now you can drain it. Go ahead and dump the whole thing on top of the other broccoli rabe. It'll get warmed up. Find the bay leaf. Discard it.

>> Place the olive oil in a large bowl. *Swirl around a bit. Look fancy.*

>> Add the garlic and lemon juice to the bowl.

>> Add the hot broccoli rabe to the bowl. Toss to lightly coat in oil and garlic. Sprinkle with salt.

>> Serve with a few shavings of Parmigiano-Reggiano alongside Toasted Penne with Chicken Sausage (page 208).

SERVES 4 (SERVING SIZE: ABOUT 1 CUP)
CALORIES 81; **FAT** 4.7G (SAT 1.2G, MONO 2.7G, POLY 0.6G); **PROTEIN** 6G; **CARB** 6G; **FIBER** 0G; **CHOL** 3MG; **IRON** 1MG; **SODIUM** 175MG; **CALC** 98MG

WHOLE-WHEAT SPAGHETTI ALLA BOTTARGA

HANDS-ON: 28 MIN. **TOTAL:** 28 MIN.

Bottarga, pressed and salted tuna or mullet roe, may be the most under-appreciated delicacy on Earth. It's expensive, but can be used in small amounts to great effect. And while whole-wheat pasta often gets panned for being coarse, it's the perfect choice here.

Food	How Much	Why
fresh breadcrumbs	¼ cup	Critical. You want irregular, fluffy breadcrumbs, not the homogenous dust found in paper canisters. Make your own in a food processor.
lemon zest	1½ tablespoons grated	Clings to the pasta as Parmesan cheese would, and is simply awesome against the bottarga.
fresh oregano	1 tablespoon chopped	An aggressive herb to bolster other aggressive flavors. There's a lot going on here.
extra-virgin olive oil	2 tablespoons	Primarily for its peppery characteristics.
butter	1 tablespoon	Adds its unique unctuous quality.
ground red pepper	¼ teaspoon	For a little capsaicin burn and a hint of smoky sweet.
garlic cloves	12, peeled, split lengthwise, germ removed	Removing the germ eliminates any bitterness from the garlic, and although we're cooking the garlic in liquid, the split cloves have a great finished look.
whole-wheat spaghetti	1 pound	The foundation.
fennel	2 cups thinly shaved	Adds substance and sweetness.
sweet onion	1 cup thinly shaved	Same as above.
Fresno or other fresh red chile	about ¼ cup very thinly sliced into rings (about ¹⁄₁₆ inch)	Lemon. Chile. Bottarga. It's magic.
fresh lemon juice	2 tablespoons	Brightness and acidity. Without it, the dish would be flat.
kosher salt	½ teaspoon	This brings the salt level where it should be.
fresh flat-leaf parsley	2 tablespoons chopped	To enliven. Provides a bright, grassy finish.
bottarga	1 ounce, finely grated using a rasp grater	The star of the dish. Don't judge. Try.

GRATE GENTLY. YOU NEED ALMOST NO PRESSURE. TUNA BOTTARGA'S HARDER TO GRATE—TRY SLICING IT FINELY WITH A KNIFE.

CONTINUED

WHOLE-WHEAT SPAGHETTI ALLA BOTTARGA

1/4 cup fresh breadcrumbs

1 1/2 Tbsp. grated lemon zest

1 Tbsp. chopped fresh oregano

2 Tbsp. extra-virgin olive oil

1 Tbsp. butter

1/4 tsp. ground red pepper

12 garlic cloves, peeled, split lengthwise, and germ removed

1 lb. whole-wheat spaghetti

2 cups thinly shaved fennel

1 cup thinly shaved sweet onion

about 1/4 cup very thinly sliced Fresno chile

2 Tbsp. fresh lemon juice

1/2 tsp. kosher salt

2 Tbsp. chopped fresh flat-leaf parsley

1 oz. finely grated bottarga

Follow These Steps:

>> In a sauté pan over medium-high heat, toast the breadcrumbs about 3 minutes, allowing a small amount to go just beyond toasted—to almost but not quite charred.

>> While the crumbs are still slightly warm, transfer to a small bowl and combine with the lemon zest and the fresh oregano.

>> Place the oil and butter in a bowl large enough to hold a pound of fully cooked pasta. Set aside for now.

COOK THE PASTA

>> Bring a large pot of water (about 12 quarts) to a full rolling boil. Add the ground red pepper. Add the garlic cloves. Yes, the garlic cloves. To the water.

>> Get the water moving with a wooden spoon. Stir to create a gentle circular current.

>> Gently slide the pasta into the pot about 1/4 pound at a time to avoid clumping.

>> Stir to ensure that the spaghetti strands are free-swimming and separated.

>> Boil the pasta vigorously (about 4 minutes, or for about half the time recommended on package).

ADD VEGGIES TO THE POT OF COOKING PASTA (FOR REAL)

>> Now, stir the fennel, the onion, and the red chile into the boiling pasta. Cook for the remaining time recommended on your pasta package, or for another 5 minutes or so.

>> Test the pasta for doneness. *Taste it. Don't throw it. That's just silly.* The finished pasta should be toothsome, meaning there's a little chew to it, not a crunch.

>> Drain the pasta and vegetable mixture into a colander. Shake once. Twice. Three times. Don't dare rinse. Please. Let it sit for 2 minutes, giving it a visit with a wooden spoon. Explore. Fold. Combine. Be gentle.

FINISH WITH A TOUCH OF FAT, ACID, HERBS, AND CRUNCH

>> Now, while the pasta is still steaming hot, transfer to the bowl containing the butter and oil. Toss well. Add the lemon juice. Toss again. Season with the salt. Toss again. *Slowly walk around your kitchen with the pasta bowl, waving the aroma toward your nose. Look serious. People will admire you.*

>> Now, add the parsley to the breadcrumbs. Toss. You're adding the parsley now so you can get the perfect juxtaposition of toasty and grassy. Otherwise, it might seem muddy. Your garnish is now ready.

>> Distribute the pasta among 6 shallow pasta bowls. *Use tongs to twirl and stack. It looks pro that way.*

>> Garnish each bowl with a small mound of the shaved bottarga, and sprinkle the breadcrumb mixture evenly among the bowls. Serve immediately. Encourage your guests to stir the garnish into their pasta before eating.

SERVES 6 (SERVING SIZE: 1 1/2 CUPS PASTA MIXTURE, 1 TABLESPOON BOTTARGA, AND 1 TABLESPOON BREADCRUMB MIXTURE)
CALORIES 378; FAT 9G (SAT 2.4G, MONO 4.6G, POLY 1.2G); PROTEIN 14G; CARB 66G; FIBER 11G; CHOL 22MG; IRON 4MG; SODIUM 262MG; CALC 73MG

CONGEE

HANDS-ON: 15 MIN. **TOTAL:** 1 HR. 15 MIN.

Chinese rice porridge can be expressed in countless ways—from nearly flavorless (expressive of rice and clean water, intended to be restorative) to full-bodied and plentiful (the accoutrements are unlimited in scope). If you can find broken rice at an Asian market, buy it, as it gives a body to congee that no other rice variety can duplicate.

Food	How Much	Why
canola oil	2 teaspoons	Facilitates the quick sauté of ginger and garlic.
green onion	2 tablespoons white part only, plus ¼ cup green onion tops, very thinly sliced, bias cut	The white part serves as a sweetener of sorts, infusing the oil, and, ultimately, the entire dish. The green tops are added at the end for color and a little bite.
fresh gingerroot	1 tablespoon peeled and grated	The bright perfume of ginger makes this congee a very satisfying dish.
white, long grain, or broken rice	1 cup	Starchy white rice gives congee its signature silky translucence. Brown rice just won't do it for this dish.
skinless, boneless chicken thighs	1 pound	It seems every culture has its own chicken and rice dish. The thighs provide depth of flavor and body.
water	8 cups	The standard water to rice ratio for congee.
kosher salt	1 teaspoon, divided	Kosher salt has a clean flavor.
white pepper	¼ teaspoon	Provides dimension.
fresh cilantro	2 tablespoons leaves torn	Adds complexity to whatever it touches.
peanuts	2 tablespoons cracked	Adds some textural interest to the dish.
Korean red pepper powder *(see page 370)*	1 tablespoon	This has an almost jammy sweetness. If it's hard to find, toss a teaspoon of powdered sugar with cayenne.
lower-sodium soy sauce	2 teaspoons	Added for the fermented flavor more than the salt.

Follow These Steps:

>> In a medium saucepan over medium heat, add the canola oil and swirl to coat.

>> Add the white parts of the green onion and the ginger. Stir, cooking for 1 minute.

>> Add the rice. Stir and cook for 2 minutes.

>> Lay the chicken thighs over the rice.

>> Add the 8 cups of water and ½ teaspoon salt. Bring to a boil, then cover and simmer for 1 hour or more, until the rice has completely lost its form.

>> Turn off the heat and remove the chicken thighs. Shred, and return to the congee.

>> Add ½ teaspoon salt and the white pepper. Stir.

>> Serve in small soup bowls garnished with the green onion tops, cilantro leaves, peanuts, red pepper powder, and the soy sauce.

SERVES 8 (SERVING SIZE: 1 CUP)
CALORIES 195; **FAT** 6.8G (SAT 1.5G, MONO 3G, POLY 1.8G); **PROTEIN** 13G; **CARB** 20G; **FIBER** 1G; **CHOL** 37MG; **IRON** 2MG; **SODIUM** 364MG; **CALC** 17MG

LEMON, FETA, AND KALAMATA OLIVE POLENTA

HANDS-ON: 14 MIN. **TOTAL:** 14 MIN.

Here in the New World, we most often associate polenta with things Italian. The Greeks also dabble in polenta, in both sweet and savory versions. The starches in cornmeal begin to gelatinize at about 200°, continuing through the boiling point. It's important to stir constantly while sprinkling in the polenta; otherwise you'll get jellylike polenta clumps filled with dry polenta. Seriously.

Food	How Much	Why
lower-sodium chicken broth	5 cups	It's a lot of liquid, and, honestly, a lot of polenta. If we didn't have you make a big batch, you'd need miniaturized cooking vessels.
lemon zest	1 teaspoon grated	The oils from the zest release in the hot cooking liquid and perfume the polenta.
kosher salt	½ teaspoon	This perfect contrast to the acid is a must. They don't make salt and vinegar chips for nothing.
egg yolk	1	To enrich, in lieu of what is typically a lot of fat.
fresh lemon juice	2 tablespoons	Bottled simply won't do, particularly here. Fresh is a must for superb flavor.
instant polenta	1 cup	Instant is a deliberate choice. For soft polenta, it's fluffier and has a luxurious mouthfeel.
feta cheese	2 ounces crumbled (about ½ cup), divided	Because my first memory of my Greek-ness is a distant relative handing me a large chunk of feta. It might be the perfect food. Briny. Acidic. Lush.
kalamata olives	2 tablespoons chopped, divided	Makes the dish almost meaty.
plain 2% reduced-fat Greek yogurt	½ cup	Pulls the acidity in multiple directions—lactic and citric (from the lemon). Makes the dish entirely more interesting. (See page 303 for more about using acids.)

Follow These Steps:

›› In a medium saucepan, bring 5 cups of chicken stock to a full rolling boil. Add the lemon zest and salt.

›› Place a small bowl on a kitchen towel to secure it. Combine the egg yolk with the lemon juice in the bowl.

›› Carefully ladle 1 cup of the hot stock into the egg yolk/lemon juice mixture while stirring the yolk mixture constantly with a whisk (you can use a fork if it's easier). *The lemon makes the yolk less likely to coagulate, so don't be overly cautious about this step.*

›› With a wire whisk in one hand, and the cup of polenta in another, slowly sprinkle the polenta into the boiling liquid and stir. *Don't pour. You'll get clumps.*

›› Turn the heat down to low. Cook for 3 minutes, stirring with a wooden spoon, being particularly attentive to the bottom of the pot.

›› Turn off the heat and let sit for 1 minute.

›› Now, fold in the yolk-lemon-stock mixture. *Normally, you'd throw a bunch of butter and cream and cheese in at this point. Not in this book.*

›› Fold in ¼ cup of the feta cheese, followed by 1 tablespoon of the kalamata olives, followed by the Greek yogurt. *Leave it a little streaky with yogurt. It eats nicely that way.*

›› Sprinkle the polenta with the remaining ¼ cup feta and 1 tablespoon olives. Either serve immediately with Greek-Style Slow-Grilled Leg of Lamb (page 362) or the 27-Hour Chicken Legs (page 298). Or chill the polenta in a loaf pan and slice it for grilling or pan-frying.

SERVES 10 (SERVING SIZE: ABOUT ½ CUP)
CALORIES 93; **FAT** 2.4G (SAT 1.4G, MONO 0.5G, POLY 0.1G); **PROTEIN** 5G; **CARB** 12G; **FIBER** 1G; **CHOL** 27MG; **IRON** 1MG; **SODIUM** 255MG; **CALC** 28MG

HARNESSING STEAM

STEAM

The fast, flexible, and flavorful method

Steam has a bland reputation in culinary circles. The problem is that it is often selected as an inappropriate substitute for other cooking methods. Monitored wisely, steam is a fabulous tool for creating vibrant, flavorful, and (thank goodness) healthful dishes. When should you steam? Consider these guidelines:

>> There's something moist and tender that you want to keep moist and tender (mussels, for instance).

>> A method that uses fat as a cooking medium would muddy or weigh down a dish.

>> You were able to get your hands on something (fish, vegetables, fruit, whatever) impeccably fresh.

>> You want to focus on the essence of the ingredients being cooked.

>> After becoming more immersed in the craft of cooking, you feel like steaming is the way to go.

LIKE THE BEET
RECIPE ON
ON PAGE 166.

Be Super Careful.

Steam is no joke. There's about 10 times more heat energy in steam than there is in boiling water, even though they're both essentially the same temperature (212°). So getting burned is a distinct likelihood if you're not careful. When you're steaming under pressure (whether in a parchment packet or a pressure cooker), remember to release steam a) gradually, and b) away from your body/face/hands/small children. When removing lids from stovetop steamer configurations, always lift the lid at an angle, slowly, away from everyone and everything. Leave the steam facials to the estheticians.

Put the Water On.

This chapter will address some of the best, easiest, and most delicious ways to leverage the power of steam. We'll speak more qualitatively about steaming, in a language that will help you get cooking, rather than overburden you with foundational scientific data that would put the eager cook to sleep. Let's get steamy.

AND ACTUALLY, REAL-DEAL STEAM CAN'T BE SEEN. WHAT YOU SEE ARE QUICKLY DISSIPATING CLOUDS OF WATER VAPOR FORMED FROM THE STEAM COMING INTO CONTACT WITH THE LOWER-TEMPERATURE AIR.

Methods

"Essential" Steam

Sometimes foods are so delicious that masking them with anything but gentle enhancements (herbs, a small pat of butter, some sea salt, a splash of wine) seems disrespectful. In this case, we'll apply steam with the intent of extracting and preserving the essence of the main ingredient. Basically, we'll use a pot, a splash of this or that, another aromatic component, a drizzle or knob of appropriate cooking fat to finish (if necessary), and something salty (salt, soy sauce, miso, fish sauce, and the like).

Mussels and clams are particularly well suited to this technique, as are shrimp (in the shell). With high-quality enameled cast-iron cookware (and its typically heavy, tight-fitting lids), it's possible to extract the liquid from the ingredient with little-to-no additional steaming liquid. Heat applied evenly to a dry pan, a lid, some mussels, some thinly sliced raw garlic, and a drizzle of olive oil makes one heck of a meal, and you can save the wine for drinking.

Steaming to Envelop

This is the garden-variety steaming technique that comes to mind when folks speak of steaming foods, particularly vegetables. Water boils in a pot below an inset colander or steamer basket. Steam is generated, the product is put in the basket, and the contraption is covered. There are myriad twists we can put on this technique, from adding aromatics to the steaming liquid to using anything-but-water as the steam source.

There's no need to shock your vegetables. Using an ice-bath for your veggies neither stops the cooking nor "locks in color." Just like you take a steak off a bit earlier than the desired temperature to let it rest, steamed vegetables (like green beans or broccoli) should be loosely placed (not packed tightly) in the basket under intense, not gentle, steam. Take the product out *before it is fully cooked,* and place in a colander or perforated drying rack with sufficient circulation to avoid eating squishy, squeaky, waterlogged vegetables. Remember, this isn't boiling, so why would we submerge anything?

Packets of Steam

The French use the term *en papillote,* or "in parchment," to describe a method of cooking that involves carefully wrapping up the food to be steamed in a sealed packet. The method and the medium need not be too precise; it's possible to use aluminum foil, parchment paper, even paper lunch bags as a means to steam. And one cool thing about using packets of steam is your ability to create sensory drama by plating the whole package and slicing it open at the table. You can go from homey to fancy using these packet-steaming methods:

» Foil Packet: The cool thing about aluminum foil is that it conducts heat well enough to transfer sufficient heat to brown the product in contact with the foil. Thus, if you want a perfect blend of roasty-toasty and steam-tender root vegetables, for instance, use foil.

» Classic en Papillote: The parchment container really ends up creating a hybrid steam-simmer environment, as juices release from the foods being cooked and pool at the bottom of the parchment pouch. Regardless, it's a great technique for things that cook fast, and cook in relative time-sync with one another. Packet cooking: the "un-braise."

CHOOSE PARCHMENT WHEN STEAMING FOODS THAT INCLUDE HIGHLY ACIDIC INGREDIENTS, SUCH AS VINEGAR, TO AVOID OFF FLAVORS CAUSED BY A CHEMICAL REACTION WITH THE ALUMINUM.

STEP BY STEP: En Papillote

1) Lay a piece of parchment or foil down, and then layer the ingredients.

2) Cover with another sheet of parchment or foil.

3) Form the packet, sealing the edges.

4) Remove or slice open the top sheet, and serve.

Stacked Steamers

Stacked steamers are indispensable in the kitchens of China and Southeast Asia. From bamboo to aluminum, these steaming configurations can be bought inexpensively in virtually any Asian food market. Bamboo is quite absorbent, so it's a great medium to use when you don't want condensed water to drip back onto the food. Different items go on different layers, and the opportunities to play are endless. And just because stackable bamboo is most often associated with the cuisines of Asia doesn't mean you have to stick to Asian cuisine when using the stacked steamer.

THIS CHAPTER GIVES FAJITAS THE STACKED STEAM TREATMENT, FOR INSTANCE. SEE PAGE 161.

Steaming to Peel

Almost all of the canned tomatoes and a significant amount of the canned fruits and vegetables on the market are peeled in powerful industrial steamers. It's quick and easy to replicate similar results at home, without the tinny taste. There are a number of benefits to peeling with steam:

» Skins and peels virtually slip off the fruit or vegetable without much work.

» The vibrant color of the fruit or vegetable under the skin is enhanced.

» You get to cook only the part that needs cooking, allowing you to use the mostly raw underlying food as you desire.

Stone fruit (peaches, plums, nectarines, apricots) and tomatoes are particularly well suited to peeling by steaming. To avoid mushy results, try to use perfectly ripe but not overripe fruits for this technique.

The photos below can guide you through the process, but here are a couple other tips: Never start an item to be steamed in a cold steamer. Always have the steam cranking before adding the food, otherwise, you'll end up with peeled mush. We're using steam as a peeling tool, not as a means of cooking.

STEP BY STEP: Peeling Tomatoes

1) Cut an "X" in the tomatoes at the bottom.

2) Steam the tomatoes. Make sure the steam clouds are vigorous.

3) Drop the tomatoes in ice water, and then remove immediately.

4) Pull away peels with a paring knife.

5) Cut in half. Squeeze out the seeds.

6) Freedom! Puree, slice, dice, or quarter as you wish.

CAST-IRON MUSSELS

HANDS-ON: 12 MIN. **TOTAL:** 12 MIN.

Few things rival the culinary euphoria that is a perfectly steamed dish of mussels with crusty bread. Often, we see mussels dressed up (Thai-style, Belgian beer, white wine and garlic, marinara), but when super-fresh ones are available, leave them alone. This recipe calls for a little bit of water, plus some butter or olive oil. That's it.

Food	How Much	Why
fresh mussels	48 (about 2 pounds), scrubbed and debearded	Because anything less than fully fresh would result in your guests (and you) ultimately making the "gross face." (See page 15.)
water	½ cup	To prevent scorching the mussels in the pan.
butter or extra-virgin olive oil	2 tablespoons	To provide a little richness. Butter is probably tastier, but you make the call.
coarse sea salt	½ teaspoon	For that photo finish. Toss it with the finished mussels.
lemon	1, thinly sliced (about 8 slices)	For some bright citrus aroma and some pleasant acidity.
fresh flat-leaf parsley	1 tablespoon quick chiffonade	For color, and a little grassy punch against the briny and highly concentrated mussel liquid.

Follow These Steps:

» Heat an enameled cast-iron Dutch oven (must have the lid) to medium-high.

» When the pan is hot, add the mussels and cover.

» Steam, covered, for about 2 minutes before checking to see if the mussels have begun to open and release some of their liquid.

» Uncover and add the water if there is not sufficient liquid (enough to coat the bottom of the pan).

» Cover the pan, and cook until the mussels begin to open.

» Turn off the heat when the mussels have peeked open, and set the pan aside, covered, for 2 minutes, to gently finish the cooking.

» Add the butter, salt, and lemon, and gently fold the mussels in the cooking juices.

» Serve in 4 wide, shallow bowls, and garnish with fresh parsley.

» *Break bread. Drink wine. Enjoy.*

SERVES 4 (SERVING SIZE: ABOUT 2 CUPS)
CALORIES 154; **FAT** 8.5G (SAT 4.2G, MONO 2.1G, POLY 0.9G); **PROTEIN** 14G; **CARB** 5G; **FIBER** 0G; **CHOL** 49MG; **IRON** 5MG; **SODIUM** 634MG; **CALC** 34MG

ROSEMARY AND SEA SALT POTATOES

HANDS-ON: 10 MIN. **TOTAL:** 40 MIN.

Upstate New York is famous for its salt potatoes, a dish in which small skin-on potatoes are cooked in super-saturated salt water. They're typically served in paper boats and are absolutely drenched in melted butter. This version of the elegant salt-steamed potato is inspired by, and is much better for you than, the aforementioned classic. They are a versatile side dish for roasted meats. They're also great turned into next-day potato salad.

Food	How Much	Why
water	3 cups	This is the steam.
sea salt	½ cup	Salty steam will leave a slight "haze" on the outside of the potato—like an ocean breeze on a spud.
fresh rosemary	3 sprigs plus 2 teaspoons chopped	The herbed steam will only delicately touch the potatoes, but it will fill your home with an absolutely inviting aroma.
fingerling potatoes	1½ pounds	Skin-on is critical; otherwise, you'll have salt-licks, not potatoes.
butter	1 tablespoon plus 2 teaspoons	Sparingly used, butter elevates the flavors of the rosemary.

Follow These Steps:

›› In a standard steamer (basket and base), combine the 3 cups water, the salt, and the rosemary sprigs. Bring to a boil over medium-high heat.

›› Place the washed potatoes in the steamer basket. Place the basket in the steamer base. Cover the steamer, reduce the heat to medium, and cook for about 30 minutes, until the potatoes are tender but not cracked.

›› Carefully remove the potatoes from the steamer and let stand 5 minutes.

›› Combine butter and chopped rosemary in a small microwave-safe bowl; microwave at HIGH 20 seconds or until butter melts.

›› Drizzle butter over potatoes. Serve.

SERVES 4 (SERVING SIZE: ABOUT 4 POTATOES)
CALORIES 162; **FAT** 5.1G (SAT 3.3G, MONO 1.3G, POLY 0.3G); **PROTEIN** 3G; **CARB** 27G; **FIBER** 3G; **CHOL** 13MG; **IRON** 1MG; **SODIUM** 188MG; **CALC** 20MG

MAD ARRAY OF VEGETABLES

HANDS-ON: VARIES **TOTAL:** VARIES

This Mad Array is an homage to simplicity. Select perfectly fresh vegetables for steaming, as you can't readily hide visual blemishes (indeed, they'll be accentuated). Each vegetable is rendered extraordinary by a focused yet thoughtful flavor treatment. Learn from this exercise in restrained cookery.

ALL SERVED HOT.
ALL SERVE 4.

RED CABBAGE

Thinly slice 1 red cabbage to yield 4 cups. Toss the raw cabbage with 2 tablespoons cider vinegar. Steam 15 minutes. Toss steamed cabbage with 2 (yes, additional) tablespoons cider vinegar, 1 tablespoon sugar, ¼ teaspoon kosher salt, and ¾ teaspoon toasted caraway seeds.

SERVES 4 (SERVING SIZE: ¾ CUP)
CALORIES 44; **FAT** 0.2G (SAT 0G); **SODIUM** 172MG

CAULIFLOWER FLORETS

Steam 4 cups for 6 minutes. Toss with a pinch of kosher salt. Divide among 4 plates and serve each with ½ tablespoon Mad Delicious Aioli (page 86).

SERVES 4 (SERVING SIZE: 1 CUP CAULIFLOWER AND ½ TABLESPOON AIOLI)
CALORIES 48; **FAT** 2.5G (SAT 0.4G); **SODIUM** 96MG

GREAT WITH A SIMPLY
GRILLED PORK CHOP.

GREEN BEANS

Steam 1 pound for 10 minutes. Toss with 16 torn basil leaves, 1 tablespoon Thai red curry paste, 2 tablespoons hot water, and 2 tablespoons chopped peanuts.

SERVES 4 (SERVING SIZE: ABOUT 1 CUP)
CALORIES 66; **FAT** 2.5G (SAT 0.4G); **SODIUM** 221MG

GREAT WITH
GRILLED SHRIMP.

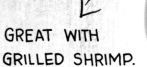

RED AND YELLOW ONIONS

Julienne 1 red and 1 yellow onion to equal 1 cup of each. Steam 12 minutes. Toss with 2 tablespoons red wine vinegar, 2 teaspoons sugar, and ¼ teaspoon kosher salt.

SERVES 4 (SERVING SIZE: ¼ CUP)
CALORIES 33; **FAT** 0.1G (SAT 0G); **SODIUM** 150MG

BEEF. PORK.
OKAY, EVERYTHING.

SUMMER SQUASH

Cut 1 large zucchini and 1 large yellow squash into 3 x ½-inch pieces to equal 2 cups of each. Steam 4 minutes. Toss with 2 tablespoons olive oil, 1 teaspoon thyme leaves, 1 grated garlic clove, and ¼ teaspoon kosher salt.

SERVES 4 (SERVING SIZE: ¾ CUP)
CALORIES 77; **FAT** 6.9G (SAT 1G);
SODIUM 150MG

BABY BOK CHOY

Cut 4 baby bok choy in half lengthwise. Steam 6 minutes. Toss with 2 teaspoons peeled, grated fresh ginger, 2 teaspoons chile oil, and 1½ tablespoons lower-sodium soy sauce.

SERVES 4 (SERVING SIZE: 2 HALVES)
CALORIES 34; **FAT** 2.4G (SAT 0.3G);
SODIUM 235MG

ENGLISH PEAS

Steam 2 cups of fresh peas for 10 minutes (or 2 cups of frozen peas for 1 minute). Toss with 1 tablespoon fresh mint (chiffonade), 3 tablespoons cream, and ¼ teaspoon kosher salt.

SERVES 4 (SERVING SIZE: ½ CUP)
CALORIES 91; **FAT** 4.4G (SAT 2.6G);
SODIUM 224MG

BROCCOLI FLORETS

Steam 4 cups for 2 minutes. Toss with 2 tablespoons olive oil, 2 minced garlic cloves, and ½ teaspoon kosher salt.

SERVES 4 (SERVING SIZE: 1 CUP)
CALORIES 82; **FAT** 7G (SAT 1G);
SODIUM 259MG

TRY WITH
ROASTED CHICKEN.

RADISHES

Cut 1 pound radishes in half. Steam for 12 minutes. Toss with 1 tablespoon butter and ¼ teaspoon kosher salt.

SERVES 4 (SERVING SIZE: ABOUT 1 CUP)
CALORIES 44; **FAT** 3G (SAT 1.9G);
SODIUM 217MG

HELLO, LAMB.

SWISS CHARD

Steam 8 cups coarsely chopped chard for 3 minutes. Squeeze chard, and toss with 1 tablespoon toasted walnut oil, 1 tablespoon fresh lemon juice, ⅛ teaspoon kosher salt, and 2 tablespoons chopped toasted walnuts.

SERVES 4 (SERVING SIZE: ⅔ CUP)
CALORIES 45; **FAT** 3.6G (SAT 0.3G); **SODIUM** 227MG

LEEKS

Julienne 3 leeks to equal 4 cups. Steam 8 minutes. Toss with 3 table-spoons cream, ¼ teaspoon kosher salt, and ½ teaspoon freshly ground black pepper.

SERVES 4 (SERVING SIZE: ½ CUP)
CALORIES 94; **FAT** 4.4G (SAT 2.6G); **SODIUM** 170MG

PAPER-THIN GOLDEN BEETS

Peel and thinly slice 1½ pounds of beets (use a man-doline or v-slicer if you have one). Steam 8 minutes. Toss with ¼ cup plain 2% reduced-fat Greek yogurt, 1 tablespoon red wine vinegar, 2 teaspoons chopped fresh thyme, and ⅛ teaspoon kosher salt.

SERVES 4 (SERVING SIZE: ABOUT 1 CUP)
CALORIES 84; **FAT** 0.6G (SAT 0.2G); **SODIUM** 211MG

DELICIOUS IN A BAKED POTATO.

SINGAPORE CHICKEN RICE

HANDS-ON: 20 MIN. **TOTAL:** 1 HR. 20 MIN.

Singapore's hawker centers were erected beginning in the 1970s in an effort to move affordable eats off the streets and into hygiene-regulated environments. Today, one can find a dizzying array of brilliantly crafted, affordable dishes of varying origin. Chicken rice, however, is a mainstay, a celebrated national dish that appeals to locals and tourists alike. It is quintessentially light (and Mad Delicious), and should immediately become part of your repertoire. It's so incredibly satisfying, you might cry. Really.

Food	How Much	Why
jasmine rice	1 cup	Jasmine rice is aromatic, has the ideal "fluff," and is what's generally used in Southeast Asia for this dish.
whole chicken	1 (5½-pound) chicken	"Chicken" rice.
coarse sea salt	a handful	It's used to scrub the chicken skin baby-smooth. It's the ultimate exfoliant.
lime	½	The acid "tightens up" the chicken skin. You'll see.
unsalted chicken stock	4 cups	Steaming with stock makes for a flavorful event.
fresh gingerroot	1 (2-inch) piece (about 2 ounces), peeled and sliced ⅛ inch thick	It's an integral part of the aromatic and flavor backbone.
garlic cloves	8, sliced	Being that the chicken is indeed steamed, garlic provides some depth of flavor and makes the chicken taste meatier.
pandan leaves (likely frozen)	2	There really is no viable substitute for pandan leaves (also known as screw pine). There are extracts available (though its usage is often questioned relative to this dish). It's unique. If you decide to go without, tell folks you're making this dish Malay-style.
kosher salt	1 teaspoon	You need salt.
green onions	8, cut into 1-inch pieces	A good section of onion is an amazingly bright and pungent foil to the deceptively rich chicken.
fresh cilantro	¼ cup chopped	It's the "caffeine" of aromatics. This enlivens the dish.

CONTINUED

SINGAPORE CHICKEN RICE

Ingredients

1 cup jasmine rice

1 (5½-lb.) whole chicken

a handful of coarse sea salt

½ lime

4 cups unsalted chicken stock

1 (2-inch) piece fresh ginger, peeled and sliced ⅛ inch thick

8 garlic cloves, sliced

2 pandan leaves

1 tsp. kosher salt

8 green onions, cut into 1-inch pieces

¼ cup chopped fresh cilantro

Follow These Steps:

>> Wash the rice (as shown on page 205). Set aside, draining.

>> In a colander, under cold, trickling water, rub the chicken skin all over with salt as to scour and smooth. Turn the water off, and rub the chicken with a half of a lime, all over the skin. *The acid serves to tighten up and firm the skin. Alternately rub with salt and lime until the skin is as smooth as, yes, a baby's bottom.*

>> Now, under fully running cold water, vigorously rub and rinse all of the salt off the bird.

STEAM THE CHICKEN

>> Configure a stovetop steamer. Pour the chicken stock into the pot. Add the ginger, garlic, and pandan leaves.

>> Raise the heat to high, tapering to medium-high when the stock comes to a boil and is steaming steadily, but not violently.

>> Put the chicken in the top steamer area and cover. *Monitor the steam from time to time to ensure that it sufficiently envelops or "clouds" the chicken.*

>> Steam for about an hour, until a thermometer inserted in the meat closest to the thigh joint of the chicken reaches 165°.

>> Save the liquid. It's incredible, and will serve as the liquid for the rice, which we'll cook next while the chicken is resting on a platter.

COOK THE RICE

>> Okay, measure the liquid remaining in the pot. It should be about 3 cups. We'll need about 2½ cups to cook the rice. Strain out and reserve the garlic and ginger. Discard the pandan.

>> There should be some visible chicken fat floating on the surface of the stock. Transfer a tablespoon or so to a small saucepan. We'll start cooking the rice in that.

>> Take a piece of the ginger and a little of the garlic (about two cloves' worth), and mash with a fork.

>> Now, heat up the saucepan to medium. Add the ginger-garlic paste. Give it a stir with a wooden spoon. Reduce heat to low.

>> Add the rice to the pot and sauté for a minute or two. Try not to brown the garlic and ginger too much. *This dish should be delicate.*

>> Cover with 2½ cups of hot stock. Cover and simmer for about 10 minutes. Then, turn off the heat but leave the saucepan on the stove, covered, for another 10 minutes. Fluff the rice.

SERVE!

>> If you didn't cut the chicken in advance, do it now. Use your Mad Skills (page 39).

>> Sprinkle the cut chicken with 1 teaspoon kosher salt, green onions, and cilantro. Serve with Hot Chile–Ginger Sauce. See the photo for serving instructions.

SERVES 5 (SERVING SIZE: 2 PIECES OF CHICKEN AND ½ CUP RICE)
CALORIES 494; **FAT** 8.6G (SAT 2.4G, MONO 2.9G, POLY 1.9G); **PROTEIN** 79G; **CARB** 21G; **FIBER** 1G; **CHOL** 198MG; **IRON** 4MG; **SODIUM** 685MG; **CALC** 58MG

HOT CHILE-GINGER SAUCE

HANDS-ON: 10 MIN. **TOTAL:** 10 MIN.

There's something glorious about the results of a mortar and pestle treatment. Intuitively, you get to decide the degree of impact, whereas there's a fair bit of heat being generated when you use something like, say, a food processor. The shaggy nature of the final sauce makes for a handcrafted look and makes the sauce more fun to eat, as you'll get spiky notes of garlic, ginger, and chile while you're enjoying your chicken. Who could complain about that?

Food	How Much	Why
fresh red Thai chiles	¼ cup coarsely chopped (about 8 small chiles)	A punch of aggressive heat is welcome against the balanced outcome of the chicken dish.
garlic cloves	4, coarsely chopped	Raw is wonderful, and layers in nicely over the sweetness of the sugar.
fresh gingerroot	about 2 tablespoons (1-inch piece, peeled, sliced, and finely slivered)	Ginger. Garlic. Geography.
sugar	1 tablespoon	For the salt.
kosher salt	½ teaspoon	For the sugar.
fresh lime juice	¼ cup	The surprising richness of the steamed chicken needs the acid.
chicken broth from Singapore Chicken Rice	¼ cup	Because it's good enough to drink.
green onions	1 tablespoon minced	It's an aroma-texture thing.
freshly ground black pepper	¼ teaspoon	This is a trick from a Vietnamese dipping sauce I once had that was made with nothing but salt, pepper, and lemon.

Follow These Steps:

>> Add the chiles, garlic, ginger, sugar, and salt to a mortar or to your smallest mixing bowl that can withstand some pounding.

>> Make fists and pound your counter so that the beat can be barely heard. *Pianissimo. Okay, you have the feel.*

>> Using a pestle or the blunt, broad end of something like a rolling pin (*be creative and look around your kitchen for something that can be used to smash things*), gently pound the mixture until it becomes shaggy in appearance, but not uniform.

>> Transfer to a good-looking dipping bowl.

>> Add the lime juice, the chicken broth, the green onions, and the black pepper; stir to combine.

SERVES 4 (SERVING SIZE: ABOUT 2 TABLESPOONS)
CALORIES 29; **FAT** 0.1G (SAT 0G, MONO 0G, POLY 0G); **PROTEIN** 1G; **CARB** 7G; **FIBER** 0G; **CHOL** 0MG; **IRON** 0MG; **SODIUM** 278MG; **CALC** 11MG

PORT-STAINED BEEF MEDALLIONS

HANDS-ON: 15 MIN. **TOTAL:** 55 MIN.

This is a counterintuitive little recipe. Indeed, you'll get some squished faces if you tell your guests you're serving them steamed beef. But this is delicious. Promise. So why are we steaming prized beef tenderloin? Because gentle steaming honors the delicate nature of the cut and the mildness of the flavor, and it allows the tender texture of tenderloin to be the lead feature in the dish. While a steakhouse char is welcome on beefier cuts, such as strip and rib-eye, the port stain gives the same visual appeal in a super-tender cut. People will ask where you hid your personal chef.

SOME TIME ON SALT WILL HELP FIRM UP THE EXTERIOR OF THE MEDALLIONS, HELPING TO CREATE THE ILLUSION OF DRY-HEAT COOKING (PAN OR GRILL, IN THE TYPICAL CASE).

Food	How Much	Why
garlic cloves	4, peeled	The perfume and flavor of garlic adds a savory note against the sweetness of port wine.
kosher salt	¼ teaspoon	To firm and flavor.
beef tenderloin	4 (4-ounce) medallions, trimmed	The star of the show.
Mad Delicious Aioli (page 86)	½ cup	The sauce.
fresh red chiles (such as Fresno chiles)	1 tablespoon finely minced	The Fresno is the ultimate utility chile. The balance of heat, sweet, and vegetal is ideal. This is a chile that lets you know it's there, but won't steal the show.
port wine	2 cups	Primarily used as a stain, the residual sugar adds contrast to the garlic-forward flavors in the aioli.
lemon zest	1 tablespoon grated	The citrusy perfume helps make the port less candy-like.
smoked paprika	1 teaspoon	A hint of fire helps complete the illusion.

CONTINUED →

PORT-STAINED BEEF MEDALLIONS

4 garlic cloves, peeled

¼ tsp. kosher salt

4 (4-oz.) beef tenderloin medallions, trimmed

½ cup Mad Delicious Aioli (page 86)

1 Tbsp. finely minced fresh red chiles

2 cups port wine

1 Tbsp. grated lemon zest

1 tsp. smoked paprika

Follow These Steps:

>> Place garlic on a cutting board; sprinkle with ¼ teaspoon salt. Chop until coarse, but consistent. Then, scrape with the flat side of knife to mash.

>> Place the beef tenderloin medallions on paper towels on a plate. Pat dry on all sides.

>> Rub the garlic mixture evenly on all 4 beef medallions. Replace the paper towels on the plate, and allow the beef medallions to quick-cure, uncovered, in the refrigerator, for about 30 minutes.

MAKE THE SAUCE

>> Blend the aioli and the chiles. Chill.

>> In a small saucepan over medium heat, bring the port wine to a boil.

>> Now, reduce heat to a gentle simmer and reduce wine to a ½ cup of liquid. It should be syrupy.

>> Remove from the heat, and stir in the lemon zest and smoked paprika. Pour the port reduction into a baking dish or shallow pan with a diameter small enough to allow the sauce to pool, yet hold all of the beef medallions.

>> Set aside.

STEAM THE MEDALLIONS

>> Ready a 10-inch stovetop steamer, filling the pot to a depth of 1 inch. I like using the bamboo steamer for this recipe. You'll only need one layer and the lid. Bring the water to a boil and get the steam going at a full (but not violent) rate.

>> Place the medallions equidistant on a small square of parchment. Cover and steam for about 6 to 8 minutes or until desired degree of doneness (the illustration on page 159 can help you determine this).

>> Remove the steaks from the steamer. Pat the tenderloin medallions dry with paper towels, and press them down into the port reduction. *Allow them to "stain" for 5 minutes on each side.*

REDUCTION IS A CHEFFY TERM THAT REFERS, SIMPLY, TO WATER BEING REMOVED BY SIMMERING OR OTHER HEAT-INDUCED EVAPORATION.

PLATE YOUR MASTERPIECE!

» Transfer the medallions to a cutting board and slice at a broad angle. You should be able to get 4 reasonably thick (about ½-inch) slices per medallion.

» Spoon 2 tablespoons of the aioli mixture on each of 4 plates and smear, running across the plate with the back of your spoon. *Snazzy.*

» Fan the medallions over the aioli performance art. Drizzle 2 tablespoons of the port reduction on the steaks to finish.

SERVES 4 (SERVING SIZE: 3 OUNCES BEEF, 2 TABLESPOONS AIOLI MIXTURE, AND 2 TABLESPOONS PORT REDUCTION)
CALORIES 323; **FAT** 17.6G (SAT 4.3G, MONO 9.5G, POLY 1.6G); **PROTEIN** 26G; **CARB** 8G; **FIBER** 1G; **CHOL** 75MG; **IRON** 2MG; **SODIUM** 298MG; **CALC** 48MG

STEP BY STEP: Staining Beef Medallions

1) The Before: You'll effectively have gray beef medallions at this juncture. Fear not. The interior is gloriously rosy.

2) The After: Drying, then "staining" will allow both the deep burgundy color and flavor of the port reduction to absorb into the exterior meat fibers, making your medallions look credibly roasted.

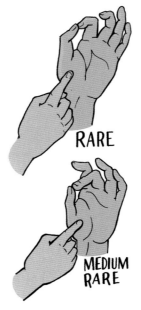

RARE

MEDIUM RARE

MEDIUM

MEDIUM WELL

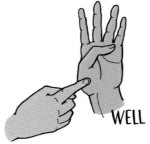

WELL

CHIPOTLE SHRIMP FAJITAS

HANDS-ON: 17 MIN. **TOTAL:** 27 MIN.

When you work with stacked steamers, you look like one serious cook. In this "I can't believe it's not Asian" creation, you'll highlight the individuality, brightness, and freshness of each ingredient rather than combining ingredients in "sizzling" fat.

Food	How Much	Why
medium shrimp	24 shrimp, peeled and deveined (about 1 pound)	Peeling and deveining make for easier eating in this dish. Make sure you take the tails off fully, too.
chipotle chiles in adobo sauce	2 chiles, finely chopped plus 2 teaspoons of the sauce	The smokiness and depth will punctuate the entire eating experience. Have beer handy.
fresh lime juice	2 tablespoons	Preferably from fresh Key (Mexican) limes.
kosher salt	3/8 teaspoon, divided	
poblano chile	1 1/4 cups thinly sliced (about 3 chiles)	For the "fajita" peppers and onions mixture.
sweet onion	1 1/2 cups thinly sliced (about 2 small onions)	The onion portion of the above. Sweet will help combat the heat from the chipotle.
6-inch corn tortillas	8	A departure from the typical Tex-Mex fajita configuration for sure, but there's something about toasty corn against chipotles that is undeniable.
beer (optional)		It's not in the recipe. It's for you. You deserve it.
Mexican hot sauce (optional)		A few dashes satisfy anyone who loves that initial tingly kiss of heat.
cilantro sprigs	16	Sprigs, not leaves. Think of cilantro as a salad green, rather than an herb, and you'll never be fussy about it again.
lime wedges	4	To bring some brightness and acidity to the final dish.

Follow These Steps:

>> Ready three layers of a classic stackable steamer (bamboo is easiest to use as a service vessel at the table).

>> Get about a quart of water in the base of your steamer to a full rolling boil.

>> Lay a small square of parchment (or a small stoneware plate) on the first bamboo steamer layer.

>> Toss the shrimp, chipotles, adobo sauce, lime juice, and 1/4 teaspoon salt together in a small mixing bowl.

>> Place the shrimp on the parchment (or plate) inside the steamer layer, and move on to the next step.

>> Toss the poblanos, onions, and 1/8 teaspoon salt in a small mixing bowl. Place directly into the next steamer layer and stack on top of the shrimp layer.

>> In the top steamer layer, *gently overlap the corn tortillas (all 8 of them), like shingles.*

>> Place all three steamer layers, with the top covered, onto the steaming water. (The order, from bottom to top, should be: shrimp, peppers and onions, tortillas.)

>> Cook for about 10 to 15 minutes, or until the shrimp are fully cooked, the onions and peppers are gently wilted, and the tortillas are soft and pliable.

>> Remove from the heat and bring the whole stack to the table.

>> *Have beer, Mexican hot sauce, and washed whole-sprig cilantro available at the table with the lime wedges.*

SERVES 4 (SERVING SIZE: 2 FAJITAS)
CALORIES 219; **FAT** 2.6G (SAT 0.4G, MONO 0.4G, POLY 0.9G); **PROTEIN** 18G; **CARB** 32G; **FIBER** 5G; **CHOL** 129MG; **IRON** 2MG; **SODIUM** 398MG; **CALC** 116MG

HERB-STEAMED WHOLE STRIPED BASS
WITH FENNEL AND SWEET ONION SOUBISE

HANDS-ON: 45 MIN. **TOTAL:** 1 HR. 20 MIN.

It's generally recognized among serious cooks that cooking anything on the bone creates a moister, more flavorful result. This whole steamed fish is bombarded with an arsenal of brightness and pungency, as it's enveloped in everything from chopped herbs to minty-lemony steam. We make our soubise sanscream, building body with fennel instead. The sauce alone will earn cheers for an encore.

SOUBISE IS A CLASSIC SAUCE BASED ON ONION PUREE COMMONLY MADE WITH CREAM OR A BÉCHAMEL (ROUX-THICKENED WHITE SAUCE) BASE, BUT NOT HERE.

Food	How Much	Why
whole striped bass	1 (3-pound) fish	It's sustainable. And delicious.
fresh mint	1 bunch	To perfume the steam.
lemon	1, thinly sliced	It softens in the simmering water and is delicious against the soubise.
green onions	2 bunches, roots trimmed and left whole	The onions diffuse the intensity of the steam on the bottom side of the fish.
fresh tarragon	2 tablespoons coarsely chopped	The second of five herbs. Mint leads, followed by this anise-like herb…
fresh Italian flat-leaf parsley	2 tablespoons coarsely chopped	…then, we add some grassiness from parsley.
fennel fronds	2 tablespoons coarsely chopped	Fennel fronds harmonize with the tarragon.
fresh thyme leaves	1 teaspoon finely minced	Thyme adds complexity and aromatic punctuation.
black pepper	¼ teaspoon	For bite.
fennel bulb	1 cup shaved razor thin (about 1 bulb)	Mellows the onions and provides further body to the sauce.
sweet onion	1 cup shaved razor thin (about 1 onion)	The foundation of the sauce.
capers	2 teaspoons	More complex than salt alone. Adds a brininess.
extra-virgin olive oil	¼ cup	Silkiness, and if of the right quality, some spice.
fresh lemon juice	1 tablespoon	One dimension of acidity.
red wine vinegar	1 tablespoon	Another dimension.
Tabasco	8 dashes	The third dimension.
arugula	4 generous handfuls	Peppery and wonderful against onion-y anything.
kosher salt	½ teaspoon, divided	To finish.

CONTINUED →

HERB-STEAMED WHOLE STRIPED BASS

1 (3-lb.) whole striped bass

1 bunch fresh mint

1 thinly sliced lemon

2 bunches green onions, roots trimmed and left whole

2 Tbsp. coarsely chopped fresh tarragon

2 Tbsp. coarsely chopped fresh Italian flat-leaf parsley

2 Tbsp. coarsely chopped fennel fronds

1 tsp. finely minced fresh thyme leaves

1/4 tsp. black pepper

1 cup razor thin fennel bulb

1 cup razor thin sweet onion

2 tsp. capers

1/4 cup extra-virgin olive oil

1 Tbsp. fresh lemon juice

1 Tbsp. red wine vinegar

8 dashes Tabasco

4 generous handfuls arugula

1/2 tsp. kosher salt, divided

Follow These Steps:

≫ Ready a stacked-style bamboo steamer. You'll need two of the layers, one for steaming the onions and fennel soft, and another for the herbs and fish.

PREP THE FISH

≫ Trim the fish per the photos on page 165.

≫ Transfer to a plate and place in refrigerator, uncovered, for a moment. *Alternatively, you can put the fish in a baking dish and cover with plenty of ice to, you know, ready the mood.*

FILL AND STACK YOUR STEAMER

≫ Fill a Dutch oven (large enough to house your steamer) about two-thirds full with water. Throw in the mint and lemon slices.

≫ Bring to a raging boil, then taper to a steady, steamy boil.

≫ For the first bamboo steamer layer, *lay down a bed of trimmed green onions as if to build a raft.*

≫ Place the fish on top of the onions.

≫ In a small bowl, toss together the chopped tarragon, the parsley, the fennel fronds, and the thyme leaves.

≫ Sprinkle in an even layer on the top side of the fish.

≫ Sprinkle with the black pepper.

≫ Top the fish with another bamboo layer, and then add the shaved fennel bulb and the sweet onion to this top steamer.

STEAM IT ALL!

≫ Cover the steamer stack, place over the simmering water, and steam for about 20 minutes before checking the fish. Depending on the size of the fish and the intensity of your steam, this can take anywhere from 20 to 35 minutes.

≫ Check the doneness of the onions and fennel. They should be soft after about 20 minutes of cooking time.

≫ When tender to the tooth, transfer to a blender and add the capers, oil, lemon juice, red wine vinegar, and Tabasco. Blend until silky smooth.

≫ In the steamer layer that contained the onions and fennel, add the arugula, then cover and return the top steamer layer to the steamer stack.

≫ Steam 15 minutes, letting the arugula wilt while the fish is finding its way to completion. Turn off the heat.

SERVE YOUR BEAUTIFUL FISH

>> *Find your most majestic serving platter*—one that has plenty of depth for sauce.

>> Once the fish is cooked through, pour half of the fennel sauce onto the base of the platter.

>> Layer the green onions over the sauce.

>> Now the fish. Then, the rest of the sauce. Sprinkle with $\frac{3}{8}$ teaspoon of the salt.

>> Top with the arugula. Hit it with the final $\frac{1}{8}$ teaspoon of salt.

>> *Laboriously remove the lemons from the hot water. Place them indiscriminately around, on, and about the fish.*

>> Use tablespoons and forks to serve the fish.

SERVES 8 (SERVING SIZE: 6 OUNCES FISH, 2 TABLESPOONS SAUCE, AND 1 TABLESPOON ARUGULA)
CALORIES 282; FAT 13.5G (SAT 2.4G, MONO 7.5G, POLY 2.6G); PROTEIN 34G; CARB 4G; FIBER 1G;
CHOL 121MG; IRON 3MG; SODIUM 282MG; CALC 174MG

STEP BY STEP: Trimming a Whole Fish

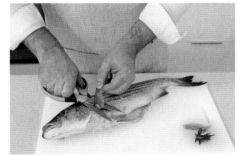

1) Using a pair of kitchen scissors, trim off the dorsal and pelvic fins.

2) Holding the edge of the pectoral fins, trim as closely to the fish's body as possible.

3) Move the fish to a cutting board, and score at a sharp angle all the way to the backbone, every inch or so.

PACKET-STEAMED BEETS
WITH TARRAGON YOGURT

HANDS-ON: 15 MIN. **TOTAL:** 1 HR. 37 MIN.

Packet-steaming in foil in an oven is a sublime way to cook root vegetables. You'll get some caramelization if you add a little fat to the packet, which is a huge flavor bonus, but the dish (and the beets themselves) will still be incredible if you choose to leave out the fat. We'll use tarragon two times: in the packet, to get the Béarnaise-like depth of the herb, and minced fresh to mix into the brightness and richness of Greek yogurt.

Food	How Much	Why
beets	2 pounds (about 7 medium beets)	Red, yellow, or both. Combining colors looks incredible. Don't worry about a little bleeding from the red ones onto the yellow. Plus, the mingling of colors looks super-cool.
toasted walnut oil or butter	1 tablespoon	If you can't find toasted walnut oil, butter is perfectly lovely. But toasted or roasted walnut oil is lively, true-to-life nutty, and tastes as expensive as it is.
fresh tarragon	4 sprigs plus 2 tablespoons minced	There's something perfect about beets and tarragon, particularly with creamy things like, in this case, Greek yogurt.
kosher salt	$^3/_8$ teaspoon, divided	To season.
white wine vinegar	2 tablespoons	To enliven the yogurt sauce.
garlic clove	1, minced	For some piquancy in the sauce.
plain 2% reduced-fat Greek yogurt	1 cup	To serve as the base of the sauce. You won't miss extra fat, as the texture of most low-fat Greek yogurt on the market is incredible (due to the fact that it's strained).

Follow These Steps:

>> Preheat your oven to 450°.

>> Trim roots and stems from beets. (See page 119 for a how-to of this process.) Pierce beets with a fork. On a sheet of foil about 24 inches long, lay down the beets, oil or butter, tarragon sprigs, and $^1/_4$ teaspoon of salt.

>> *Drape another sheet of the same length on top of the beets, and seal the packet around all four sides, turning inward toward the beets to crowd them together.*

>> Place the packet directly on the oven rack, leaving the packet in the oven for about an hour (more or less, depending on the size of the beets).

>> When the beets can be easily pierced with a fork, remove the packet from the oven. Set aside for 20 minutes to rest.

>> Unseal the packet, and peel the beets with a spoon, paper towel, or dull knife. The skins should slip right off.

>> On a cutting board, quarter the beets, and place in a bowl.

>> In a small bowl, combine the vinegar and the raw garlic. Allow to steep for 2 minutes.

>> Add the Greek yogurt to the garlic and vinegar. Stir well, finally folding in $^1/_8$ teaspoon salt and the minced tarragon.

>> Either mix the beets with the yogurt sauce (*á la* potato salad), or dollop the yogurt on plates next to the steamed beets. This is a great side dish for whole roasted fish or chicken.

SERVES 6 (SERVING SIZE: ABOUT 5 BEET WEDGES AND ABOUT 2$^1/_2$ TABLESPOONS YOGURT SAUCE)
CALORIES 112; **FAT** 3.3G (SAT 0.8G, MONO 0.6G, POLY 1.5G); **PROTEIN** 6G; **CARB** 16G; **FIBER** 4G; **CHOL** 3MG; **IRON** 1MG; **SODIUM** 251MG; **CALC** 54MG

A SAVORY IDEA:

LIGHTY FORK-CRUSH THE
PEACHES & SERVE ALONGSIDE
GRILLED MEATS. **AMAZING.**

BOURBON-STEAMED PEACHES

HANDS-ON: 11 MIN. **TOTAL:** 30 MIN.

No one's complaining about peaches, bourbon, and sugar. This recipe allows you some practice with your steam-peeling technique and provides a little nip of whiskey if you don't get it perfect the first time. This dish is amazing when turned into a browned butter blender sauce (see Brown-Buttered Mango Coulis, page 72) or when served with grilled meats or roasted chicken. It also makes a killer accompaniment to ice cream.

Food	How Much	Why
ripe peaches	5	Because you'll mess one up the first time and will feel terrible giving someone the ugly peach. If you have extra, chop them coarsely and lay the pieces on each dish as a foundation for the other, beautifully peeled peach halves.
dark brown sugar	1 cup	Use dark in this case, because we'll actually be steaming with a simple syrup made from this sugar, and a little extra molasses kick is all the more delicious.
water	2 cups	This is the precursor to steam.
bourbon	½ cup	For aroma and depth of flavor.
kosher salt	⅛ teaspoon	To enliven the nuances of the ripe peaches.
fresh lemon juice	1 tablespoon	A little acid balance makes for empty plates. Promise.

Follow These Steps:

≫ Wash and dry the peaches.

≫ Score the bottoms of each peach with a ½-inch "X."

≫ In the pot that underlies your standard steamer configuration, combine the sugar, 2 cups water, bourbon, salt, and juice. *Go ahead and throw the halved lemon in the syrup for a little bitter punctuation if you are so inclined; otherwise discard it.*

≫ Bring the syrup to a full rolling boil.

≫ Place the peaches in the steamer basket, scored side up, and cover the steamer. Steam for 3 minutes, or until the peel starts to "open" up away from the score marks.

≫ Remove the steamer basket from the steamer configuration (leave the peaches in it), and set aside to cool for a few moments, until the peaches can be handled safely.

≫ Back at the stove, the syrup should be rolling away at a boil (and some lovely peach juices should have dripped into it).

≫ Over medium-high heat, reduce the syrup 5 minutes, until it coats the back of a spoon and is about the consistency of real maple syrup at room temperature.

≫ Turn off the syrup and let it rest.

≫ The peaches should be cool enough to peel. With clean hands, peel from the "X" toward the stem end of the peach. *You should be able to remove the peel in 4 easy "fillets."*

≫ Using a paring knife, halve the peaches. Then tumble them in the syrup to coat.

≫ Serve the peaches, slightly warm or at room temperature, with about 2 tablespoons of the reduced syrup.

SERVES 4 (SERVING SIZE: 1 PEACH AND 2 TABLESPOONS SYRUP)
CALORIES 269; **FAT** 0.4G (SAT 0G, MONO 0.1G, POLY 0.1G); **PROTEIN** 1G; **CARB** 63G; **FIBER** 2G; **CHOL** 0MG; **IRON** 0MG; **SODIUM** 73MG; **CALC** 9MG

PAN COOKING

Sweating, searing, sautéing, pan roasting, frying, and braising

In professional kitchens, the sauté station (you probably call it the stove) is the holy grail, the place from which, if you succeed, you just might graduate to chef-dom. For the budding home cook, regulating burners is the hard part of cooking. Learning to combine ingredients and harmonize flavors makes you a credible *food person,* for sure, but mastering the application of heat, particularly at the stove, makes you a *cook.*

Pan cooking is about control. The recipes in this chapter require your attention and your sensibility. This isn't a pop-it-in-the-oven-for-20-minutes-come-back-and-dinner-is-ready chapter. These recipes are for the person who likes to cook, who wants to become one with dinner. Let's start by outlining cooking methods typically associated with the pan.

(MOSTLY) DRY-HEAT METHODS FOR PAN COOKING

If food isn't steamed or submerged in a water-based liquid, it's a dry-heat method.

"Barely" or Gently Cooking

There are foods that benefit from very gentle cooking, where simply being *kissed* by heat is enough to coax them to perfection. Twice-Cooked Garlic Shrimp (page 177) leverages this method; we slowly raise the temperature on the shrimp so its structure is respected, its moisture is left largely within, and its freshness is honored. If we say gentle and the recipe calls for a pan, then it's the Gently Cooked Method.

IF A FISH CAN BE CONSUMED RAW DELICIOUSLY, THEN IT IS A CANDIDATE FOR THE GENTLY COOKED METHOD.

Sweating

Sweating is a method intended to soften and intensify without browning. Think onions, garlic, small-diced vegetables, and the like—as little as a teaspoon of fat, super-low heat. Sweat vegetables to help them taste just like the vegetable where browning would muddy things. If there's sizzle, it's not sweating. If you're super-patient, you can sweat vegetables all the way soft and turn them into a puree. Try it with garlic. You'll thank me.

Sautéing

I'm not a big fan of being constrained by terminology (silly me, here I am, writing a book, outlining things by terms). Instead, I advocate having broad frames of reference and learning to navigate the temperature continuum ranging from very cold to very hot. The frames of reference give you a general sense of what to do. Use them as a starting point. Cooking sensibility has set in when you know how to work flexibly around a given temperature reference point. In the case of this technique, the word sauté is based on the French word for "to jump." It involves a hot pan, a little fat, and food in motion. It generally happens quickly and involves food that has been cut to a uniform thickness and size to ensure it cooks evenly. There are a few techniques that are cousins of sautéing:

>> **Pan Searing:** A proper sear would see the food sliding around on a hot, slick pan like an air-hockey puck glides across the playing table. The pan is typically a little hotter, the fat amount is a little more restrained. Sear: chicken, beef medallions, block-cut fish (like tuna or halibut). If you're searing scallops, dry the scallops. Put the scallops in the pan. Let the heat do the work.

>> **Pan Charring:** This is wanton sautéing with unrestrained high heat—burning bits permitted. This is a fantastic light cooking trick, because you can coax a ton of flavor from nearly any food with just a touch of (or barely any) fat. If it contains water, proteins, and sugar (which is everything, really), you can play with charring. Make the Pan-Charred Green Beans with Tarragon recipe (page 196). It won't be the last time you do.

>> **Stir Frying:** This is Asian sautéing. It typically refers to a more varied (and populated) pan of scattered ingredients being rapidly lifted and tossed, but not really "stirred." Anything that can be cut into bite-sized pieces is a candidate for this method, like broccoli florets, morsels of chicken thigh, quartered baby bok choy. Heat here is generally close to unrestrained.

>> **Pan Roasting:** This is the most mindful cooking technique, requiring the most masterful of heat regulation. Pan roasting requires you to become a Master of Medium Heat—modulating between medium-low, medium, and medium-high—to ensure you cook the food through to the center without drying out the exterior, achieve a lovely, even crust-meets-lacquer exterior, and control the rendered fats and juices so they don't burn. The thing to be cooked is typically a larger item—like a small beef tenderloin or a chicken breast. You baste. You monitor. You turn (the food) often for evenly applied Maillard magic.

>> **Pan Toasting:** This is usually a prelude to a moist cooking method, where you're trying to evoke some roasted and toasted notes from whatever will soon be soaked, usually something starchy, such as pasta or rice. You'll taste what I mean when you try the Toasted Penne with Chicken Sausage (page 208).

>> **Pan Frying:** Typically, this involves a pool of temperature-controlled fat or oil to cook partially submerged breaded or coated or starchy things. The idea is to evenly crisp whatever hits the fat. If portions are controlled and draining is done on a rack (not paper towels, please), frying can make an occasional visit to the light cooking kitchen. Choose oils with a higher smoke point, such as grapeseed, peanut, or canola. They'll be more stable, and your fried bits and pieces will be more evenly cooked.

PAN SEARING

PAN CHARRING

STIR FRYING

PAN ROASTING

PAN TOASTING

PAN FRYING

MOIST METHODS FOR PAN COOKING

If water is employed (in the form of a broth, stock, steam, etc.), it's a moist-heat method. Steep. Poach. Simmer. Boil. Steam. All moist.

Quasi-Braises

Where a sautéed item sees a brief simmer in some sauce.

Pan Sauces

When you've controlled a pan's heat properly, there are often tasty, unburned bits left behind that serve to flavor your sauces when "deglazed" with plenty of liquid (as in the Chicken-Pecan Meatballs on page 247). With the Sautéed Cod with Tomatoes, Piquillos, and Olives (page 250), we've opted to finesse both components, focusing on an evenly browned, (good) restaurant-caliber sauté. The pan sauce utilizes the browned bits that remain behind.

The Hydration of Starchy Things

The culmination of a pan toast and a patient simmer—perfectly illustrated in the risotto-inspired Toasted Penne with Chicken Sausage (page 208).

HYBRID METHODS FOR PAN COOKING

These are your inspirations to break "the rules." The method for Carnitas de Pollo (page 255) is a hybrid of a confit, a braise, and a pan-fry. Watch the pan. Observe the transformation. Play around with your own combination of techniques. Share the results. Blog about them.

STEP AWAY FROM THE RECIPE

While following well-written recipes can inform your cooking style and ensure consistent results, little is more freeing than hitting the market, grabbing the freshest/best/most interesting/tastiest ingredients, and crafting a meal on the fly.

Use this five-step thought process when you want to play with your pans and break free from the confines of the recipe. (I provide a sample answer for each question from my imaginary shopping trip. You should get the gist.)

FOND

"FOND" IS FRENCH FOR BACKGROUND, BOTTOM, OR SUBSTANCE. IN CULINARY PARLANCE, IT REFERS TO THE DELICIOUS "STUFF" ON THE INSIDE BOTTOM OF PANS—JUST BEGGING FOR YOU TO RELEASE IT (DEGLAZE) WITH WINE, STOCK, OR EVEN WATER.

» **What are you cooking?** Vegetables? Meats? Starchy items? A combination of the aforementioned? In small pieces? Medium? Large? Is it a singular item? A smattering of items? This will help you select a technique or variation/hybrid of a technique. *I just got back from the market and bought these peeled early Vidalia onions, with beautifully trimmed green tops. They're gorgeous!*

» **Now choose the cooking fat.** Smoke point is a concern. So is flavor. The amount of fat correlates to the technique. Also, remember this is, technically speaking, a dry-heat cooking method, so you'll want to pat wetter ingredients dry—because they'll brown easier and more evenly—and because spattering oil hurts. A lot. *While I love a bit of butter for flavor, I know that butter can burn easily, so I'll use this peanut oil. I can always swirl in a nib of butter for flavor at the end.*

» **Choose the pan.** The above decision should be made in concert with your choice of pan. Wok-like? Cast iron? Fancy heavy-bottomed cookware? Enameled Dutch oven? All-purpose skillet? Is it a complex recipe? Will you be working with two pans? *Because I'm cooking large onion halves, this'll need something that distributes heat evenly over longer cooking times: cast iron.*

» **Contemplate heat regulation.** Will you need the heat level to fluctuate up and down—with you in control? Raging, unrestrained heat? Perfectly monitored, constant, steady heat? This decision is interconnected with your choice of pan. A quick lesson: One thing to remember when you're cooking with pans at the stove is **the pan is not glued to the stove.** In addition to regulating the heat, you can lift the pan from the burner when cooking, lightly agitating it in the air to allow things to cool off. You can even have a small pitcher of water around to dose (not *douse*, and carefully, please) the pan a bit if you've taken the heat too far. You don't have to stand there and watch things burn. Get a hold of your-self. And your pans. And that poor chicken. *Okay, so I'm not cooking chicken, but these onions need some low and slow, well-monitored cooking. I'll start at medium-high to build some color, but once that happens, I'll taper it down to low so I can get those onions tender all the way to the center.*

» **Think about building fonds and deglazing.** Assuming you have a fond (see page 174) that is pleasantly browned and not charred, you can begin layering in the wetter things along with the ingredients that will render liquid when heated. Also, think about acids and sauces built atop your pan-cooked item, and make sure you chose the right pan. *I like glaze-y onions, but you've told me to focus on balancing flavors. How about this: a tablespoon honey, one half of lemon, squeezed, and a pinch of salt? And I know thyme works with almost everything. I'll toss in a sprig. And that nib of butter. Mmm.*

Easy, right? Now, let's pan cook.

WE'RE TALKING **DRY-HEAT** METHODS HERE. AT THE END OF THE CHAPTER, WE'LL TALK MOISTURE— DISCUSSING BRAISES, PAN SAUCES, AND HYBRID METHODS.

TWICE-COOKED GARLIC SHRIMP

HANDS-ON: 25 MIN. **TOTAL:** 25 MIN.

*Shrimp benefit from delicate cooking, as sharp, aggressive heat cooks them unevenly, yielding
a seized, rubbery exterior. This recipe is an exercise in patience, and illustrates that part one
of great cooking is mastering the application of heat. Part two is the mindful harmonizing of
flavors. Always get fresh shrimp if you can. Its texture and flavor are unparalleled (think lobster).*

Food	How Much	Why
cooking spray	to coat the pan	To prevent the shrimp from sticking to the pan.
jumbo (21-25) shrimp	24 (about 1 pound), peeled and deveined	This size is ideal for this technique. Anything smaller won't endure the second, more aggressive pan-cooking treatment.
toasted walnut oil	1 teaspoon	When cooking garlic soft, but not browned, adding a toasted nut oil helps provide welcome earthiness.
garlic cloves	4, slivered	The flavor in focus. The reason we're not browning it is that burned edges become inevitable if the heat isn't handled just so. Let's take baby steps.
butter	½ tablespoon	For roundness and mouthfeel.
fresh lemon juice	3 tablespoons	Everything thus far is round, warm, or earthy. This peps things up.
fresh flat-leaf parsley	1 tablespoon chiffonade	And this enlivens to finish.
kosher salt	a pinch	It might need it. It might not. It's all in the shrimp selection.

Follow These Steps:

>> Spray a cool, 12-inch skillet with cooking spray. Lay the shrimp in a single layer in the pan.

>> Turn the fire on the lowest flame/heat setting possible. Let the pan get progressively hot to the touch. If you want to work like a chef, tap the bottom of the pan with the tip of your finger. It'll burn a little, but not a lot. Slowly raise the heat to medium-low. Controlling the heat is critical here. Don't let the shrimp sizzle. Watch the edges of the shrimp gradually brighten in color.

>> When the edges of the shrimp turn from gray to bright orange (after about 6 minutes), *turn them over, one by one, maintaining the soldier-like layout in the pan.*

>> Similarly cook the other side of the shrimp until the bottom edges brighten in color, about 4 minutes.

>> Turn off the heat. Transfer the shrimp to a mixing bowl. *Allow them to mingle and "carry over."*

>> Make sure all remaining ingredients are within arm's reach.

>> Bring the pan, unwashed, back to the flame. Swirl in the walnut oil. Bring the heat to medium-high. Get the oil hot, but don't let it smoke. There's not much fat in the pan, and you don't want it to scorch. *Now, pour in the shrimp, and sauté like a rock star, facilitating the "jump"* (see illustration).

>> Cook for 45 seconds. Lower the heat all the way to low. In fact, depending on what "low" looks like on your cooktop, you might be able to turn the heat off at this point. It all depends on the quality of your cookware and the nature of your cooktop.

>> Add the garlic. Toss the mixture a few times. Let the garlic soften, but not brown. Add the butter, lemon juice, and parsley. Now taste. You might not need the salt. If you do, add it now.

SERVES 4 (SERVING SIZE: ABOUT 6 SHRIMP)
CALORIES 150; **FAT** 4.3G (SAT 1.2G, MONO 0.8G, POLY 1G); **PROTEIN** 24G;
CARB 3G; **FIBER** 0G; **CHOL** 218MG; **IRON** 1MG; **SODIUM** 288MG; **CALC** 100MG

POTATOES BOULANGÈRE

HANDS-ON: 10 MIN. **TOTAL:** 50 MIN.

Chefs have taken this simple potato dish in every direction imaginable. This pan-roasted version has stuck, becoming a new classic. Pan roasting requires your focus and attention, and this recipe allows you to work on developing finesse—evenly browning potatoes, making sure you don't burn the bacon, and bringing the onions to caramelized perfection. Practice makes perfect potatoes. Get to work.

Food	How Much	Why
bacon	2 ounces, cut into 1/8-inch-wide pieces	You can render enough fat out of just a couple of ounces to give real depth to the dish.
yellow onion	2 cups julienne	We'll be sweating them first. Sweating is cooking something that can render liquid over very low heat in a very little bit of fat. That treatment readies the onions to be very evenly browned while the dish cooks "down."
water	1/4 cup	Helps to even out the caramelization and browning of the onions.
butter	1 tablespoon	Because we used so little bacon, we can soften the flavor with a little butter.
fingerling potatoes	1 pound, halved lengthwise	They have a tight flesh that helps them hold shape. Plus, they're cute.
kosher salt	1/4 teaspoon	The bacon by itself doesn't lend enough salt.
garlic clove	1, peeled and smashed	Why not?
fresh thyme	2 sprigs	If you have bacon and onions, use thyme. Your inner French chef will be pleased.
unsalted chicken stock	1/4 cup	The lore that's been passed down suggests that the baker put the potatoes under the rack where the chicken was cooking. That's so romantic. And delicious.

Follow These Steps:

>> Heat a heavy-bottomed skillet over medium heat. Add the bacon to the pan. Cook until crisp, about 5 minutes.

>> Turn off the heat. Then, using a slotted spoon, remove the bacon. Leave the fat in the pan. Make sure the bacon fat is evenly distributed throughout the pan, and add the onions.

>> Put the pan on a very low heat and patiently allow the onions to sweat, avoiding any browning at this juncture.

>> Fold the onions from time to time, allowing them to collapse. They should be very soft. This should take 20 minutes or so.

>> Add 1/4 cup water to the pan. The moisture from the onions should be sufficient to fully deglaze the pan. Using a wooden spoon, stir and scrape up any fond (see page 174) before transferring the onions to a bowl.

>> Add the butter to the pan and melt it to the point of frothiness. *You'll know when you're there.* Low to medium-low heat.

>> Add the potatoes to the pan and tumble until they are evenly coated in butter. Hit the potatoes with salt. Tumble again.

>> Raise the heat to medium and cook the potatoes for 15 to 20 minutes, or until they are evenly browned. *Lift and turn them occasionally, treating each potato as an equal. Don't flop them about in an indiscriminate mass. That's not cool.*

>> Now, add the garlic and the thyme. Cook for about 3 to 5 minutes, or until the thyme is fragrant and the garlic is toasty-brown.

>> Add the chicken stock, the onions, and the bacon, and crank up the heat to super-high.

>> *Stir and fold gently while the chicken broth reduces away to a glorious glaze.* Turn off the heat about 1 minute before the liquid is fully reduced. Serve.

SERVES 4 (SERVING SIZE: 3/4 CUP)
CALORIES 202; **FAT** 9.5G (SAT 4G, MONO 3.6G, POLY 0.9G); **PROTEIN** 5G; **CARB** 25G; **FIBER** 3G; **CHOL** 17MG; **IRON** 1MG; **SODIUM** 284MG; **CALC** 33MG

SEE PAGE 373 FOR A
BLOOPER FROM THIS RECIPE.

RED SAUCE JOINT PEPPERS AND EGGS HERO

HANDS-ON: 25 MIN. **TOTAL:** 25 MIN.

*At Long Island pizzerias, it isn't uncommon to see a hot peppers and eggs hero on
the menu. It's economical and satisfying. Cooks often just give peppers and onions
a quickie sauté, leaving them raw-crunchy. As for the eggs, they work better when tender.*

Food	How Much	Why
whole-wheat hero (hoagie) rolls	6 (2-ounce) rolls, halved lengthwise	Whole wheat is better for you, generally speaking. That's the last time we'll talk about it.
hot Italian turkey sausage	2 (4-ounce) links, casings removed	A little crumbled hot sausage with peppers and eggs needs no reason.
olive oil	2 tablespoons	Flavor. Mouthfeel. There's something delightfully slippery about good olive oil.
red bell pepper	3 cups sliced	Along with the onions, these are a focal point of the dish. Slice them thinly so they collapse and almost "melt" into the eggs.
green bell pepper	1 cup sliced	As contrast. Even with one's eyes closed, they taste "green," and in this case, that makes for a more complex-tasting dish.
onion	2 cups sliced	For the peppers. They're friends.
garlic cloves	4, sliced	Forever inspired by garlic, onions, and peppers sweated in olive oil. To honor tradition.
large eggs	4	To envelop the pepper mixture and to fill you up.
large egg whites	4	To bulk up the eggs enough to create an abundant, light hero.

Follow These Steps:

>> Preheat the broiler. Pop the hoagie rolls in the oven, cut sides up, on a baking sheet. Broil them for 1½ minutes or until toasted. *If you allow for some random charring, you have soul.* Set the rolls aside.

>> Heat a large, flat-sided skillet over medium-high heat.

>> Add the sausage to the pan and cook 3 minutes or until browned, stirring to crumble. Remove the sausage from the pan.

>> Add the olive oil and swirl.

>> Add the bell peppers and the onion. Sauté for about 7 minutes, until the vegetables collapse and become tender. Add the sausage and the garlic.

>> Now, reduce the heat to low and sweat further for about 5 minutes, stirring occasionally.

>> Combine the eggs and egg whites in a bowl with a fork.

>> Pour the eggs into the peppers and onions.

>> Using a heatproof silicone spatula, gently scramble the eggs into the peppers and onions, scraping in long strokes along the bottom of the pan, folding with each scrape.

>> Turn off the eggs when they are still moist and glistening, after 1 minute. They'll carry over.

>> Spoon about ⅔ cup egg-pepper mixture into each of the rolls and serve hot. Immediately.

SERVES 6 (SERVING SIZE: 1 HERO)
CALORIES 406; **FAT** 17.7G (SAT 3.2G, MONO 6.2G, POLY 3.3G); **PROTEIN** 26G; **CARB** 38G; **FIBER** 6G; **CHOL** 175MG; **IRON** 3MG; **SODIUM** 782MG; **CALC** 105MG

MUSHROOM TARTE FLAMBÉE

HANDS-ON: 45 MIN.   **TOTAL:** 1 HR. 15 MIN.

*This flatbread's flavor is built around duxelles, a steady sauté of mushrooms and shallots
(here, we layer in garlic) where the fine mince results in so much surface area being exposed
to the hot pan that it's possible to reduce away most of the ingredients' moisture.
The resultant rich, concentrated "paste" makes for a fantastic filling, spread, and topping.*

Food	How Much	Why
refrigerated fresh whole-wheat pizza dough	12 ounces	For ease.
cooking spray		To keep the dough from annoyingly sticking to the bowl.
butter	1 tablespoon	Butter's flavor matches well with mushrooms.
mushrooms	1 pound, finely chopped	White mushrooms have a ton of flavor to unlock, particularly with this method.
shallot	1, minced	To honor tradition. You could use onion, too.
garlic cloves	2, minced	A bridge to the rosemary, coming later.
kosher salt	½ teaspoon, divided	Some to draw out moisture from the duxelles. The rest is for seasoning the onions.
yellow onion	2 cups julienne	Julienne onions collapse evenly in the skillet. The burnt edges of the tips (after baking) provide some character.
riesling or other fruity white wine	¼ cup	This is a very Alsatian dish. They have a way with riesling. Use some here, and then drink the rest.
fresh rosemary	2 teaspoons minced	Rosemary's piney flavor is superb against Gruyère.
black pepper	¼ teaspoon	For some bite.
Gruyère cheese	3 tablespoons finely shredded	To keep everything light, we pushed forward onion and tapered the typical quantity of cheese.

Follow These Steps:

>> Preheat the oven to 475°.

>> Let the pizza dough sit at room temperature (this is called proofing) for about 30 minutes in a large bowl coated with cooking spray.

>> In a large skillet over medium-high heat, add the butter and let it melt. Add the mushrooms, the shallot, the garlic, and ¼ teaspoon of the salt.

>> Cook, stirring frequently, for about 15 minutes, or until most of the moisture has been evaporated from the mushrooms. *It should be a deep, dark-colored paste.* Allow to cool to room temperature.

>> Heat another large skillet over medium heat. Spray with cooking spray.

>> Add the onions and sweat for 20 minutes or until soft and translucent.

>> Add the riesling, raise the heat to medium-high, and stir 30 seconds or until the wine has fully evaporated.

>> Fold in the rosemary. Season with ¼ teaspoon salt and pepper.

>> Stretch the pizza dough quite thinly, as to make a cracker-bread, until it is about ⅛ inch to ¼ inch thick.

>> Lay the dough on a perforated pizza pan. If you don't have one, use a baking sheet. The crust will be a tad less crisp.

>> Spread the mushroom mixture in an even layer on the dough, leaving a 1-inch border. Top evenly with the onions, and finish with the cheese.

>> Bake at 475° for 15 minutes, or until the dough is completely crisp.

SERVES 6 (SERVING SIZE: 2 SLICES)
CALORIES 204; **FAT** 5.3G (SAT 1.9G, MONO 0.9G, POLY 0.3G); **PROTEIN** 9G; **CARB** 35G; **FIBER** 6G; **CHOL** 9MG; **IRON** 2MG; **SODIUM** 443MG; **CALC** 72MG

BUTTER-SEARED SEA SCALLOPS
WITH PAN-FRIED SWEET CORN HASH

HANDS-ON: 25 MIN. **TOTAL:** 25 MIN.

A properly browned scallop is one of the wonders of cookery, because getting it perfect isn't easy. First, scallops are crazy-wet, and moisture fights against browning. You can get a pocket of water trapped between the pan surface and the scallop, thus inhibiting the temperature rise needed for browning. Secondly, butter, while delicious, adds a higher degree of difficulty than vegetable oils, as its solids are prone to burning and its smoke point is fairly low. Master this and you'll be able to sear anything well.

Food	How Much	Why
Pan-Fried Sweet Corn Hash (*page 187*)	2⅔ cups	Corn and scallops have complementary sweetness profiles and allow for myriad directions with acid, spice, and salt sources (soy sauce, miso, fish sauce, and, of course, salt).
very fresh, dry-packed, chilled sea scallops U-10	1 pound	I specify very fresh, because sometimes "not frozen" is marketed as fresh. Fresh scallops should smell sweet and have a tight structure (not torn and fibrous). Ask to make sure they have been very recently harvested.
butter	2 tablespoons, melted	The flavor works best, it facilitates (and contributes further) browning, and will challenge your mastery of pan cooking. Butter is sensitive and delicate.
cooking spray		For help.
kosher salt	¼ teaspoon, divided	
freshly ground white pepper	¼ teaspoon, divided	More than anything, it's to help highlight your newfound, amazing pan skills.

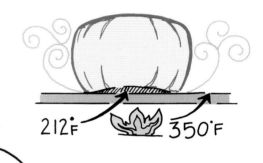

212°F   350°F

U-10 IS SEAFOOD INDUSTRY LINGO FOR THE SIZE OF SCALLOPS. THERE WILL BE APPROXIMATELY, BUT NOT EXACTLY, 10 SCALLOPS PER POUND.

CONTINUED

BUTTER-SEARED SEA SCALLOPS

2²/₃ cups Pan-Fried Sweet Corn Hash

1 lb. sea scallops

2 Tbsp. melted butter

cooking spray

¹/₄ tsp. kosher salt, divided

¹/₄ tsp. freshly ground white pepper, divided

Follow These Steps:

>> Make the Pan-Fried Sweet Corn Hash, and keep it warm while you sear the scallops.

PREP THE SURFACE OF THE SCALLOPS

>> Dry the well-chilled sea scallops with paper towels. Get them really dry. And well-chilled should be about 34°—the temp in your fridge.

>> Brush the scallops evenly with the butter on all sides. The butter should solidify on the sides of the scallops if they are properly chilled and dried.

>> Heat a large heavy-bottomed sauté pan over medium heat for 3 minutes.

>> Spray the pan evenly, but lightly, with cooking spray.

>> Raise the heat to medium-high.

PUT THE SCALLOPS IN THE PAN

>> Slide half the scallops into the pan, one by one. *If the pan has been heated properly, the scallops will slide like an air-hockey puck in an arcade.* Just like that.

>> *Try sliding the scallops around in the pan. Cool, right?* Gently press the scallops against the hot pan surface to "pop" out any water/steam pockets.

>> Season with ¹/₁₆ teaspoon salt and ¹/₁₆ teaspoon pepper. Use your fingers.

LET 'EM SEAR

>> Now, let the scallops sear. The edges will brown. *Doneness is a matter of taste, for sure, but 2 minutes and a flip, followed by 1 minute on the non-presentation side should be great.*

>> Season the other side of the scallops.

>> Using a fish spatula or tongs (but be gentle with tongs), transfer the scallops to a plate.

>> Repeat the procedure to sear the remaining scallops.

>> Divide the scallops among 4 plates. Top each serving evenly with the Pan-Fried Sweet Corn Hash. Don't be too fussy.

SERVES 4 (3 OUNCES SCALLOPS AND ²/₃ CUP CORN HASH)
CALORIES 359; **FAT** 16.2G (SAT 5.8G, MONO 4.4G, POLY 1.8G); **PROTEIN** 25G; **CARB** 34G; **FIBER** 4G; **CHOL** 61MG; **IRON** 1MG; **SODIUM** 650MG; **CALC** 61MG

IN PRO KITCHENS, COOKS DECIDE WHICH SIDE OF THE FOOD HAS THE BEST VISUAL APPEAL. COOK THE PRESENTATION SIDE FIRST. IT'LL CREATE SOME WOW ON THE PLATE BEFORE YOUR GUESTS TAKE A BITE.

PAN-FRIED SWEET CORN HASH

HANDS-ON: 35 MIN. **TOTAL:** 35 MIN.

Next time you hear someone tell you, "That's not technically a [insert rule/technique/style here]," kindly ask them to open their mind to variations on theme, and furthermore, to the enjoyment of life. This is kind of a pan-fry. Play with your words. And your food.

Food	How Much	Why
butter	1 tablespoon	Because the solids brown, and its fat is round and tasty.
canola oil	1 tablespoon	Some additional fat to facilitate the pan-fry. We have enough butter flavor with a tablespoon.
fresh sweet corn	2 cups cut off the cob (about 4 ears)	Fresh, in this case, relies on the corn being raw (where canned and frozen have seen heat processing), thus snappier.
red bell pepper	¾ cup diced small	It's pretty. Choose a ripe one.
Yukon gold potato	1 cup diced small	Yukons hold their shape well when they're scattered in a dish such as this.
yellow onion	¾ cup	To help provide savory depth.
fresh thyme leaves	1 teaspoon	Thyme provides great contrast against sweet corn and scallops.
garlic cloves	2, peeled and thinly sliced	Friend of onion and bell pepper.
sugar	1 teaspoon	I'm a big proponent of layering Maillard browning and actual sugar caramelization. It makes for happy mouths.
kosher salt	½ teaspoon	Necessary. There's a lot of sweet in here.
ground red pepper	⅛ teaspoon	To harmonize and provide some smoky depth. Against hot fat, it provides an unparalleled liveliness and fullness.
cider vinegar	1 tablespoon	A delicate acidity to balance the other flavors.
fresh flat-leaf parsley	2 tablespoons rough chopped	With everything else spending time bouncing around on heat, this offers a welcome final lift and separation.

Follow These Steps:

» Heat a cast-iron skillet or other heavy-bottomed pan over medium-high heat.

» Add the butter and the oil. Swirl. Let the butter melt.

» Add the sweet corn and bell pepper, and raise the heat to high. Fry, stirring occasionally, for about 4 minutes, allowing the corn to get slightly browned.

» Lower the heat to medium-high and add the potato. Cook, stirring frequently, for about 4 minutes.

» Lower the heat to medium-low, and add the onion, thyme, and garlic.

» Sprinkle in the sugar, the salt, and the ground red pepper. Stir. Cook 3 minutes or until the potatoes are tender.

» *Crank the heat to high for a minute or two, stirring frequently, to give the dish a final browning.*

» Turn off the heat and stir in the cider vinegar. Fold to coat.

» Finish with the parsley. Serve over Butter-Seared Sea Scallops.

SERVES 4 (SERVING SIZE: ⅔ CUP)
CALORIES 204; **FAT** 9.1G (SAT 2.1G, MONO 3G, POLY 1.2G); **PROTEIN** 6G; **CARB** 31G; **FIBER** 4G; **CHOL** 8MG; **IRON** 1MG; **SODIUM** 271MG; **CALC** 21MG

COCOA-CRUSTED NEW YORK STRIP

HANDS-ON: 15 MIN. **TOTAL:** 20 MIN.

Cocoa powder is barely sweet, mostly bitter, and intensely earthy. For pan cooking, it's functionally appealing as well, because it has some fat, is velvety, coats things fully, and absorbs moisture like flour. When cooked in a pan with a bit of cocoa, your steak will mimic the legendary American steakhouse crust. Buy good beef. Amaze your guests. Consider serving with Pan-Roasted Radishes (page 207) and some fresh watercress spritzed with lemon and sprinkled with coarse salt.

Food	How Much	Why
cocoa powder	1 tablespoon	The myriad reasons above. Also, it asked not to be typecast anymore.
kosher salt	½ teaspoon	Steak needs salt.
ground red pepper	¼ teaspoon	Red pepper pops through the cocoa.
New York strip steak	1 pound, trimmed	It has just enough fat to create a succulent experience, and little enough to make it a *Cooking Light*-worthy dish.
cooking spray	to coat the pan	That's all you'll need. Fat will render from the steak to assist the cooking.

THIS CUT CAN BE EASILY OVERCOOKED.
USE THE TOUCH TEST (PAGE 159),
& MAKE SURE TO PULL IT OFF ONE LEVEL
OF DONENESS PRIOR TO YOUR PREFERENCE.
A GOOD CARRY-OVER REST ON A CUTTING
BOARD WILL GET IT TO (YOUR) PERFECT.

COCOA-CRUSTED NEW YORK STRIP

1 Tbsp. cocoa powder

½ tsp. kosher salt

¼ tsp. ground red pepper

1 lb. New York strip steak, trimmed

cooking spray

Follow These Steps:

COAT THE STEAK

≫ In a small bowl, combine the cocoa, salt, and red pepper.

≫ Transfer the mixture onto a plate in an even layer, ready for the steak.

≫ Dredge the steak in the mixture. *Lift up an edge and look to see if it's evenly coated. If not, do some massage work.*

≫ Flip and similarly dredge the other side. The steak should take on nearly everything on the plate. If there's some remaining cocoa mixture, roll the edges of the steak in it.

CREATE A TASTY CRUST

≫ Preheat a cast-iron skillet or heavy-bottomed sauté pan. Medium-high heat.

≫ Spray the surface evenly with cooking spray.

≫ Let the pan *begin* to smoke.

≫ *Gently lay the steak into the pan—roll it away from you chivalrously, as if to gesture to let someone pass through a doorway.*

≫ Let it smoke and sputter and scream. You're building a crust, and that takes fire.

≫ Using a firm but not aggressive touch, press the steak surface with four fingertips to make sure that all the surface area of the steak is in contact with the pan. Otherwise, you'll get gray pockets, and *that's not pro.* Cook for about 3 minutes. More for rare-o-phobes.

≫ Using tongs, flip the steak. Repeat the same cooking process with the other side. Test for doneness.

A LITTLE BIT OF SMOKE IS OKAY.

FINISH COOKING THE STEAK

≫ Turn off the heat. Remove the steak to a plate. Let the steak rest for 3 minutes or so at room temperature.

≫ *Now, assuming the steak is still very rare (it is), bring it back to the same pan, now warm, and raise the heat to medium. Cover the pan. Yep, cover it.* Cook for 1½ minutes to get it to medium-rare. Now, remove the pan lid (away from you to avoid a steam burn).

≫ Flip the steak. Cook 1½ minutes on the other side. Take those juices that drained off onto the plate and pour them over the steak in the pan. Now, it's likely medium-rare to medium (depending on the thickness of the steak). Place the steak on the plate again.

≫ Okay, one last time: Let it rest for 2 minutes or so.

≫ Now, on the bias or straight-cut steakhouse style, slice the steak against the grain so that you get 12 to 16 slices. *Tilt it and fan it while you carve. Just because.*

SERVES 4 (SERVING SIZE: 3 OUNCES STEAK)
CALORIES 185; **FAT** 8.1G (SAT 2.8G, MONO 3G, POLY 0.3G); **PROTEIN** 26G; **CARB** 1G; **FIBER** 1G;
CHOL 75MG; **IRON** 2MG; **SODIUM** 357MG; **CALC** 35MG

STEP BY STEP: Straight Cut and Bias Cut

1) The choice behind the cut is all about what you're serving the steak with. With sides that have some heft and thickness, like hearty oven-roasted potatoes and thick asparagus, go straight cut.

2) With more delicately textured foods like wilted spinach, soft polenta, and pan jus, go with the bias cut so the textures play off each other nicely.

WONDRA IS SUPER COOL. IT'S A BLEND OF WHEAT FLOUR & MALTED BARLEY FLOUR THAT'S HAD ITS STARCHES "PRE-HYDRATED." THINK: INSTANT WHITEWASH. IT CREATES SUPER CRISPY COATINGS & SILKY SMOOTH SAUCES. STOCKPILE IT.

CORIANDER-DUSTED SNAPPER
WITH FENNEL, SAFFRON, AND LEMON

HANDS-ON: 25 MIN. **TOTAL:** 25 MIN.

This dish is a nod to quick-moving sauté cooks everywhere—the ones you love to watch in open kitchens. It's your turn. Use a mandoline or V-slicer to cut the fennel bulb and sweet onion like a pro.

Food	How Much	Why
fresh lemon juice	3 tablespoons	Enlivens the sauce. Is mostly water, so it's a fine choice for blooming the saffron.
saffron threads	1/8 teaspoon	For a hint of Provence.
Wondra flour	1/2 cup	It's *the* dusting flour of culinary champions.
ground coriander	1 tablespoon	The pine-meets-citrus flavor pairs well with saffron and acid.
ground red pepper	1/2 teaspoon	To wake up the tomatoes.
snapper fillets	4 (6-ounce) fillets	This is a good size for dusting and sautéing. Try to buy them all around the same thickness.
olive oil	2 tablespoons	A flavorful oil works here.
butter	1 tablespoon	Helps with browning and enriches things.
fine sea salt	1/2 teaspoon	Fish from sea. Salt from sea.
fennel bulb	1 1/2 cups shaved razor thin	Shaving it thin makes for a very professional look and mouthfeel.
sweet onion	1 1/2 cups shaved razor thin	It cooks relatively quickly, and many of the flavors are soft, so sweet onions are an easy choice.
garlic cloves	2, peeled and thinly sliced	When you slice 'em you can see 'em. That's nice here.
yellow tomato	1 cup diced	Softer in flavor than most red varieties.
fresh flat-leaf parsley	2 tablespoons roughly chopped	Parsley provides fresh pine-meets-lemon flavors.

Follow These Steps:

➤ In a small bowl, combine the lemon juice and the saffron. This process is called "blooming" and allows the saffron to open up in flavor and color. Set aside.

➤ Heat a skillet large enough to hold all four fillets. Medium heat.

➤ In a bowl, combine the flour, coriander, and red pepper.

➤ Dredge the fish fillets in the flour and fully dust off, as if to try to remove almost all of the flour. Transfer back and forth between your hands, gently patting. If you've ever seen a tortilla made by hand, use that same motion.

➤ Add the olive oil and butter to the pan. Swirl and warm the butter until its aroma is toasty and starts to foam.

➤ Gently slide the fillets into the pan, skin sides down, leaving a fair amount of space between them.

➤ Now, don't move the fillets until the edges start to brown a bit, like a properly made pancake. This should take about 4 minutes. *It's better to adjust the flame than to rustle with the fish. I promise.*

➤ Using a thin fish turner, flip the fillets. Season with salt. *Cook for another 2 minutes or so, or until one sacrificial piece (yours) flakes off nicely, but is still translucent.* Transfer the fillets to a plate for a moment while you cook the vegetables.

➤ Add the fennel, onion, and garlic to the pan. Cook 1 minute. Turn the heat to low and continue to stir and sweat the vegetables until translucent, about 2 more minutes.

➤ Now, add the tomato and saffron mixture. Raise the heat to medium, stir, and sauté until saucy. Sprinkle with the parsley.

SERVES 4 (SERVING SIZE: 1 FILLET AND ABOUT 1/2 CUP VEGETABLES)
CALORIES 364; **FAT** 12.5G (SAT 3.3G, MONO 6.1G, POLY 1.7G); **PROTEIN** 39G;
CARB 24G; **FIBER** 4G; **CHOL** 71MG; **IRON** 2MG; **SODIUM** 457MG; **CALC** 117MG

CAST-IRON EGGPLANT AND WALNUT BRUSCHETTA

HANDS-ON: 30 MIN. **TOTAL:** 45 MIN.

Eggplant is a tricky ingredient. Anyone can cook it, but not everyone can coax it toward luxurious-ness. It rewards the patient cook, the one who would not dare serve it with even a tinge of spongy nakedness. Eggplant deserves constant, controlled heat, and will yield at just the perfect moment.

Food	How Much	Why
eggplant	4 cups peeled and diced	It's peeled because we want it to fully collapse when cooking, and the skin can be a nuisance in creamy, fully cooked eggplant.
kosher salt	½ teaspoon	To season the eggplant and draw out some water before cooking. The "it draws out bitterness" thing? Not so much.
olive oil	2 tablespoons	It's peppery, vegetal, and flavorful. Eggplant likes that.
yellow onion	1 cup diced	For some body and some textural contrast.
garlic cloves	4, sliced	It's a mouthfeel and visual thing.
sugar	1 tablespoon	Some will char a bit. Some will caramelize. Some will dissolve.
sherry vinegar	2 tablespoons	Sherry vinegar has a deep, layered flavor, and a just-perfect acidity.
fresh thyme	2 teaspoons minced	Where there is sherry vinegar, bring thyme.
whole-grain artisan-style bread	8 (½-inch-thick) slices, cut in half	With the walnuts in the formula, the complexity of whole grain is welcome.
walnuts	½ cup large pieces	Broiled, they give a campfire quality to the dish.
fresh flat-leaf parsley	¼ cup chopped	The ubiquitous, yet perfectly appropriate fresh finish.
fresh pecorino Romano cheese	2 teaspoons grated	A tad saltier than Parmigiano-Reggiano, plus the walnuts give this all the nuttiness the dish needs.

Follow These Steps:

➤➤ Preheat your broiler.

➤➤ Toss the eggplant with the salt. Place in a colander over a bowl to catch any liquid run-off. Tumble occasionally. Let the eggplant sit for 10 minutes or so before using.

➤➤ Heat a large cast-iron or other heavy-bottomed skillet over medium-high heat. Add the olive oil and swirl.

➤➤ *When the oil wrinkles into a semi-psychedelic haze, just before it reaches the smoke point, add the eggplant in a single layer.* Let cook for 2 minutes before attempting to stir.

➤➤ Now grab a wooden spoon. Sauté the eggplant for about 5 minutes or until well browned and tender, stirring occasionally. Add the yellow onion and the garlic. Stir.

➤➤ Lower the heat to medium-low. Add the sugar, sherry vinegar, and thyme. Fold to integrate, and cook over low heat for 10 minutes, until the mixture softens and becomes unified.

➤➤ Turn off the heat. *Let the eggplant mixture rest for a few minutes—right there in the pan.*

➤➤ Place the bread slices on a baking sheet and broil until slightly charred on both sides, 1 minute per side. Remove the bread. Put the walnuts on the baking sheet in a single layer.

➤➤ Broil the walnuts until the first sign of char appears on a single nut piece. Remove from the oven and fold into the eggplant mixture. Add the parsley to the eggplant mixture.

➤➤ To serve, spoon a generous amount of eggplant mixture on the bread slices. Sprinkle evenly with the pecorino Romano.

SERVES 8 (SERVING SIZE: ½ CUP EGGPLANT MIXTURE AND 2 BREAD HALVES)
CALORIES 150; **FAT** 10.4G (SAT 1G, MONO 3.8G, POLY 3.4G); **PROTEIN** 5G;
CARB 15G; **FIBER** 4G; **CHOL** 0MG; **IRON** 1MG; **SODIUM** 197MG; **CALC** 38MG

PAN-CHARRED GREEN BEANS
WITH TARRAGON

HANDS-ON: 11 MIN. **TOTAL:** 11 MIN.

*Vegetables such as green beans are typically given the moist-heat treatment
(steaming, boiling, blanching), but they end up being uncommonly intense in
flavor when their built-in water content is manipulated via a dry-heat method like
pan charring. Wonderful friends of mine took me to a Chinese restaurant in Bangkok
famous among locals for its amazing ways with vegetables. This dish is a
Western daydream of that establishment's pan-cooking mastery.*

Food	How Much	Why
cooking spray		To facilitate blistering of the beans. It's a fry/char instead of a burn/char. You'll see.
fresh green beans	8 ounces, washed and tipped	They can handle the heat, and become gloriously wilted while retaining a perfect snap.
butter	½ tablespoon	The "sauce" is a riff on béarnaise. That needs butter...
cider vinegar	1 tablespoon	...and vinegar...
kosher salt	¼ teaspoon	...and salt, of course...
fresh tarragon	2 teaspoons chopped	...and is finished with fresh tarragon.

BÉARNAISE IS CLASSICALLY MADE WITH EGG YOLKS
& A LOT MORE BUTTER THAN WE'RE USING HERE.
FRET NOT. WE'RE MAXIMIZING FLAVOR.

Follow These Steps:

》 Place a medium-sized skillet over high heat. Let it heat
for about 2 minutes.

》 Spray the pan evenly with cooking spray.

》 Add the green beans to the pan, shaking them into a single
layer, and letting them char slightly before tumbling.

》 Once you achieve the first signs of charring, continue to
tumble over high heat for about 5 minutes. *Bring the pan on
and off the heat to control. Don't fuss with the flame/controls.*

》 Turn the heat off. Let the beans rest for 1 minute.

》 Add the butter. Tumble to melt and distribute.

》 Add the cider vinegar. Tumble. *Raise the heat if necessary
to evaporate off most of the liquid. You shouldn't need to.*

》 Season with salt and tarragon, tumble once more, and serve
immediately. Try tossed with Georgia Peanut-Fried Chicken
(page 224) or a drizzle or two of Warm Tomato Vinaigrette
(page 85).

SERVES 4
CALORIES 37; **FAT** 2.1G (SAT 1G, MONO 0.8G, POLY 0.2G); **PROTEIN** 1G;
CARB 4G; **FIBER** 2G; **CHOL** 4MG; **IRON** 1MG; **SODIUM** 164MG; **CALC** 23MG

SRIRACHA-SPIKED TURKEY
WITH BIBB WRAPS

HANDS-ON: 20 MIN.　**TOTAL:** 20 MIN.

Sriracha has become a phenomenon for good reason. It's a malleable little condiment, and the California-made version is a masterpiece of flavor harmonization. Here, we give it a tomato paste-ish treatment by toasting it in oil before building the addictive turkey mixture. Flag this page.

Food	How Much	Why
Mad Fresh Sriracha *(page 58)*	2 tablespoons	Because you took the time to make your own, you should use it liberally. You can use the bottled stuff.
grapeseed oil	1 tablespoon	Its neutral flavor allows the onion and ginger flavors to really shine.
onion	½ cup minced	The base.
fresh gingerroot	1 tablespoon grated	The resonant flavor. It also provides some residual sugar, which toasts up nicely against high heat.
ground turkey	1 pound	The protein of choice.
green onions	¼ cup sliced	For a bright, nearly raw onion-y finish.
fresh lime juice	3 tablespoons	The preferred acid of Southeast Asian–inspired foods.
dry roasted peanuts	2 tablespoons chopped	They're fun.
fish sauce	1½ tablespoons	It adds a pleasant "funki-ness" that you can't get from any other ingredient.
Thai chiles	2, minced	Yes, for heat, but their flavor is quite distinct and marries well with fish sauce.
Bibb lettuce	8 leaves	The container.
cucumber	1 cup cut into matchsticks	A delightful counterpart to chiles.
carrot	1 cup cut into matchsticks	For crunch.
fresh cilantro leaves	½ cup	Its perfume "wraps up" all the flavors like a blanket.

Follow These Steps:

》 Combine sriracha and oil in a 12-inch skillet over medium-high heat. Cook 3 minutes or until mixture begins to bubble.

》 Add the onion and ginger. Stir for a minute.

》 Add the turkey. Raise the heat to high. Cook 6 minutes, stirring until the meat is scattered throughout the pan. Keep stirring. *So long as nothing's burning, keep the heat cranked and the turkey moving.*

》 When the turkey is cooked through and slightly crisped, turn off the heat. Toss in the green onions, the lime juice, the peanuts, the fish sauce, and the Thai chiles. Fold to combine.

》 Divide the turkey mixture evenly among the lettuce leaves. Top each leaf with 2 tablespoons cucumber, 2 tablespoons carrot, and 1 tablespoon cilantro.

》 Serve with fresh lime wedges, if desired.

SERVES 4 (SERVING SIZE: 2 LETTUCE WRAPS)
CALORIES 269; **FAT** 15G (SAT 3G, MONO 4.7G, POLY 5.7G); **PROTEIN** 25G; **CARB** 11G; **FIBER** 3G; **CHOL** 78MG; **IRON** 2MG; **SODIUM** 556MG; **CALC** 65MG

THAI-STYLE WATER SPINACH
(PAD PAK BOONG)

HANDS-ON: 16 MIN. **TOTAL:** 16 MIN.

I've had the joy of visiting Thailand numerous times in recent years. During one visit, I fell in love with a vegetable they call pak boong, or morning glory. It's also known as water spinach, and I must confess it may be slightly harder to find in the States. Ask around, though. Asian markets usually have it and you can, of course, order it online. Use hearty varieties of Chinese broccoli, watercress, or bok choy so you can learn the technique. This dish is about putting raging heat under your command.

Food	How Much	Why
red and green Thai bird chiles	6	Their fragrance is unique—floral, citrusy, with a bracing flavor.
sugar	1 tablespoon	We're going for hot-salty-sweet with the ground pork. Sugar helps this along.
garlic cloves	6 of the smallest cloves possible, preferably not pre-peeled, coarsely chopped	In Thailand, the native garlic has tiny, almost uniform cloves that have a much more distinct flavor than much of what's available in the U.S. Reach for smaller cloves; they're more intense in flavor. The pre-peeled stuff just tastes off.
ground pork	4 ounces	Makes the dish so complete, so wonderful.
canola oil	2 tablespoons	It's neutral and can handle the heat.
pak boong, gai lan (Chinese broccoli), watercress, or bok choy	1½ pounds, cut into 3-inch sections	The centerpiece.
oyster sauce	1 tablespoon	It's for umami, the ever-so-satisfying "fifth taste."
fish sauce	1½ teaspoons	Depth and salt.
lower-sodium chicken broth	¼ cup	For steam and some additional savory overtones.

Follow These Steps:

≫ Using a mortar and pestle, roughly smash the chiles with the sugar and the garlic. The chiles should be bruised, but still whole. The garlic should turn slightly translucent from the pounding, but should not be turned into a paste. *You're simply looking to release flavor, not make a uniform mixture.*

≫ Heat a wok or large, flat-sided fry pan to the highest heat your stove can handle. Before cooking, back it off a bit—to medium-high heat.

≫ Add the pork to the pan. Stir-fry until well browned and crispy, about 4 minutes. Using a slotted spoon, transfer the pork to a small bowl, leaving the little remaining fat behind.

≫ Now, add the canola oil. Swirl and scrape. This should take about 15 to 20 seconds.

≫ Add the smashed garlic and chile mixture. Stir for 15 seconds.

≫ Raise the heat back to high. Add the greens. Pour in the oyster sauce and the fish sauce.

≫ *Think in this cadence: Wilt. Stir. Wilt. Stir. Wilt. Turn off. Rest.* Let each "round" take about 20 to 30 seconds, for a total of about 2 minutes, depending upon the intensity of your heat.

≫ Add the pork and broth, and toss.

≫ Transfer to a serving platter or shallow bowl. Spoon any remaining sauce over the greens. Serve immediately.

SERVES 6 (SERVING SIZE: 1 CUP)
CALORIES 145; **FAT** 6.6G (SAT 1.1G, MONO 3G, POLY 1.4G); **PROTEIN** 9G;
CARB 14G; **FIBER** 2G; **CHOL** 14MG; **IRON** 1MG; **SODIUM** 266MG; **CALC** 57MG

SPICY CRAB FRIED RICE

HANDS-ON: 20 MIN. **TOTAL:** 60 MIN.

Daydreaming yielded this idea for a hybrid between fried rice and a sushi-joint hand roll.
It turns out that making fried rice from short-grain, sushi-style rice is fantastic,
as it stands up to agitation quite well and lends an almost meaty quality to the final dish.

Food	How Much	Why
avocado	1, diced	It's certainly not uncommon to see this in a sushi roll, but crab and avocado are perfect mates.
fresh lime juice	2 tablespoons, divided	Some for the avocado, some to brighten the fried rice.
uncooked short-grain white (sushi) rice	1½ cups	It is chewy and aesthetically fantastic when stir-fried, the grains all separate and toasty.
water	2 cups	The cooking liquid for the rice.
grapeseed oil	2 tablespoons	Handles high heat well.
fresh gingerroot	1 tablespoon grated	Garlic's friend in perfuming the rice.
garlic cloves	3, grated	We're adding it in high heat so you'll experience garlic's less subtle flavors. Some will char; some will brown.
Thai bird chiles	2, minced	Honestly, because you probably have some in your fridge if you've been using this book. Serranos are okay, too.
togarashi (Japanese red chile seasoning)	1 tablespoon, divided	Citrus, chile, nori, and sesame flavors predominate. It's really wonderful against things like avocado—or mayonnaise-dressed crab.
large eggs	2, beaten	To coat the grains and to provide richness.
soy sauce	2 tablespoons	It's your seasoning.
rice vinegar	1 tablespoon	So far, everything is very savory-round. This enlivens.
sugar	2 teaspoons	This balances the vinegar/lime addition.
green onions	½ cup sliced	For a fresh finish.
lump crabmeat	1 cup	Get the jumbo size. Anything smaller just wouldn't have the desired bite.
mayonnaise	1 tablespoon	Sushi chefs use really good mayo to add depth to their creations.
nori	1 sheet, cut into fine julienne	Umami, in sheet form.

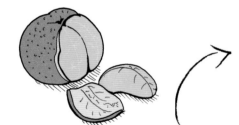

SHICHIMI TOGARASHI IS A BLEND
OF SEVEN "FLAVORS," INCLUDING
DRIED CHILE, ORANGE PEEL, SESAME,
GINGER & NORI (DRIED SEAWEED).

CONTINUED →

SPICY CRAB FRIED RICE

1 avocado, diced

2 Tbsp. fresh lime juice, divided

1½ cups uncooked short-grain white (sushi) rice

2 cups water

2 Tbsp. grapeseed oil

1 Tbsp. grated fresh gingerroot

3 garlic cloves, grated

2 Thai bird chiles, minced

1 Tbsp. togarashi, divided

2 large eggs, beaten

2 Tbsp. soy sauce

1 Tbsp. rice vinegar

2 tsp. sugar

½ cup sliced green onions,

1 cup lump crabmeat

1 Tbsp. mayonnaise

1 sheet nori, cut into fine julienne

Follow These Steps:

>> Toss the diced avocado in a tablespoon of the lime juice. Set aside.

WASH, COOK, AND COOL THE RICE

>> Place the rice in a bowl about four times the volume of the rice. Place the bowl in a clean sink. Slowly run cold water into the rice while washing the rice with your hands.

>> Run the water and wash the rice until the water runs nearly clear. Drain well and return the rice to the bowl.

>> Place the rice in a rice cooker and add the 2 cups of water. Cook per the machine's instructions. If you don't have a rice cooker, bring the water to a boil in a medium saucepan; add the rice. Cover, reduce heat, and simmer 20 minutes or until the liquid is absorbed.

>> Remove the rice from the rice cooker and spread the cooked rice evenly on a large baking sheet. Cool to room temperature.

FIRE UP YOUR WOK AND STIR-FRY!

>> Heat a wok over high heat.

>> Add the grapeseed oil, followed by the rice. Use a turner designed for your wok, if possible. Stir-fry the rice, spooning it off the surface of the wok rapidly using a scoop-and-fold motion.

>> Keep cooking the rice until the grains stay reasonably separated and are well toasted, about 8 minutes.

>> Add the ginger and garlic. Keep stirring.

>> Add the chiles and ½ tablespoon of the togarashi.

>> Make a well in the center of the rice. *Pour in the beaten eggs. Scoop and fold rapidly, imagining every grain of rice evenly coated with egg. It won't be, but you'll be close. You're gunning for golden-hued rice with some scattered bits of egg, not chunks.*

>> Turn off the heat.

SEASON AND FINISH THE DISH

>> Add the soy sauce, the rice vinegar, 1 tablespoon of the fresh lime juice, and the sugar. Stir it.

>> Fold in the green onions. Let rest for a moment.

>> Combine the crab, the mayonnaise, and ½ tablespoon of the togarashi.

>> Serve the rice steaming hot topped with the crab mixture, avocado mixture, and nori.

SERVES 6 (SERVING SIZE: 1 CUP)
CALORIES 352; **FAT** 12.7G (SAT 1.9G, MONO 4.9G, POLY 4.8G); **PROTEIN** 11G; **CARB** 49G; **FIBER** 6G; **CHOL** 74MG; **IRON** 3MG; **SODIUM** 554MG; **CALC** 44MG

HOW TO MAKE MAD DELICIOUS FRIED RICE

RINSE THE RICE. WHY? THERE IS STARCH ON THE SURFACE OF THE RICE. IF YOU DON'T REMOVE THAT BY RINSING, IT WILL HYDRATE BEFORE THE STARCHES IN THE RICE GRAINS HYDRATE & YOU'LL END UP WITH GLUEY, PASTY RICE.

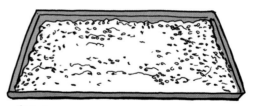

SPREAD OUT THE RICE & COOL IT QUICKLY.

INTRODUCE GINGER & GARLIC, LIFTING & FOLDING CONSTANTLY. NOW'S A GOOD TIME TO ADD DRY SEASONING AND OTHER FLAVORFUL BITS.

USE COMMANDINGLY HIGH HEAT. KEEP THE RICE MOVING.

MAKE A WELL IN THE CENTER OF THE RICE. MOVE FAST. COAT RICE GRAINS WITH EGG.

SEASON WITH SOY, VINEGAR, FRESH LIME & SUGAR. FINISH WITH GREEN ONION.

THE FRENCH, AND THOSE TAUGHT BY THE FRENCH,
CALL THIS BROWNED BUTTER "BEURRE NOISETTE."

PAN-ROASTED RADISHES

HANDS-ON: 15 MIN. **TOTAL:** 15 MIN.

Ah, the radish. Its American history has it thin-sliced and tossed among mismatched vegetables and iceberg lettuce as an inconsequential splash of color. It's time to right generations of oversight of this marvelously delicious vegetable. Radishes of all kinds can stand up to fairly aggressive dry-heat cooking methods like pan roasting, as they contain plenty of water to help regulate their internal temperature during cooking. You will make this dish regularly, for the honor of radishes everywhere.

Food	How Much	Why
cooking spray		To help blister the outside of the radishes. Only a spritz of fat is needed to start the process.
red radishes, any shape	1 pound (about 3 bunches), halved lengthwise	It's time to eat radishes in larger quantities. Repeat after me: Roasted. Radishes.
butter	½ tablespoon	This is the "sauce." It will brown slightly when cooked. That's delicious.
fresh thyme	2 whole sprigs	Thyme has a number of flavor compounds that are fat soluble—so the thyme effectively perfumes the butter.
garlic clove	1, smashed with a knife	When it's smashed, and not minced, you're less likely to burn the garlic and get "off" flavors.
kosher salt	⅛ teaspoon	To finish.

Follow These Steps:

》 Fire up a large skillet. Medium-high.

》 Spray evenly with cooking spray.

》 Add the radishes. Using a wooden spoon, tumble the radishes in the pan while blistering and browning, about 1 minute. *There are plenty of natural sugars to play with in those radishes.*

》 When the radishes look toasted in areas and slightly pan-charred in others, lower the heat somewhere between medium-low to low (essentially, we want the radishes to sweat now, not roast, so low and controlled is the answer).

》 Tumble again. *Monitor while the radishes collapse a bit. You'll see them getting tender before your eyes.* Cook for about 6 minutes, tumbling occasionally.

》 Pierce one with a fork, not a knife. *If it's tender, pick it up ceremoniously. Wave it in the air to cool it down. Sway your hips, too. It's cool to dance when you cook. Now, taste.* You'll want to experience this flavor, even pre-seasoned.

》 Hopefully, they're not quite ready yet. Add the butter, the thyme sprigs, and the smashed garlic clove to the pan. Raise the heat to medium-high. Tumble for about 1 minute, allowing the garlic to toast. Season with salt.

》 Now here's a meal: Serve hot alongside the Cocoa-Crusted New York Strip (page 188) and Maria's Cilantro Cebollas (page 79).

SERVES 4 (SERVING SIZE: 4 OUNCES)
CALORIES 32; **FAT** 1.6G (SAT 1G, MONO 0.4G, POLY 0.1G); **PROTEIN** 1G; **CARB** 4G; **FIBER** 2G; **CHOL** 4MG; **IRON** 0MG; **SODIUM** 117MG; **CALC** 32MG

TOASTED PENNE
WITH CHICKEN SAUSAGE

HANDS-ON: 55 MIN. **TOTAL:** 55 MIN.

*Dry pasta lends itself to a variety of cooking techniques, so let's toast it, and then cook
it risotto-style to build a creamy sauce from the noodles. I learned this method from a
chef who was from Togo but apprenticed in Italy. It was what the kitchen staff ate for
lunch. He called it "Toast Pasta." Here, it's presented with browned chicken sausage.
Chop and add the Spicy Broccoli Rabe for an impressive and very complete meal.*

BRONZE-DIE CUT PASTA HAS A
ROUGHER EXTERIOR (THINK SANDPAPER)
- ONE THAT ADHERES WELL TO SAUCES.
THE MASS- PRODUCED STUFF FLIES OUT
OF TEFLON- COATED DIES, MAKING
FOR A MORE SLIPPERY PASTA SURFACE.

Food	How Much	Why
unsalted chicken stock	6 cups	For richness. Water could be used, for sure.
extra-virgin olive oil	2 tablespoons, divided	It's chosen here for its flavor more than its function.
Italian-style chicken sausage	4 links (13 ounces), casings removed	Try to get Italian-style, because the (typically added) fennel seed is perfect against the toasted overtones of the pasta.
sweet onion	1 cup thinly sliced	Onion is a common counterpart to sausage, its flavors blossoming when slow-cooked in fat.
uncooked penne pasta	2 cups (8 ounces)	Make sure it's dry pasta. With the penne being the focal point of the dish, splurging on a rustic, Old World–style variety would be worth every cent.
kosher salt	½ teaspoon	For the pasta, not the "water."
Spicy Broccoli Rabe *(optional, page 126),* **at room temperature**	1 recipe, cut into 1½-inch pieces	This is an optional component to the dish, but really enlivens the whole thing. Cutting it makes the dish easier to eat—plus the whole thing will look very abundant.
fresh lemon juice	2 tablespoons	You have fat from olive oil and sausage. The ingredient flavor profiles are quite round. They need an acid.
Calabrian chiles	1 tablespoon minced	Okay, they're mad-trendy, but are perfectly balanced for this dish. A splash of fashion never hurt a meal. Alternatively, buy hot cherry peppers (in a jar).
Parmigiano-Reggiano cheese	½ ounce grated	Again, this is a simple dish, so using the best ingredients will show. The nuttiness of Reggiano is ideal against this ingredient list.

CONTINUED →

TOASTED PENNE WITH CHICKEN SAUSAGE

6 cups unsalted chicken stock

2 Tbsp. extra-virgin olive oil, divided

4 links Italian-style chicken sausage, casings removed

1 cup thinly sliced sweet onion

2 cups uncooked penne pasta

½ tsp. kosher salt

1 recipe Spicy Broccoli Rabe, cut into 1½-inch pieces (optional)

2 Tbsp. fresh lemon juice

1 Tbsp. minced Calabrian chiles

½ oz. grated Parmigiano-Reggiano cheese

Follow These Steps:

>> *First, think risotto, not pasta. Your brain will thank you.*

>> Bring the stock to a simmer in a saucepan. Hold it hot. You'll be using it…like…for…risotto (but for pasta).

>> Place a high-sided 12-inch skillet (probably your largest, right there, stored underneath everything) on medium heat.

COOK THE SAUSAGE AND ONION

>> Add 1 tablespoon of olive oil to the skillet. Add the sausage and onion. Cook over medium heat, stirring occasionally, until sausage is done and onion is golden brown.

>> Remove sausage mixture with a slotted spoon, leaving drippings in pan. Set aside.

TOAST THE PENNE

>> Return the pan to medium heat and add the remaining olive oil. Swirl into an even layer. Give it about 30 seconds. If the oil starts to smoke too fast, turn down the heat—we want this to be a slow, even heat.

>> Add the dry pasta to the pan. Shake. Toss. Stir. Tumble. Observe the transformation.

>> The more controlled the heat, the more evenly the pasta will be toasted. This is a matter of taste. I happen to like the pasta to be unevenly toasted, even charred, in places. It makes for a more complex dish, particularly against a slightly bitter vegetable such as broccoli rabe.

>> When the pasta has transformed in color from its original pale khaki color to something resembling a better beer, about 5 minutes, add the sausage mixture. Sauté for about 2 minutes.

HYDRATE THE PENNE

>> *Now, add a cup of stock. Stir. Stir. You'll see the starch begin to integrate with the pasta water. That's a good thing.*

>> Lower the heat to a slight simmer, and keep stirring.

>> Reduce the liquid until it is almost fully absorbed, about 5 minutes. It will look like you threw a pat of butter or two into finished pasta.

>> Add stock 1 cup at a time, stirring all the while and observing for the right amount of reduction.

>> Repeat this step progressively until you have creamy, saucy, tender pasta (about 30 minutes total).

SEASON AND FINISH

» Now add the salt. Stir. You may not use all of the stock if you've simmered slowly. *You may need a cup of water or so if you let it bubble more aggressively. Either way, it will be spectacular.*

» If you've opted to do the broccoli rabe thing, add it now, gently stirring and folding to incorporate, until the vegetable is warmed throughout. Taste it.

» Finish with lemon juice, chiles, and grated cheese.

SERVES 4 (SERVING SIZE: 1²/₃ CUPS)
CALORIES 355; **FAT** 13.8G (SAT 3.5G, MONO 5.4G, POLY 0.9G); **PROTEIN** 24G; **CARB** 36G; **FIBER** 2G;
CHOL 51MG; **IRON** 3MG; **SODIUM** 678MG; **CALC** 77MG

STEP BY STEP: Toasting Penne

1) Add the uncooked penne to the preheated pan.

2) Stir infrequently. It's okay to have some unevenness in the char.

3) Allow as much browning and char as your taste buds prefer. Go deep. The liquid will "wash" much of the char into the resultant sauce.

YOU CAN TRY THIS METHOD WITH ANY OF YOUR FAVORITE SMALL PASTAS.

PAN-TOASTED CHICKPEA GNOCCHI
WITH BEANS AND GREENS

HANDS-ON: 50 MIN. **TOTAL:** 1 HR. 10 MIN.

*This was one of those recipes that sounded way better than its early results. But the
ever-so-patient Cooking Light Test Kitchen team trudged along with me through myriad failures
and half-baked ideas, believing that, conceptually, this could be good. So there we were, in
Birmingham, Alabama. And on the shelf, in the land of biscuits, was a bag of self-rising flour. Eureka!
We discovered that it's possible to use protein-rich chickpea flour in gnocchi and still get
a light, fluffy result. High five. This is one balanced, nutritious, and delicious meal.*

Food	How Much	Why
Chickpea Gnocchi (page 214)	1 recipe	The base.
butter	2 tablespoons	Helps to brown the gnocchi. It also browns itself and yields what might be the most magical and versatile of all flavors: browned butter.
olive oil	2 tablespoons	To keep the butter from burning and to add another layer of flavor.
green beans	1 cup cut into 1-inch pieces	There's a three-bean salad riff in here.
canned unsalted chickpeas (garbanzo beans)	1 cup rinsed and drained	Part two.
canned unsalted kidney beans	½ cup rinsed and drained	And the kidney bean. There it is. Good for you.
canned diced tomatoes	½ cup drained	Make sure you drain 'em. We just want the little jammy bits of tomato; otherwise you'll get strangely juicy gnocchi water.
garlic cloves	2, sliced	For the look and the texture.
escarole/curly endive head	1 medium head, chopped	It's a quick-cooking, mild-flavored choice.
fresh lemon juice	2 tablespoons	You have lots of round flavors in this dish. Acid is needed.
kosher salt	¼ teaspoon	We've gone with lower-sodium selections throughout so you can evenly salt the dish.
Romano cheese	⅓ ounce shaved	The tang of Romano is the perfect choice here.

CONTINUED

PAN-TOASTED CHICKPEA GNOCCHI

1 recipe Chickpea Gnocchi

2 Tbsp. butter

2 Tbsp. olive oil

1 cup green beans cut into 1-inch pieces

1 cup canned unsalted chickpeas, rinsed and drained

½ cup canned unsalted kidney beans, rinsed and drained

½ cup canned diced tomatoes, drained

2 garlic cloves, sliced

1 medium head escarole/ curly endive, chopped

2 Tbsp. fresh lemon juice

¼ tsp. kosher salt

⅓ oz. shaved Romano cheese

Follow These Steps:

>> Remove the gnocchi from the refrigerator. Uncover.

>> Warm a heavy-bottomed skillet over medium heat.

TOAST THE GNOCCHI

>> Add the butter to the pan, swirl, melt, and bring to the foaming point.

>> Add the gnocchi, and sauté for about 5 minutes, turning periodically, until evenly toasted.

>> Transfer the gnocchi to an oven-safe plate while you cook the escarole. Hold them in a warm place, preferably in a warm oven.

MAKE THE GREENS AND BEANS "SAUCE"

>> Raise the heat in the pan to medium-high and add the olive oil.

>> Add the green beans to the pan. Stir to deglaze the browned bits left behind by the gnocchi. Cook 2 minutes. *The beans will retain a bit of a crunch.*

>> Add the chickpeas, the kidney beans, the tomatoes, the garlic, and the escarole, and stir until the beans are heated through and the escarole has wilted, about 2 minutes.

>> Turn off the heat. Sprinkle the bean and endive mixture with lemon juice and salt.

>> Serve on a platter, with the greens and beans on the base and the gnocchi on top, with a sprinkling of Romano cheese.

SERVES 4 (SERVING SIZE: 1¼ CUPS)
CALORIES 496; **FAT** 18.3G (SAT 6.1G, MONO 7.8G, POLY 2.1G); **PROTEIN** 18G; **CARB** 67G; **FIBER** 15G; **CHOL** 109MG; **IRON** 5MG; **SODIUM** 716MG; **CALC** 209MG

CHICKPEA GNOCCHI

HANDS-ON: 40 MIN. TOTAL: 1 HR. 20 MIN.

Food	How Much	Why
baking potato	18 ounces (1 potato)	Because we want to yield a pound of flesh.
kosher salt	½ teaspoon	Without salt, this would be completely bland. It needs to be incorporated in the dough.
chickpea flour	3 ounces (about ½ cup plus 1 tablespoon), divided	It adds a good dose of high-quality protein, and toasts up nutty and rich.
self-rising flour	1.4 ounces (about ¼ cup)	The answer to our leaden failures.
large egg yolks	2	To bind and enrich.
cooking spray		

Follow These Steps:

» Place a large pot of water on medium-high heat. Bring to a boil.

» Pierce the potato with a fork. Place the potato on a microwave-safe plate, and microwave at HIGH about 8 minutes or until tender.

» Split the potato and let the potato rest until it can be safely handled, about 5 minutes.

» Scoop the flesh into a stainless steel mixing bowl. *Using a fork, break up the structure of the potato, as to attempt to break it into a loose pile of dry, almost granular potato bits.* Add the salt.

» Gradually work ½ cup of chickpea flour and the self-rising flour into the potato until well combined.

» Add the egg yolks and mix either by hand or with a sturdy wooden spoon to create a smooth-looking and feeling dough.

» Dust a cool counter surface with some additional self-rising flour. I've been told the motion is like feeding chickens (but I have yet to feed a chicken).

» Divide the dough into 4 equal parts and roll as shown at right into ropes that are ⅝ inch thick (about 1.5 centimeters) and about 19 inches long. *Cut into 1¼-inch lengths. Use a ruler. Look serious.*

» Roll the gnocchi off the tines of a lightly floured fork with your thumb if you so desire. I don't.

» Place the gnocchi on a baking sheet coated with cooking spray. Coat a jelly-roll pan or a second baking sheet with cooking spray, too.

» The water should be at a full rolling boil at this point. Gently add a quarter of the gnocchi to the boiling water and cook until they float and are cooked throughout. This should take about 1½ to 2 minutes, tops. Taste one to be sure.

» *Using a slotted spoon or skimmer that can be used to "fish out" the gnocchi, go get 'em and shake off all the excess water without breaking up the gnocchi.* Be just firm enough.

» Place the gnocchi in a colander to drain.

» After draining, transfer the gnocchi to the jelly-roll pan in a single layer. Place the pan in the refrigerator between batches. Repeat the cooking procedure with the rest of the gnocchi, working in batches.

» When all four batches are complete, refrigerate, uncovered, for about 20 minutes.

» Remove the gnocchi from the refrigerator and gently tumble them in a stainless steel bowl with 1 tablespoon of chickpea flour. It'll help keep them from sticking and help the gnocchi brown as you cook them for the finished dish.

» Lay the gnocchi on a plate in a single layer, covered, until you're ready for them in the final recipe. This isn't one to keep around for more than a day or so.

SERVES 4 (SERVING SIZE: ABOUT 15 GNOCCHI)
CALORIES 248; **FAT** 4.5G (SAT 1G, MONO 1.3G, POLY 1.1G); **PROTEIN** 9G; **CARB** 43G; **FIBER** 4G;
CHOL 92MG; **IRON** 2MG; **SODIUM** 391MG; **CALC** 59MG

STEP BY STEP: MAKING GNOCCHI

1) Using a dough scraper, cut the dough into four equal, manageable parts.

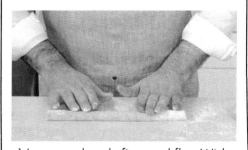

2) Lay your hands firm and flat. With even, gentle pressure, roll from the center to the outside and back to center again, shaping the rope evenly as you roll.

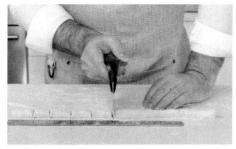

3) Cut the gnocchi into even lengths as shown.

ISAN-INSPIRED LARB

HANDS-ON: 25 MIN. **TOTAL:** 30 MIN.

Food	How Much	Why
sugar	1 tablespoon	To facilitate the mashing of the garlic and to contribute sweetness against the punchy heat of this dish.
garlic cloves	3	Essential in this style of larb.
jasmine rice	2 tablespoons, uncooked	For crunch. You'll see.
cooking spray		
ground pork	2 ounces	For some fat and additional flavor.
white mushrooms	1 cup minced	To bulk up the meat mixture and lend some earthiness. Serves to balance.
ground turkey	3/4 pound	The main substance.
fresh lime juice, preferably from small Key or Mexican limes	3 tablespoons	Mexican or Key limes simply taste different. The larger Persian limes commonly sold in supermarkets have their place, for sure, but not here. We need the boldness here.
fish sauce	1 1/2 tablespoons	For salt and to offer depth of flavor.
shallots	4, very thinly sliced	Shallots offer some welcome pungency.
Thai bird chiles	3, minced	The right kind of chile for larb.
napa (Chinese) cabbage	2 cups chiffonade	Its ruffled texture traps liquids beautifully.
green onions	1/2 cup cut into 1/4-inch dice	Now, we're building the "salad."
green beans	1/2 cup trimmed and cut thinly on the bias	Crunch.
cucumbers	2, peeled and cut julienne	Relief.
fresh mint leaves	1 bunch	This is critical, and is absolutely incredible against fish sauce and the toasted rice.
Thai basil leaves	1 bunch, torn	Movement No. 2 of this herb symphony.
fresh cilantro	1/2 bunch	Ties the herbs together in one big flavorful knot. It's a lovely trio.
Thai-style or other dry crushed chiles	1 teaspoon	Adds a toasty capsaicin punch. As the salad is mixed, it rehydrates and announces its presence forcefully.
Key limes	2, cut "seviche-style" (see page 27)	For a dose of freshness, *à la minute*.

Larb has its origins in Laos, though variations of the dish— basically a minced meat salad— have been popularized from Northeast Thailand, known as the Isan region, down through Bangkok. This version makes use of what should be commonly available in your food market. Feel free to ramp up the chiles if you like a less restrained salad. The Isan people would smile upon you.

CONTINUED

ISAN-INSPIRED LARB

1 Tbsp. sugar

3 garlic cloves

2 Tbsp. jasmine rice, uncooked

cooking spray

2 oz. ground pork

1 cup minced white mushrooms

¾ lb. ground turkey

3 Tbsp. fresh Key lime juice

1½ Tbsp. fish sauce

4 shallots, very thinly sliced

3 Thai bird chiles, minced

2 cups napa (Chinese) cabbage chiffonade

½ cup green onions cut into ¼-inch dice

½ cup green beans trimmed and cut thinly on the bias

2 cucumbers, peeled and cut julienne

1 bunch fresh mint leaves

1 bunch Thai basil leaves, torn

½ bunch fresh cilantro

1 tsp. Thai-style crushed chiles

2 Key limes, cut "seviche-style"

Follow These Steps:

>> Using the side of a chef's knife, mash the sugar and the garlic to a fine paste. Set aside.

TOAST AND CRUSH THE RICE

>> Heat a heavy-bottomed skillet to medium-high. Let heat for a minute before adding the dry rice to the pan.

>> Toast the rice in the pan, stirring periodically. As you stir the rice, you'll find the hot spots in your pan, and smell varying degrees of toastiness. *A slightly uneven toast will make for a more complex final dish. A slight char on a few grains isn't a bad thing.*

>> Transfer the toasted rice to the bowl of a small food processor.

>> Pulse until the rice grains are the consistency of coarse cornmeal. Alternatively, you can hand-crush the rice with a mortar and pestle.

CREATE A TEXTURALLY PLEASING MEATY BASE

>> Wipe the pan you cooked the rice in with a paper towel, and bring it back to the heat. Medium-high.

>> Spray the pan evenly with cooking spray.

>> Add the ground pork. Cook until nearly crisp.

>> Leave the fat in the pan. Add the minced mushrooms.

>> Cook the mushrooms until they have browned and the majority of the moisture has been reduced. Add the turkey.

>> Stir the meat and mushroom mixture in between surface brownings: Essentially, let the bottom layer crisp up a bit (about 4 minutes), then stir like mad.

>> Repeat the process twice more, or until the meat mixture is the perfect blend of crisp and moist. *Tasting the mixture along the way will help with determining doneness.*

>> Turn off the heat.

ADD FLAVOR. LET IT SEEP IN

>> Transfer the meat mixture to a mixing bowl.

>> Add the garlic paste, the lime juice, the fish sauce, the shallots, and the minced chiles. Combine and let rest at room temperature.

>> Toss in half of the ground toasted rice. Reserve the rest for garnishing.

FINISH WITH HERBS, FRESH GREENS, AND CRUNCHY RICE

» Combine the napa cabbage, the green onions, the green beans, and the cucumbers in a mixing bowl. Toss evenly.

» Grab a good-looking platter.

» Lay the cabbage mixture on the base of the platter.

» Now, getting back to the meat mixture, check for temperature. Just beyond room temperature is perfect for this dish. If it is so, toss in the mint leaves, the Thai basil, and the cilantro.

» Pour the meat mixture over the cabbage "salad."

» Garnish with more toasted rice, a sprinkling of crushed chiles, and the Key limes.

SERVES 4 (SERVING SIZE: 3¼ CUPS)
CALORIES 257; **FAT** 10G (SAT 2.6G, MONO 3.3G, POLY 2.4G); **PROTEIN** 23G; **CARB** 20G; **FIBER** 3G;
CHOL 68MG; **IRON** 3MG; **SODIUM** 607MG; **CALC** 89MG

BASIL GLOSSARY

SWEET BASIL
DELICATE SWEET FLAVOR, SLIGHTLY FLORAL. THE MOST FAMILIAR BASIL IN THE U.S.

DARK OPAL BASIL
SLIGHTLY SPICY WITH A HINT OF LICORICE.

THAI BASIL
MINTY, LICORICE FLAVOR

LEMON BASIL
LOVELY LEMON FRAGRANCE. OFTEN ADDED AT THE END OF COOKING TO PROTECT ITS DELICATE FLAVOR.

LESS BUTTER CHICKEN

HANDS-ON: 45 MIN. **TOTAL:** 1 HR. 30 MIN.

Butter Chicken (Murgh Makhani) is a classic Indian dish that warrants more exploration by the serious home cook. It is a beautiful study in spice harmonization, and while tomatoes make up the bulk of the sauce, the flavors of toasted spice and butter predominate. Here we introduce beurre fondue, a quickie water-butter preparation that helps carry the butter flavor throughout the dish while using less butter than you'd normally find in classic butter chicken.

Food	How Much	Why
raw cashews	2 tablespoons	When ground and simmered into the sauce, add body and creaminess.
coriander seed	2 teaspoons	Lends floral and citrus notes.
cumin seed	1 tablespoon	Adds warmth and gently bitter undertones.
kosher salt	½ teaspoon	Needed for balance.
red pepper flakes	½ teaspoon	For neutral, penetrating heat.
white peppercorns	6	Slightly musky, they provide some pungency that is gentler than black pepper.
methi (dry fenugreek leaves)	1 tablespoon	Slightly bitter, it has the aroma compound sotolone, which is also found in burnt sugar and aged rum. It also provides some toastiness.
skinless, boneless chicken thighs	6	A great choice for braising and simmering, thighs cook up fork-tender.
cooking spray		All the fat we need to brown the chicken.
tomatoes	3 cups steam-peeled, seeded, and chopped	This is the bulk of your sauce. Remember the passata you made on page 30? When you peel, seed, and chop, that's called concasse.
red onion	1 cup roughly chopped	They provide the savory-sweet foundation to the dish and are essential to the sauce's texture.
water	1 cup, divided	Some to thin out the tomatoes, some to make a quick butter sauce.
fresh gingerroot	1 tablespoon grated	An aromatic powerhouse, this gets simmered with the tomatoes.
fresh garlic	1 tablespoon minced	Another component of the tomato sauce. It's minced because it goes straight into liquid.
serrano chile	1, minced	For penetrating chile heat.
butter	1 tablespoon	See recipe name.
crème fraîche	1 tablespoon	You'll often see yogurt or double cream used in butter chicken recipes. This splits the difference, being both tangy and rich.

ONIONS ARE SO IMPORTANT TO INDIA & MOST REGIONAL CUISINES THAT PRICE & POLITICS SURROUNDING THE ONION MARKET CAN IMPACT ELECTIONS.

CONTINUED

LESS BUTTER CHICKEN

2 Tbsp. raw cashews

2 tsp. coriander seed

1 Tbsp. cumin seed

½ tsp. kosher salt

½ tsp. red pepper flakes

6 white peppercorns

1 Tbsp. methi

6 boneless, skinless chicken thighs

cooking spray

3 cups tomatoes, steam-peeled, seeded, and chopped

1 cup roughly chopped red onion

1 cup water, divided

1 Tbsp. grated fresh gingerroot

1 Tbsp. minced fresh garlic

1 serrano chile, minced

1 Tbsp. butter

1 Tbsp. crème fraîche

Follow These Steps:

» *There are four distinct building blocks to this dish: the spices, the chicken, the sauce, and the finish. Let's start with the spices.*

TOAST THE SPICES

» In a small sauté pan over medium heat, toast the cashews, the coriander, the cumin, the salt, the red pepper flakes, and the white peppercorns.

» *Toast until someone in the next room asks what you're cooking—2 minutes.* Remove from the heat.

» Transfer the toasted cashews, spices, and the methi to a mortar and pestle, a mini food processor, or a coffee grinder. Crush or process the spice mixture until it's finely ground.

SEASON AND SEAR THE CHICKEN

» Rub the spice mixture into the chicken thighs. Let them soak up the flavors for about 3 to 4 minutes.

» Heat a large, high-sided pan appropriate to handle the rest of this braising process. You're cooking 6 thighs and well over a quart of "stuff." Medium-high heat.

» Spray the pan evenly with cooking spray.

» When the pan has that hot, hazy look, add the chicken thighs in a single layer.

» Sear for 2 minutes on each side. Turn off heat and transfer the chicken to a plate.

START THE TOMATO SAUCE

» Add the tomatoes, the red onion, ½ cup of water, the ginger, the garlic, and the chile. Turn the heat back on and stir to deglaze. (See photos at right.)

» Simmer for 30 minutes, covered, over low heat.

» While the sauce is cooking, let's learn something. Grab a small saucepan.

MAKE A BEURRE FONDUE

» Heat up the other ½ cup of water to about 190°. *Those little bubbles form on the bottom of the pot, but no bubbling takes place per se. Makes sense?* Now, turn off the heat.

» Now, using a small wire whisk, stir in the butter, followed by the crème fraîche. This is a version of beurre fondue, an emulsified butter and water "sauce" popularized by Thomas Keller when he wrote his *French Laundry Cookbook*. *The crème fraîche makes it a quickie cream sauce. Have fun with that.*

» Let that sauce hang out for a minute.

COMBINE SAUCES

»» Now, go blend the tomato mixture. You can use an immersion blender, but ideally you'll use a standard blender, if you promise to be careful.

»» Pour the tomato mixture into the blender, put the lid on, and remove the center piece. Further cover with a tea towel, and give a couple of quick pulses. *Now, progressively raise the speed, clicking through all the buttons like a 5-year-old, until you get to "frappé or liquefy," favorite 1970s kitchen blender terms.*

»» With the motor running, remove the lid. You're safe. The blender has created a vortex.

»» Pour in the cream sauce. Blend for another minute or two. The color will get paler. That's simply from aeration.

CENTER PIECE REMOVED.
GOOD

CENTER PIECE NOT REMOVED
BAD

BRAISE THE CHICKEN

»» Put the sauce back in your braising pan and add the chicken thighs. Cook over the lowest heat setting for about 30 minutes, or until the thighs can be "pulled" with tongs.

»» Serve, preferably over simply cooked basmati rice. A good store-bought naan is quite delicious—and just what you want to sop up the last of your masterful sauce.

SERVES 6 (SERVING SIZE: 1 THIGH AND ABOUT ⅓ CUP SAUCE)
CALORIES 195; **FAT** 10.7G (SAT 3.7G, MONO 3.7G, POLY 1.7G); **PROTEIN** 16G; **CARB** 10G; **FIBER** 3G; **CHOL** 58MG; **IRON** 2MG; **SODIUM** 269MG; **CALC** 40MG

STEP BY STEP: Deglazing

1) Dry-heat cooking leads to lovely crusty bits on the pan.

2) You don't necessarily have to add a liquid to start the deglazing process—just something wet (like these tomatoes).

3) Allow the heat to cook down the vegetables, releasing their moisture, and gently scrape the bottom of the pain while you stir. Voilà.

GEORGIA PEANUT–FRIED CHICKEN

HANDS-ON: 15 MIN. **TOTAL:** 20 MIN.

J.C. and Jo Bell revolutionized peanut butter a few years back when they were charged with creating something amazing from America's massive peanut surplus. PB2, a powdered peanut butter, is a culinary dream ingredient. Cut 50/50 with Wondra flour (it's the superfine sugar of flours, see page 192), it makes for an unparalleled dredge for chicken. This dish retains the gentle sweetness of peanut, and has most of the crunch of true-to-form fried chicken.

Food	How Much	Why
skinless, boneless chicken thighs	8 thighs (about 1 pound)	It's a mouthfeel thing. This is fried chicken. It should be rich and unctuous. Thighs help that along.
PB2 Powdered Peanut Butter *(see Resources, page 370)*	½ cup	It's neat. You can get it online, but both natural stores and mainstream supermarkets are catching on, too.
Wondra flour	½ cup	It doesn't clump, and it allows for a very even dredge.
kosher salt	¼ teaspoon	It's fried chicken. You're craving salt. Make sure you get all the dredge onto the chicken, as this is a small amount of added salt.
ground red pepper	¼ teaspoon	With the sweetness from the peanut butter, a little heat is welcome.
grapeseed oil	¼ cup for frying	It's neutral and has a fairly high smoke point. It's great for frying.

Follow These Steps:

❯❯ Place a wire rack over a sheet pan and set it aside. *You'll transfer your just-fried chicken here. None of this paper-towel stuff, please.*

❯❯ Rinse the chicken thighs and pat them dry. Set aside on a plate.

❯❯ Combine the PB2, the Wondra, the salt, and the ground red pepper in a mixing bowl. Stir to mix all ingredients very evenly.

❯❯ In a small sauté pan, add the grapeseed oil. *Raise heat to medium, and allow the oil to develop a look similar to the haze on a highway on a hot, steamy day. You know that look. It's a bendy swirl.*

❯❯ Now, lower the flame to medium-low. That should hold the heat steady (though you may have to teeter between low and medium-low, depending on the reliability of your stove and the thickness of your pan's bottom).

❯❯ Sprinkle a tiny pinch of the flour mixture into the oil. If it sizzles, start cooking.

❯❯ Dredge the thighs in the PB2 mixture, one by one, before adding to the pan. *Be sure to cook only one or two thighs at a time, otherwise you'll crowd the pan, cool down the oil too quickly, and end up with soggy chicken. No one wants that.*

❯❯ Cook for 4 minutes on each side. Then, using spring-loaded tongs, transfer the fully cooked chicken thighs to the elevated wire rack.

❯❯ Rest for 5 minutes before slicing, and then serve with Pan-Charred Green Beans with Tarragon (page 196).

SERVES 4 (SERVING SIZE: 2 THIGHS)
CALORIES 355; **FAT** 23.3G (SAT 3.8G, MONO 6.3G, POLY 11.7G); **PROTEIN** 25G; **CARB** 12G; **FIBER** 2G; **CHOL** 74MG; **IRON** 1MG; **SODIUM** 248MG; **CALC** 10MG

RINSING AND DRYING THE CHICKEN CREATES A VERY
EVEN SURFACE FOR DREDGING. IT'S NOT DONE TO RINSE
OFF BACTERIA; INSTEAD, RINSING REMOVES THE SLICK,
JELLY-LIKE SUBSTANCE, SO YOU GET ONLY THE MOISTURE
THAT "SURFACES" AFTER PATTING THE CHICKEN DRY. YOU
WON'T GET CLUMPS OF BREADING FALLING OFF THE CHICKEN
IF YOU FOLLOW MY INSTRUCTIONS. I PROMISE.

LOWER EAST SIDE BRISKET

HANDS-ON: 50 MIN. **TOTAL:** 3 HR. 35 MIN.

Although many, if not most, Americans' first experience with brisket is in the form of barbecue, mine was in a Lower East Side apartment complex—on Passover. I was 17. It was my first experience with sweet and tangy slow-cooked brisket. Variations on home-cooked brisket are as varied as the Yiddish slang that peppers the Tri-State area. This recipe, reconstructed from memory, is a perfect entry-point into braising. Brisket has relatively flat, even surfaces, making browning easy. Pomegranate molasses and tomato paste give you a jump on enriching the sauce. So long as you don't cook at too high a heat, you'll yield a moist and tender brisket worthy of serving to anyone's bubbie.

A CUTE NICKNAME FOR A JEWISH GRANDMOTHER

Food	How Much	Why
beef brisket	2 pounds, trimmed	It's a brisket recipe.
freshly ground black pepper	1 tablespoon, divided	Some to rub into the brisket. Some to finish. The grandmother who cooked this had zero fear of pepper.
kosher salt	1¼ teaspoons, divided	This is a more tapered amount of salt than what's generally used in brisket, but it's plenty flavorful. This recipe is an exercise in making a little go a long way—and using salt where it makes the biggest impact.
canola oil	1 tablespoon	To sear the brisket.
onion	2 cups chopped	Become part of the body of the sauce. They're also the foundational aromatic vegetable in here.
carrot	1 cup chopped	For sweetness.
celery	1 cup chopped	For more body.
garlic cloves	4, smashed	Onions and garlic are almost ubiquitous pan-fellows. Without garlic in this dish, the pomegranate molasses might tilt it a bit toward being too sweet.
tomato paste	¼ cup	It gets browned along with the mirepoix, providing depth of flavor. It thickens the sauce, too.
unsalted beef stock	2 cups	Beef in pan. Beef stock.
pomegranate molasses	¼ cup	It's essentially a reduction of pomegranate juice and sugar, but it's more tangy than sweet. Some folks use ketchup. It seems prudent to take this back to the Old World.
fresh thyme	2 teaspoons chopped	Inspired by mirepoix, above. Common in a braise.
fresh bay leaves	2	It has eugenol, which is clove-like. It also has eucalyptus-like perfume. That works in a slightly sweet braise.
cider vinegar	2 tablespoons	To spike the acid levels. It helps prevent the need for the whole bottle of pomegranate molasses. This is efficient.
fresh flat-leaf parsley	2 tablespoons chopped	Fresh to finish.

CONTINUED →

LOWER EAST SIDE BRISKET

2 lb. trimmed beef brisket, trimmed

1 Tbsp. freshly ground black pepper, divided

1¼ tsp. kosher salt, divided

1 Tbsp. canola oil

2 cups chopped onion

1 cup chopped carrot

1 cup chopped celery

4 garlic cloves, smashed

¼ cup tomato paste

2 cups unsalted beef stock

¼ cup pomegranate molasses

2 tsp. chopped fresh thyme

2 fresh bay leaves

2 Tbsp. cider vinegar

2 Tbsp. chopped fresh flat-leaf parsley

Follow These Steps:

» Preheat your oven to 275°.

» Heat a Dutch oven over medium-high heat.

SEASON AND BROWN THE BRISKET

» Season the brisket with 2 teaspoons of the black pepper and ¾ teaspoon salt. Rub the seasoning into the flesh.

» Add the oil to the Dutch oven. Swirl and look for the haze.

» Brown the brisket for about 8 minutes on each side. We're looking for a thick, deep, crusty exterior (see photos at right). Transfer the brisket to a platter for a moment.

USE A MIREPOIX TO START THE BRAISING LIQUID

» Reduce the heat to medium-low and add the onion, carrot, celery, and garlic. Cook for about 5 minutes, stirring occasionally.

» Add the tomato paste. Stir to incorporate, and cook 1 minute.

» Add the beef stock, the pomegranate molasses, the thyme, and the bay leaves. Stir.

CAN BE FOUND IN MOST MIDDLE EASTERN STORES & OFTEN WHERE KOSHER OR HALAL FOODS ARE SOLD.

BRAISE!

» Return the brisket to the Dutch oven, tumble once, and cover.

» Place the Dutch oven in the 275° oven and cook for about 2½ hours. Turn it halfway through the cooking time. *You have to be careful with the leaner "first cut" (that's the cut without the fatty cap), as it can shred to a dry oblivion if left unmonitored. It should be quite tender, but not fall-apart tender.*

» *Cheat. Take a paring knife and saw off a small piece near the tip. That's yours to savor and evaluate.*

» It should be done. Take it out of the oven.

REST THE BRISKET

» Splash in the vinegar, and, using a wooden spoon, swirl it into the pan sauce.

» Let the brisket rest in the sauce for about 15 minutes, out of the oven and off the heat.

» Transfer the brisket to a cutting board. Ready a platter.

» Back to the Dutch oven: Remove the bay leaves from the sauce.

TURN THE BRAISING LIQUID INTO A TASTY SAUCE & SERVE

» Skim the sauce of any surface fat and blend smooth using an immersion blender (if you have one; a standard blender works, too).

» Now, slice the brisket into ½-inch slabs, against the grain, and fan onto a platter.

» Season with the remaining 1 teaspoon pepper and ½ teaspoon of salt.

» *Douse with lots and lots of the sauce. Okay, all of the sauce.*

» Garnish with parsley.

» Share.

SERVES 8 (3 OUNCES BEEF AND ABOUT ½ CUP SAUCE)
CALORIES 228; FAT 6.3G (SAT 1.8G, MONO 3G, POLY 0.7G); PROTEIN 27G; CARB 15G; FIBER 2G;
CHOL 74MG; IRON 3MG; SODIUM 586MG; CALC 60MG

STEP BY STEP: Creating a Crusty Exterior

1) Season the meat with the spice mixture. This is the start of your crust.

2) Add the oil. You can't see the haze easily in the photo, but you'll notice an immediate viscosity breakdown— that's why it'll look all swirly.

3) Brown the brisket to the perfect color.

FENNEL AND KALE–STUFFED
PORK BRACIOLE

HANDS-ON: 1 HR. 40 MIN. **TOTAL:** 2 HR. 10 MIN.

Food	How Much	Why
olive oil	2 tablespoons, divided	Some to sauté the vegetables, some for browning the braciole.
fennel	2 cups julienne cut, divided	The sauce has lemon and wine. Fennel preparations are made better with acid.
onions	2 cups julienne cut, divided	For body in the stuffing. Plus, fennel alone would be overpowering.
garlic cloves	6, minced and divided	It's Italian-American. Hello.
lemon zest	2 tablespoons grated	The juice comes later. This perfumes the stuffing.
kale	4 cups chopped	Kale holds up to the not-so-short cook time.
kosher salt	1¼ teaspoons, divided	Some for the stuffing, some to sprinkle on at finishing time.
whole-grain bread	2 (1-ounce) slices, diced	The nuttiness adds welcome depth to the stuffing.
large egg white	1	To bind.
milk	¼ cup	To soften the bread in making the panade.
fresh pecorino Romano	2 tablespoons grated, divided	Its salty, sharp flavor is brilliant with lemony things.
pork cutlets	4 (8-ounce) cutlets	From the leg, if possible. You'll be pounding them thinly.
twine for tying		Without it, the whole thing unravels.
Wondra flour	¾ cup	It's the ultimate dusting flour. See page 192.
fresh lemon juice	6 tablespoons	See fennel.
white wine	1 cup	Choose something unoaked, like a pinot grigio or sauvignon blanc. We're looking for a bright, citrusy sauce.
unsalted vegetable stock	2 cups	Flavorful. Neutral.
crushed red pepper	1 teaspoon	This dish is screaming for a little red sauce joint heat.
fresh rosemary	1 sprig	Its pine-like aroma takes well to lemon.
fresh flat-leaf parsley	2 tablespoons coarsely chopped	For a colorful and grassy finish that lends itself well to acid-forward dishes.

It's known in Italy as involtini, but in Italian-American pork stores (and homes), particularly in cities that have a Little Italy, it's probably called braciole [BRAH-ZHOWL]. Thin slices, often pork leg or beef top round, are stuffed with whatever makes sense. We use soft cooked fennel and onions with plenty of the power-nourisher, kale. This recipe uses a panade (see page 243), as it deftly binds up the moist stuffing ingredients. It's lemony, it's soulful, it's whatever you want to stuff it with—it's braciole.

CONTINUED

FENNEL AND KALE-STUFFED PORK BRACIOLE

2 Tbsp. olive oil, divided

2 cups julienne cut fennel, divided

2 cups julienne cut onions, divided

6 garlic cloves, minced and divided

2 Tbsp. grated lemon zest

4 cups chopped kale

1¼ tsp. kosher salt, divided

2 (1-oz.) slices whole-grain bread, diced

1 large egg white

¼ cup milk

2 Tbsp. grated fresh pecorino Romano, divided

4 (8-oz.) pork cutlets

twine for tying

¾ cup Wondra flour

6 Tbsp. fresh lemon juice

1 cup white wine

2 cups unsalted vegetable stock

1 tsp. crushed red pepper

1 fresh rosemary sprig

2 Tbsp. fresh flat-leaf parsley

Follow These Steps:

>> Heat a large skillet over medium heat. Add 1 tablespoon olive oil, and swirl to coat.

MAKE THE FILLING

>> Add 1 cup each of the fennel and the onions. Spread them out evenly. Good.

>> Stir frequently and cook for precisely 13 minutes or until they are both golden brown and translucent.

>> Add 3 of the minced garlic cloves and the lemon zest. Cook 1 minute, stirring to incorporate.

>> One cup at a time, add the kale and cook 10 minutes, stirring and folding until the greens collapse and become incorporated with the onion-fennel mixture.

>> Monitoring closely, raise the heat to high, and stir frequently, so that the mixture is moist, but not watery. *Encourage evaporation by stirring and resting—in waves.*

>> Season with ½ teaspoon of the salt.

>> Turn off the heat and transfer the mixture to a mixing bowl. Refrigerate for now, uncovered. It'll only be in the fridge for a few minutes.

>> In a separate mixing bowl, combine the bread, the egg white, the milk, and 1 tablespoon pecorino. Using your hands, squeeze, mash, and stir to combine into a uniform mixture. This is a panade.

>> The kale mixture will likely still be warm. *That's okay. Make sure it's not super-hot.*

>> Fold the panade into the kale mixture, creating a well-bound stuffing. You should be able to compress it into a uniform mass with your hand without it falling apart. Refrigerate, covered, until well chilled.

PREP THE PORK FOR THE FILLING

>> On a butcher block or resilient kitchen surface, lay down four broad sheets of plastic wrap—one for each pork cutlet. You'll be pounding the pork cutlets on this foundation.

>> Lay down the pork cutlets on top of the plastic wrap.

>> Now, top each pork cutlet with another broad piece of plastic wrap.

>> Using a mallet, small heavy skillet, or old-school rolling pin, pound steadily but gently—tearing is a bad thing—until the pork is a thin, flat sheet, not quite translucent, about ¼ inch thick.

>> Remove the top sheets of plastic wrap and discard them. Sprinkle the cutlets evenly with ½ teaspoon salt.

STUFF AND ROLL BRACIOLE

>> Take the kale mixture from the refrigerator, and distribute the stuffing evenly among the 4 pounded cutlets: Use about ½ cup per cutlet and spread it over the pork, leaving a ½-inch margin around the outside edges.

>> Roll and tie the cutlets.

DREDGE AND BROWN THE PORK

» Spread the Wondra flour on a pie pan or plate. Dredge the cutlets evenly.

» Bring a Dutch oven to medium heat. Add the other tablespoon of olive oil and heat for about 2 minutes, or until the oil "breaks" into a haze, but not a smoke.

» Brown the rolled and stuffed cutlets on all sides, about 5 minutes total for all "four sides," assuming you'll get some slight flattening as you cook the cutlets.

» Remove the rolled and stuffed cutlets to a plate for a moment. Reduce the heat to medium-low.

BUILD A TASTY COOKING SAUCE

» Add the remaining 1 cup of fennel and 1 cup onions to the Dutch oven. Stir frequently and cook until very soft, about 15 minutes.

» Add the 3 minced garlic cloves, the lemon juice, the white wine, the vegetable stock, the crushed red pepper flakes, and the rosemary sprig.

» Now, return the rolled and stuffed cutlets to the Dutch oven.

» Raise the heat until the liquid bubbles intermittently, but not any more frequently. Boiling is not beneficial here.

» Braise the braciole for about 30 minutes.

» Turn off the heat. Let the braciole stand in the Dutch oven for 30 minutes. *Braciole, if handled improperly, can end up dry. This step lets everything seek equilibrium, allowing the meat to reabsorb any moisture it may have lost in the cooking process. It's a gentle bath.*

» Carefully transfer the braciole to a small heatproof pan or casserole dish. Snip and discard the twine. Keep the braciole warm.

» Ladle a few ounces of liquid over each braciole while you finish the sauce.

COMPLETE AND SERVE THE DISH

» Raise the heat on the sauce that remains in the Dutch oven to high. Bring to a boil and cook for about 3 minutes more.

» Turn off the heat.

» Carefully blend the sauce using an immersion blender, or by carefully blending in small batches using a standard tabletop blender (see page 223). Blend until smooth.

» Ladle the sauce on a platter in an even layer.

» To present, slice each braciole into 8 slices, each slice about ³⁄₄ inch thick. Fan over the sauce.

» Garnish with the fresh parsley, the remaining salt, and 1 tablespoon pecorino.

SERVES 8 (SERVING SIZE: ABOUT 3 OUNCES COOKED MEAT AND ¹⁄₃ CUP SAUCE)
CALORIES 307; **FAT** 10.3G (SAT 2.1G, MONO 4.1G, POLY 1G); **PROTEIN** 30G; **CARB** 24G; **FIBER** 3G;
CHOL 74MG; **IRON** 3MG; **SODIUM** 590MG; **CALC** 118MG

SPICY BRAISED CALAMARI

HANDS-ON: 15 MIN. **TOTAL:** 1 HR. 30 MIN.

*You've likely heard that calamari needs to be cooked for a minute—or for a very long time.
Here's why: When you cook squid rapidly (just to heat it through), you're not doing
much to transform the collagen from its tender native state. If you cook it just a moment
too long, the collagen starts to denature, strands unravel, and you get rubber bands.
At this point, you must shift to a longer cooking mode. Add some acid from tomatoes,
and a long, low and slow braise, and you get hydrolyzed, tender collagen. And that's delicious.*

Food	How Much	Why
squid	2 pounds, tubes cut into ¼-inch slices and tentacles	Calamari recipe. You can use pre-cut rings here instead, if you like.
olive oil	2 tablespoons, divided	You're cooking the calamari twice. In the first cook, you'll sauté it, in two batches.
sweet onion	1 cup julienne cut	Sweet, to contrast the acidity of the tomatoes. Julienne, so it dances well with the squid.
garlic cloves	3, sliced	Sliced garlic holds up and provides some visual contrast. Don't be afraid to rough-cut this. The texture is welcome.
Fresno chile or other mild red chile	2, thinly sliced	Go for round slices that mimic the shape of the squid. The Fresno adds just enough bite, so that the dish retains its elegance.
red wine, fruity, but not sweet	1 cup	For depth.
diced tomatoes	1 (14-ounce) can	Its acidity, along with the heat, helps transform and tenderize the collagen.
lemon zest	1 tablespoon	When cooking anything from the sea in tomatoes, a little lemon zest softens the nose of the sauce.
crushed red pepper	1 teaspoon	It offers a raisiny contrast to the Fresnos.
kosher salt	³⁄₈ teaspoon	The tomatoes aren't salt-forward enough to get the dish where it needs to be.
thin spaghetti	8 ounces	The perfect strand.
lemon juice	2 tablespoons	Brightens.
Italian parsley	2 tablespoons coarsely chopped	Fresh to finish.
black pepper	½ teaspoon	Why not?

DON'T GO WITH ANGEL HAIR, AND DON'T GO WITH THICK. YOUR PERFECTLY COOKED SQUID WILL SHINE THROUGH.

CONTINUED

SPICY BRAISED CALAMARI

2 lb. squid, tubes cut into ¼-inch slices and tentacles

2 Tbsp. olive oil, divided

1 cup julienne-cut sweet onion

3 garlic cloves, sliced

2 Fresno chiles, thinly sliced

1 cup red wine

1 (14-oz.) can diced tomatoes

1 Tbsp. lemon zest

1 tsp. crushed red pepper

⅜ tsp. kosher salt

8 oz. thin spaghetti

2 Tbsp. lemon juice

2 Tbsp. coarsely chopped Italian parsley

½ tsp. black pepper

Follow These Steps:

SAUTÉ THE SQUID

» Dry the squid well on paper towels.

» Heat a Dutch oven to medium-high for about 3 minutes. *A constant, well distributed medium-high is always better and more controllable than screaming high heat.*

» Add 1 tablespoon of olive oil, and immediately add half of the squid.

» Sauté for about 2 to 3 minutes, stirring frequently, almost as if to stir-fry. Get some color on them.

» Place cooked squid in a large Dutch oven.

» Cook the rest of the squid: Add 1 tablespoon of olive oil to the skillet, and sauté 2 to 3 minutes.

» Move the second batch of cooked squid to the Dutch oven.

USE VEGETABLES TO CREATE A SAUCE

» Return the pan to the heat and reduce the temperature to medium. Add the onion, the garlic, and the chiles. Stir and cook for 2 minutes or until slightly soft.

» Add the wine to the pan. Cook 3 minutes or until reduced by half.

» Add the reduced wine to the squid, along with the tomatoes, the lemon zest, the red pepper, and the salt. Stir to incorporate.

BRAISE

» Bring the squid mixture to a boil. Only for a moment.

» Reduce the heat to low, cover the pot, and simmer, but don't boil, for an hour and 15 minutes.

COOK THE PASTA

» While the squid is simmering, cook the spaghetti for 6 minutes. Drain it well. There's plenty of sauce, and you don't want to dilute it.

» Add the pasta to the squid for the last 5 minutes of its cooking time.

» The squid should be tender at this moment. Turn off the heat.

» Stir in the lemon juice, half of the parsley, and the black pepper. Transfer to a serving platter, sprinkle with the remaining half of the parsley, and serve while still piping hot.

SERVES 6 (SERVING SIZE: ⅔ CUP PASTA AND 1 CUP SQUID MIXTURE)
CALORIES 362; FAT 7.3G (SAT 1.4G, MONO 3.5G, POLY 1.3G); PROTEIN 30G; CARB 41G; FIBER 3G; CHOL 352MG; IRON 3MG; SODIUM 663MG; CALC 81MG

FAY-ZHOWA-DA FEIJOADA LEVE
(BRAZILIAN BLACK BEAN STEW)

HANDS-ON: 35 MIN. **TOTAL:** 1 HR. 52 MIN.

Feijoada is, by most accounts, the recognized national dish of Brazil. Stories often call the dish "simple," tying it to a history of slaves and struggle, with the black bean being an ingredient relegated to the underclass. Studied Brazilians would push back, pointing out that feijoada has been a celebrated menu item for all the people of (and visitors to) Brazil to enjoy since at least the 1800s. And then there's cassoulet from France, and cozido from Portugal, dishes where Europe embraced and dressed up the bean. Surely some cross-pollination occurred during settlement. Honor feijoada's long and storied history by recognizing that it's a dish as lively, gracious, and ever-evolving as the Brazilian people.

Food	How Much	Why
olive oil	1 tablespoon	For browning the ribs.
pork back ribs	12-bone rack, cut into single ribs	In searching for the right cut of pork to keep this dish light, the back rib won for its meatiness, look, and flavor.
Italian chicken sausage	4 (2-ounce) links	Classic feijoada uses quite a bit of pork. This lighter version leverages chicken sausage.
yellow onion	2 cups diced	Part of the aromatic base of the dish.
garlic cloves	8, minced and divided	Some is used in the braise and some to perfume the rice.
unsalted chicken stock	3 cups	The cooking liquid. It's neutral, yet flavorful.
lager beer	12 ounces	A little extra cooking liquid is needed.
lower-sodium black beans	2 (14-ounce) cans, rinsed and drained	Canned beans make the dish snappier to prepare.
carne seca or buffalo jerky	2 ounces	Online purveyors of Brazilian foods offer up their version of carne seca. It's different from jerky and the much drier Machaca (also called carne seca), which is an easy find.
bay leaves	2	To perfume the whole pot.
kosher salt	¾ teaspoon, divided	A must.
black pepper	½ teaspoon	For some piquancy.
unsalted chicken stock	2 cups	We're going for richness in flavor. Water would detract here.
uncooked white rice	1 cup	Use long grain. Fluffy rice is nice with beans.
butter	1 tablespoon	Because butter has delicious solids for toasting.
yellow onion	2 tablespoons minced	For some pilaf-like texture.
uncooked farina (such as Cream of Wheat)	¼ cup	It goes from grain to crunch in brown butter in a matter of seconds. Brazilians use manioc meal. If you can find it, use it.
oranges	2, peeled and sliced ¼ inch thick	A not-uncommon accompaniment.

CONTINUED

FEIJOADA LEVE

Ingredients

1 Tbsp. olive oil

12-bone rack of pork back ribs, cut into single ribs

4 (2-oz.) links Italian chicken sausage

2 cups diced yellow onion

8 garlic cloves, minced

3 cups unsalted chicken stock

12 oz. lager beer

2 (14-oz.) cans lower-sodium black beans, rinsed and drained

2 oz. carne seca or buffalo jerky

2 bay leaves

¾ tsp. kosher salt, divided

½ tsp. black pepper

2 cups unsalted chicken stock

1 cup uncooked white rice

1 Tbsp. butter

2 Tbsp. minced yellow onion

¼ cup uncooked farina

2 oranges, peeled and sliced ¼ inch thick

Follow These Steps:

>> Fire up a Dutch oven over medium heat.

>> Add the olive oil and swirl.

BROWN THE MEATS

>> Dry the ribs with paper towels. Add half the ribs to the Dutch oven and cook 6 minutes, browning them as evenly as possible on all sides.

>> Remove the ribs and set aside. Repeat the process with the remaining 6 ribs.

>> Add the chicken sausage to the Dutch oven and brown evenly on all sides, about 5 minutes.

>> Remove the chicken sausage and set aside.

CREATE A FLAVORFUL LIQUID FOR COOKING THE BEANS

>> Now, add the 2 cups onion and stir until translucent, about 5 minutes.

>> Add 6 garlic cloves. Cook 1 minute.

>> Add the 3 cups chicken stock and beer, and stir until combined.

>> Reduce heat to medium-low. Add the black beans. Stir to incorporate.

ADD THE MEATS TO THE STEW AND SIMMER

>> Return the chicken sausage and ribs to the pot.

>> Add the carne seca or jerky, the bay leaves, ½ teaspoon salt, and the pepper.

>> Monitor the pot until it comes to a slight simmer. **Don't let it bubble fiercely.**

>> Reduce the heat to low, cover the pot, and simmer for 1 hour, until the ribs are still moist but cooked through.

>> Remove the sausages and let them stand for 5 minutes.

>> Cut them into a total of 12 (½-inch) pieces. Return them to the pot.

>> Remove the carne seca or jerky, shred it, and stir the meat back into the stew.

MAKE THE RICE

>> Bring the 2 cups chicken stock and ⅛ teaspoon of the salt to a full rolling boil in a small saucepan.

>> Add the rice and 2 garlic cloves. Stir to combine.

>> Reduce heat to very low and cover.

>> Cook for 12 minutes.

>> Remove the pan from the heat, and, leaving the pan covered for another 10 minutes, let it stand and allow the rice to continue cooking from carry-over heat.

STEP BY STEP: Preparing Farofa

1) Warm the skillet. Melt the butter.   2) Sweat the onion.   3) Toast the farina.

PREPARE THE FAROFA

>> Heat a small skillet over medium heat.

>> Add the butter and warm until it foams. Swirl.

>> Add the 2 tablespoons onion and cook 2 minutes, until translucent.

>> Add the farina and ⅛ teaspoon of the salt, and stir frequently to toast, 3 minutes.

AND SERVE!

>> Fluff the rice with a fork and spoon it evenly among 12 shallow bowls.

>> Top each serving with ⅔ cup of the feijoada and 1 rib, and sprinkle each evenly with farofa.

>> Serve with the orange slices.

SERVES 12 (SERVING SIZE: ¼ CUP RICE, ⅔ CUP BEAN STEW WITH 1 RIB, AND 2 TABLESPOONS FAROFA)
CALORIES 395; **FAT** 17.7G (SAT 6.1G, MONO 6.3G, POLY 2.3G); **PROTEIN** 30G; **CARB** 31G; **FIBER** 4G;
CHOL 88MG; **IRON** 4MG; **SODIUM** 638MG; **CALC** 88MG

CHICKEN-PECAN MEATBALLS

HANDS-ON: 37 MIN. **TOTAL:** 1 HR. 50 MIN.

Food	How Much	Why
fresh breadcrumbs	made from 4½ (1-ounce) slices white bread	Chicken is pretty moist stuff. This scatters throughout the ground chicken when you fold it, and it helps bulk it up a bit.
ground chicken	2 pounds	Don't use all-white-meat ground chicken. Please. Fear not some tasty schmaltz.
fresh goat cheese	4 ounces, divided	It's acidic, soft, and can be easily blended. As a finish, its zesty flavor serves as a contrast to the rich flavor of the meatballs.
sweet onion	½ cup grated and squeezed of excess juice	It's a great little technique for distributing maximum onion flavor while focusing on creating a velvety-textured interior.
pecan pieces	⅓ cup, divided (¼ cup finely chopped, the rest for garnish)	It might be because this book was written in Georgia. Wait. Yes. It is.
fresh chervil	1 tablespoon minced	Chervil is delicate, yet intoxicating. Substitute 1 teaspoon tarragon and 2 teaspoons parsley if no chervil is available.
brown sugar	1 tablespoon	Some molasses-y love, and a little help with the browning/caramelizing process.
kosher salt	½ teaspoon	
black pepper	½ teaspoon	Black pepper with brown sugar: It works.
garlic cloves	2, minced	These might be flat without some garlic.
whole-grain bread	1.5 ounces, diced	Because bread should be a shout-it-out-loud component of a meatball.
buttermilk	¼ cup	Why not soften the binding agent with something delicious and tangy?
hot sauce	3 dashes	More for perfume than for spice.
egg whites	2, lightly beaten	For binding.
cooking spray		To coat the pan.
unsalted chicken stock	1 cup	The backbone of the sauce.
Charred Peach Passata *(page 30)*	2 cups	The body of the sauce.
bacon	1 ounce, cooked and crumbled	Lends a favorable smoky finish.
lemon or lime wedges	6	A squirt balances the sweetness from the passata and the meatballs.

Bread makes for a good meatball. Ground chicken is a little wetter than beef, so this creation borrows two common practices: the addition of breadcrumbs (though you'll take the time to make fresh) and the building of a panade, which is essentially really, really soggy bread. The flavor profile nods to the South, but this recipe is a play on an everyday Mad Delicious meatball. Tinker with ingredients. Make this recipe yours.

CONTINUED

CHICKEN-PECAN MEATBALLS

fresh breadcrumbs, made from 4½ (1-oz.) slices white bread

2 lb. ground chicken

4 oz. fresh goat cheese, divided

½ cup grated sweet onion, squeezed of excess juice

⅓ cup pecan pieces, divided (¼ cup finely chopped)

1 Tbsp. fresh chervil

1 Tbsp. brown sugar

½ tsp. kosher salt

½ tsp. black pepper

2 garlic cloves, minced

1.5 oz. whole-grain bread, diced

¼ cup buttermilk

3 dashes hot sauce

2 egg whites, lightly beaten

cooking spray

1 cup unsalted chicken stock

2 cups Charred Peach Passata

1 oz. bacon, cooked and crumbled

6 lemon or lime wedges

Follow These Steps:

>> Set up a food processor. Tear up the white bread, and throw it in. *Pulse. Pulse. Pulse. One more time. That's good.*

FLAVOR AND SHAPE THE MEATBALLS

>> In a chilled bowl, combine the chicken, 2 ounces of the goat cheese, the fresh breadcrumbs, the onions, ¼ cup of the finely chopped pecans, the chervil, the brown sugar, the salt, the black pepper, and the garlic. *Don't mash, just gently fold with your fingertips.*

>> In another bowl, combine the diced whole-grain bread, the buttermilk, the hot sauce, and the egg whites. Let soak.

>> Fold the bread mixture into the ground meat mixture. *Don't try to create a homogenous mass; the pockets of moistened bread in the final meatball are glorious.*

>> Start rolling meatballs to about 1 inch in diameter. You should get around 32.

BROWN THE MEATBALLS

>> Heat a large skillet over medium heat. Coat with cooking spray.

>> Add half the meatballs, leaving about an inch between them, one by one. Let them brown on one side for about 4 minutes, controlling the heat, before turning.

>> Remove the first batch of meatballs. You'll get them done in batches, browning all around as discussed.

>> Lower the heat. *Do some pan maintenance by scraping with a wooden spoon and discarding little crispies. Snack. Make more.*

SIMMER THE MEATBALLS IN A TASTY SAUCE

>> All the meatballs should be outside the pan. (Somewhere away from extra pairs of hands.) Now, deglaze the pan with the chicken stock—add the stock to the pan and scrape it with a wooden spoon to get all those browned bits.

>> Add the peach passata. Add all the meatballs. Bring to a simmer. Cover.

>> Simmer the meatballs for about 10 to 12 minutes. Turn off the heat and hold them warm.

>> To serve, ladle about ⅓ cup of passata into a soup bowl, followed by 4 meatballs.

>> Garnish the meatballs with 2 ounces crumbled goat cheese, crisped bacon, and a few pecan pieces.

>> Serve with a wedge of lemon or lime.

SERVES 8 (SERVING SIZE: 4 MEATBALLS AND ABOUT ⅓ CUP SAUCE)
CALORIES 364; FAT 18.5G (SAT 5.8G, MONO 7.7G, POLY 3.2G); PROTEIN 29G; CARB 22G; FIBER 3G; CHOL 109MG; IRON 2MG; SODIUM 558MG; CALC 81MG

MAD GUIDE TO MAKING MEATBALLS

MAKE YOUR OWN BREADCRUMBS. IT REALLY DOES MAKE A DIFFERENCE.

BE DELICATE WHEN WORKING WITH THE MEAT MIXTURE. OVERHANDLING CREATES TOUGH, DENSE MEATBALLS.

THIS IS THE PANADE.

DON'T TRY TO MAKE A HOMOGENOUS MASS; THE POCKETS OF MOISTENED BREAD IN THE FINAL MEATBALL ARE GLORIOUS.

THE MEATBALLS SHOULD BE ROLLED TO A CONSISTENT SIZE SO THEY BROWN & COOK EVENLY.

MAD LIGHT SUNDAY GRAVY

HANDS-ON: 40 MIN. **TOTAL:** 2 HR. 10 MIN.

Gravy means different things to different people—it depends on where you call home. For "New Yawkers," particularly ones with Italian ancestry, "gravy" is a tomato ragù typically made of beef and pork, that almost universally includes meatballs and sausage. It's traditionally shared on Sundays, where family and friends come and go at will, serve themselves up some gravy, and show respect to the cook. Under slow, even heat, chicken thighs break down similarly to pork shoulder, so texturally, this version of Italian-American Sunday Gravy is right on the money.

THE FLAVOR OF FRESH BASIL DISSIPATES OVER TIME, SO DON'T BE AFRAID TO KEEP SOME EXTRA AROUND FOR DOSING THE POT LATER.

Food	How Much	Why
whole-wheat bread	2 (1½-ounce) slices, diced	For the panade, the moistened bread mixture that gives body and unctuousness to the meatball without a ton of extra fat.
garlic cloves	8, finely chopped and divided	Italian-American fare. Meatballs. Garlic.
milk	2 tablespoons	To moisten the bread.
ground turkey	1 pound	Makes a good meatball.
onion	¾ cup finely chopped, divided	Some to add moisture and body to the meatballs. Some is for the sauce.
fresh flat-leaf parsley	¼ cup chopped	Brightens up the meatballs.
pecorino Romano	1 tablespoon grated	A blend of dry cheeses isn't uncommon in Italian-American meatball making.
Parmigiano-Reggiano	1 tablespoon grated	Because you can say you used the good stuff.
egg whites	2	To bind the meatballs.
olive oil	2 tablespoons, divided	For browning. And flavor.
skinless, boneless chicken thighs	2 pounds	Cooks up a lot faster than pork shoulder, and is a bit lighter.
Italian chicken sausage	4 (2-ounce) links	Saving you some fat calories here.
chicken necks	4	For lip-smacking mouthfeel. You'll hydrolyze some collagen, so the sauce will be richer.
whole plum tomatoes	1 (28-ounce) can	Because you get some straight juice, and you can crush the tomatoes to your preference.
tomato paste	2 tablespoons	To thicken and embolden.
dried oregano	1 teaspoon	Dry is more appropriate here. The deep woodsiness of dry oregano is a better fit for gravy. We're going fresh with basil for contrast, too.
kosher salt	½ teaspoon	It needs it.
fresh basil leaves	24	The leaves wilt on contact with the gravy, offering up their perfume immediately.

CONTINUED →

MAD LIGHT SUNDAY GRAVY

2 (1½-oz.) slices whole-wheat bread, diced

8 garlic cloves, finely chopped and divided

2 Tbsp. milk

1 lb. ground turkey

¾ cup finely chopped onion, divided

¼ cup chopped fresh flat-leaf parsley

1 Tbsp. grated pecorino Romano

1 Tbsp. grated Parmigiano-Reggiano

2 egg whites

2 Tbsp. olive oil, divided

2 lb. skinless, boneless chicken thighs

4 (2-oz.) links Italian chicken sausage

4 chicken necks

1 (28-oz.) can whole plum tomatoes

2 Tbsp. tomato paste

1 tsp. dry oregano

½ tsp. kosher salt

24 fresh basil leaves

Follow These Steps:

>> *It's Louis Prima time. Your favorite Internet music source has it. This is a must.*

MAKE MEATBALLS

>> Moisten the bread and 4 garlic cloves with the milk in a large bowl.

>> Add the ground turkey, ¼ cup of onion, the parsley, both cheeses, and the egg whites to the bread mixture. Don't mix yet.

>> *Combine well, without mushing it.* The meat is already ground, and it's turkey, a more pasty product than beef or pork. Make 16 small, 1-inch meatballs.

>> Refrigerate in a single layer, uncovered, while you brown the other meats.

BROWN THE CHICKEN, SAUSAGE, AND MEATBALLS

>> Heat a Dutch oven on the stovetop on moderate heat. *Let the gravy begin.*

>> Add 1 tablespoon of the olive oil and swirl to coat. Add the chicken thighs and cook 3 minutes per side, until brown. Set aside on a platter.

>> Add the chicken sausage and necks and cook 5 minutes, browning them on all sides. Cook the sausages to about 155°. *Remember, this will be simmered again, so slightly undercooked is okay.* Set aside on a platter.

>> Add 1 tablespoon oil to the Dutch oven.

>> Now, add half the meatballs and cook 5 minutes, browning them on two sides. *Don't roll them about; simply turn once.* They'll cook through in the gravy.

>> Remove them to the platter, and repeat with the remaining meatballs.

MAKE A SAUCE—ITLL BRING THE GRAVY TOGETHER

>> Add 4 cloves of garlic and ½ cup of onion to the pot. Stir 2 minutes, until they're slightly browned and translucent.

>> Now, add the tomatoes to the Dutch oven, juice and all, and the tomato paste and oregano. Bring to a boil. Scrape the bits off the bottom of the pot with a wooden spoon.

>> Gently add all of the chicken, the meatballs, the sausage, and the salt. Cover, reduce the heat to medium-low, and simmer for an hour and a half or more, until the chicken thighs pull apart with a pair of tongs.

FINISH AND SERVE

>> Remove the meat to a platter. Cut the sausages into 1-inch pieces on the bias. Cut the necks in half.

>> Add the basil to the gravy. Stir.

>> To serve, arrange the chicken thighs, sausage, necks, and meatballs on a platter. *Spoon just enough tomato over to enrobe, but not drench. This is Gravy.*

SERVES 10 (SERVING SIZE: ABOUT 1¼ CUPS)
CALORIES 303; **FAT** 12.9G (SAT 3.1G, MONO 4.5G, POLY 2.4G); **PROTEIN** 35G; **CARB** 10G; **FIBER** 2G; **CHOL** 132MG; **IRON** 3MG; **SODIUM** 592MG; **CALC** 101MG

SAUTÉED COD
WITH TOMATOES, PIQUILLOS, AND OLIVES

HANDS-ON: 25 MIN. **TOTAL:** 35 MIN.

Sometimes a dish is created based on a beautifully haunting, years-old memory of a meal. This is one of those. A recreation of an unforgettable Basque piperrada (or pipérade). Gloriously mellow Castelvetrano olives were on the table. Espelette pepper–spiced something, I'm sure. You're jumping into two-pan territory here.

Food	How Much	Why
olive oil	2 tablespoons, divided	We're building a piperrada. Olive oil is the fat of choice.
yellow onion	1½ cups sliced	Part one of the piperrada.
green bell pepper	1 cup sliced	Part two.
garlic cloves	5, sliced	This is a lot of garlic, but it's also getting a dose of Espelette (spicy, sweet, almost smoky flavor).
whole canned piquillo peppers	1 cup sliced	Piquillos have this magnificently dense flesh, like soft leather. It raises the bar on piperrada.
whole plum tomatoes	1 (14.5-ounce) can, undrained and chopped	To envelop the sautéed vegetables in an acid-forward sauce.
cod	4 (6-ounce) fillets	Cod is a great choice for this preparation because of its broad, meaty flake.
kosher salt	⅛ teaspoon	
Espelette pepper	½ teaspoon	This becomes the dominant fragrance in the dish. It emboldens, but also softens and unifies.
Castelvetrano olives	12, sliced	I like this olive against the boldness of the sauce. It's meatier and mellower than most varieties.
fresh flat-leaf parsley	1 tablespoon chopped	A last-minute refresher.

Follow These Steps:

» Ready a fairly large heavy-bottomed skillet and accompanying lid. This is for the vegetables. Heat the pan to medium-high.

» Now, start the vegetables. Add 1 tablespoon olive oil to the pan. Add onion, bell pepper, and sliced garlic. Sauté 6 minutes or until the vegetables are lightly browned and wilted.

» Lower the heat to medium-low. Add the piquillos and the tomatoes. Cover and cook for about 20 minutes.

» Heat a medium-sized skillet to medium-high. Pat the cod fillets dry with paper towels. Season with the salt.

» Add 1 tablespoon olive oil to the medium-sized skillet, and add the seasoned fillets to the pan. ***Press gently to ensure that the surface area of the fish touching the pan is free of air pockets.*** Cook for about 3 minutes before attempting to turn.

» Cook the flip side of the fish roughly 5 minutes, depending upon thickness, just until fish flakes evenly when tested with a fork but retains some translucency—a glisten. ***Cod is a fish that can carry-over cook quite fast, and if you cook it 100% through at the stove, it will be dry at the table. For sure.*** Turn off the heat and let the cod rest in the pan.

» When the vegetables are tender, remove the lid and raise the temperature to high. Reduce most of the liquid out of the pan. It should glisten and be almost jammy in texture. Now, fold in the Espelette pepper and the olives.

» Raise the heat on the cod pan to low. Spoon the entire tomato-pepper-olive mixture over the cod fillets and warm the pan until it bubbles and/or sizzles. Sprinkle with parsley. Serve.

SERVES 4 (SERVING SIZE: 1 FILLET AND ⅔ CUP SAUCE)
CALORIES 282; **FAT** 9.1G (SAT 1.2G, MONO 5.1G, POLY 1.2G); **PROTEIN** 33G;
CARB 16G; **FIBER** 2G; **CHOL** 73MG; **IRON** 2MG; **SODIUM** 635MG; **CALC** 65MG

THE ONLY THING OMITTED FROM THIS RECIPE IS THE GREAT WINE, BECAUSE, WELL, WE DRANK THAT. YOU SHOULD, TOO.

MAD RISOTTO, LOBSTER EDITION

HANDS-ON: 45 MIN. **TOTAL:** 45 MIN.

We often hear that risotto is a dish to be constantly stirred. I guess that's okay if you have the time and want to be intimate with your rice, but it's not necessary. What you're looking to do is cook the rice until the starches are ready to be manipulated by human, spoon, and liquid. That can happen toward the end of the cooking process, giving you time to make a lovely little lobster ragout.

Food	How Much	Why
plum tomatoes	1 (28-ounce) can, undrained and chopped	They're lush, ripe, and delicious.
unsalted chicken stock	3 cups, divided	It's mellow and neutral.
olive oil	2 tablespoons, divided	Some to start the risotto and some to start the ragout.
Arborio or other medium- or short-grain rice	1 cup	Arborio, Carnaroli, Vialone Nano, heck, even Calasparra or Calrose make a nice risotto. Fire up your search engine.
onion	1 cup diced and divided	Risotto typically begins similarly to pilaf, with some onion sweated in fat. The rest of the onion is for the lobster preparation.
garlic cloves	4, smashed and divided	We're going for a bulb-y flavor with this dish. Onion, garlic, fennel.
fennel bulb	1 cup diced	See above.
crushed red pepper	2 teaspoons	Punches through tomatoes quite well.
serrano chiles	2, minced	Crushed red pepper on its own provides a generic pop of heat, but not the depth of some additional chile.
cooked lobster meat	2 cups (about 13 ounces), cut into ³/₄-inch pieces	Because you're worth it.
butter	1 tablespoon	Lobster. Butter.
salt	½ teaspoon	

Follow These Steps:

➤➤ Drain the tomatoes in a colander over a bowl, reserving the tomato liquid. Coarsely chop the tomatoes. Add ³/₄ cup of the chicken stock to the tomato liquid.

➤➤ Heat a medium-sized saucepan over medium-high heat for the risotto. Add 1 tablespoon of olive oil to the pan and swirl.

➤➤ Add the rice and stir to toast, about 2 minutes. Add ½ cup of the onion and 2 of the garlic cloves. Stir until translucent.

➤➤ Add 2 cups of the stock. Bring it to an immediate boil, then reduce to a simmer. Cook for about 15 minutes on the lowest possible heat setting.

➤➤ Now, you should be able to get the rest of the dish ready while the rice is cooking. **Let's go.**

➤➤ In another skillet, heat the other tablespoon of olive oil. Medium heat.

➤➤ Add the fennel bulb, ½ cup of the onion, and 2 cloves of garlic. Stir to brown gently.

➤➤ Add the tomatoes, the crushed red pepper, and the minced chiles. Sauté and stir for about 4 minutes.

➤➤ Add a few tablespoons of the reserved tomato juice mixture and ¼ cup stock to moisten. Fold in the lobster, reduce heat to low, and warm the lobster chunks through, about 2 minutes.

➤➤ Now, return your attention to the risotto. It's time to stir and gradually add liquid, one ladleful of the remaining tomato juice mixture at a time. *Stir until quite creamy, but still toothsome.* Add the butter and salt, and stir to finish.

➤➤ Serve the risotto in shallow bowls, with a generous spoonful of the lobster ragout on top.

SERVES 8 (SERVING SIZE: ABOUT ⅓ CUP RISOTTO AND ½ CUP RAGOUT) **CALORIES** 216; **FAT** 5.5G (SAT 1.5G, MONO 2.9G, POLY 0.5G); **PROTEIN** 14G; **CARB** 28G; **FIBER** 3G; **CHOL** 37MG; **IRON** 2MG; **SODIUM** 541MG; **CALC** 78MG

FOLD THE LOBSTER RAGOUT INTO THE RISOTTO OR USE IT AS A TOPPING. YOUR CALL.

CARNITAS DE POLLO

HANDS-ON: 35 MIN. **TOTAL:** 2 HR. 5 MIN.

Carnitas are often celebrated for their fat-forward technique and texture. But is it really the fat? Probably not. Successful carnitas are revered more for the crisp exterior texture and the fork-tender interior. Here, we take a leaner approach with chicken thighs, going a bit more complex with some citrus and beer, and pulling off a miracle of fat restraint. Serve these with Maria's Cilantro Cebollas (page 79). The tangy, crisp, and bright flavors are a perfect foil to the rich carnitas.

Food

Food	How Much	Why
skinless, boneless chicken thighs	2 pounds	Fatty and unctuous enough to be credible "carnitas."
kosher salt	1 teaspoon	To firm and season the thighs.
cooking spray		
yellow onion	2 cups sliced (about 1 large)	When slow-cooked and fully collapsed, onions are as soft and slippery as bone marrow. This is a good thing inside a warm tortilla.
garlic cloves	6, halved	We're leaving them whole to provide some textural variation in the finished dish.
water	2 cups	The cooking liquid.
light beer	1 (12-ounce) bottle	For some bread-y aroma. Don't use hoppy stuff.
fresh orange juice	½ cup	Reduces, gets syrupy, and is the backbone of the glaze.
fresh lime juice	¼ cup	Your sole acid in the dish. Provides balance and brightness.
brown sugar	1 tablespoon	Helps the glaze along. Provides some color depth.
corn tortillas	12 (6-inch) tortillas	Corn tortillas add depth of flavor that flour tortillas can't contribute here.
limes	2, cut "seviche-style" (see page 27)	While there is fresh lime in the onions, a little table-side squeeze is welcome.

Follow These Steps:

» On a cutting board, rub the chicken thighs with the salt. Transfer to a plate momentarily.

» This is a time to break out your top-quality Dutch oven or heavy-bottomed pot. Heat the Dutch oven over medium-high heat and spray evenly with cooking spray.

» Lay down the chicken thighs in a single layer, and cook 12 minutes or until they're well browned before turning. Flip the thighs over and cook 8 minutes or until browned. *You want them to be quite crusty, to the point of almost seeming overcooked. Fret not, you'll add some liquid to rehydrate the dish in a moment.*

» *When the chicken thighs resemble roasted chicken that's been accidentally left in the oven overnight with the pilot light on, they're ready for the onions and the garlic.* Tumble about for a minute or so.

» Add 2 cups water and the beer, and bring to a simmer. Lower the heat and simmer robustly at a steady, constant bubble for about an hour and 20 minutes, uncovered, or until the liquid is about ¼ cup from being fully evaporated.

» Now, add the orange juice, lime juice, and brown sugar, and continue to cook and turn the thighs, about 2 minutes or until the chicken pieces are nicely glazed and nearly falling apart. Turn off the heat.

» After about 10 minutes, when the chicken is cool enough to handle but still quite warm, remove the chicken and tear it into bite-sized pieces. Combine the pulled chicken with the cooked onions and soft garlic.

» Platter and serve with warm corn tortillas and lime wedges.

SERVES 6 (SERVING SIZE: ½ CUP CHICKEN, 2 TORTILLAS, AND 1 LIME WEDGE)
CALORIES 333; **FAT** 7.8G (SAT 1.8G, MONO 2.2G, POLY 2.2G); **PROTEIN** 33G; **CARB** 31G; **FIBER** 4G; **CHOL** 125MG; **IRON** 2MG; **SODIUM** 549MG; **CALC** 74MG

IN THE OVEN

Baking, roasting, broiling, finishing, and warming

Ovens. They take the lead in cooking. Whereas in most other techniques, you'll spend a lot of time monitoring things, with ovens, they are at the ready to do most of the work for you. The recipes in this book are tooled for a standard everyday conventional oven—no forced air circulation, no steam-injected, combination-cooking, computerized fancy-pants "oven." But ovens aren't ideal for cooking everything, so what follows are some of the cooking techniques, environmental situations, and dishes that call for you to put yours to work.

Toasting

In the recipes ahead, you'll be toasting nuts, and chickpeas, and things with bread. Pay careful attention to the recommended temperatures, as attempts to rush the toasting process (thinking you'll be able to do it at higher heat in less time) yield disastrous results. Regardless of what you're preparing, make sure you have separation between the "pieces" of food (whatever they are), and use the center rack so each piece will toast evenly. If you have a convection oven, your toasted results will be deeper and more even, and will require less tinkering/handling.

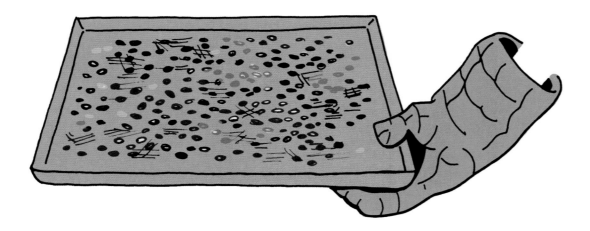

Roasting

We do a lot of roasting in the pages ahead—that is, cooking food in the oven on an uncovered pan. With large items, there's usually a benefit in adjusting the temperature as the dish cooks, applying high heat to create a deeply browned exterior, and then turning down the heat so the item cooks at a lower, more controlled temperature to ensure an even, moist interior. It really doesn't matter which order you choose, only that you're monitoring interior temperatures as recommended in the recipes.

Note that some items, like root vegetables, benefit from a touch of moist heat (steaming, poaching, boiling, simmering, etc.) before roasting. With these harder, longer-cooking vegetables (carrots, turnips, fennel, and similar), roasting alone can sometimes yield a leathery result, but the combination packet-steam/roast method yields a tender, jammy interior and (because of the moisture added during the steaming process) an item that can handle a much higher oven temperature, which creates a more deeply browned and even exterior.

DON'T CROWD THE PAN, OR YOU'LL JUST BE STEAMING IN YOUR OVEN. GIVE THE SMALL PIECES ROOM TO BREATHE, AND MAKE SURE TO GIVE THINGS A TUMBLE PERIODICALLY.

Broiling

Broiling—cooking foods in the oven under an intense heat source—is an under-utilized technique in the home. If you haven't already, adopt it. Next time you hit up a full-service restaurant with an open kitchen, observe that big slab of fire-breathing stainless steel above the range. (They call it a salamander—it's a broiler.) There are things going in and out of it constantly. It's not just convenient, it's essential.

When should you use it? Where moisture is plentiful in the recipe/collection of ingredients to be broiled, the dish *might* be a candidate for start-to-finish broiling, like with the Clam Shack–Style Broiled Fish (page 309). Alternatively, the broiler is an incredible finishing tool, and can be used to bring some depth of color and Maillard-imposed flavor (normal people call it browning), or can add a bruléed finish to glazed items like the Sorghum-Roasted Salmon (page 310).

Your Stovetop Is Packed and/or You Can't Maintain Low Heat

Remember, an oven blasts heat at/on things. If it can be cooked low and slow and covered on a stove, it can go into the oven, too. So next time you're cooking multiple dishes for a fiesta and you run out of stove space, cover that pot/pan and get it in the oven. If the recipe calls for an item to be covered and cooked on low on the stovetop, a general guideline is to put it in the oven, covered, somewhere between 250° and 300°. The 27-Hour Chicken Legs (page 298) can go either way.

THERE'S MORE ROOM IN HERE.

It's Really Cold Outside

Sometimes, you'd love to fire up that grill, but then, well, you're not so ready to brave the outdoors. Instead, preheat that oven. Outdoor cooking recipes that call for indirect heat with the grill covered are perfect candidates for combination oven-cooking methods, like the oven-packet-steam/broil method for the Peanut and Peppercorn Pork Back Ribs (page 306). Broil more aggressively, ramping up the char level, to evoke the outdoors.

Savory Baking/Casserole-y Things

Here you have the items where either a) there are so many ingredients that require mingling under consistent, uniform heat that the oven is the ideal place for their cooking, and/or b) the item to be cooked is simply too large to be cooked anywhere but an oven. And anything with a bread/bread-y component is a candidate for a trip behind the oven door.

Remember this: The oven is just another tool with which you can apply heat. It's that simple. The recipes that follow show the range of things your oven can do.

PUN INTENDED.

CRUNCHY CHICKPEAS

HANDS-ON: 10 MIN.   **TOTAL:** 1 HR. 15 MIN.

Chickpeas, often celebrated for their protein content, have a significant amount of starch as well. It's the amylose content that helps provide the structure that leads to the crazy-crunchy final result. Sumac, a maroon-red berry that's dried and crushed, contributes a pronounced tartness to the spice blend from significant levels of malic acid (think green apple, rhubarb). The tiny bit of vinegar sprinkled on the chickpeas helps some of the spice adhere to your fingers, giving you a second chance to enjoy the salty-spicy-sumac blend.

Food	How Much	Why
unsalted chickpeas (garbanzo beans)	2 (15-ounce) cans, rinsed and drained	They're easy, they're consistent, and we can control the salt level.
ground sumac	1 tablespoon	For its unique tang.
popcorn salt or other fine salt	½ teaspoon	Because we selected the no-salt-added chickpeas, the salt can be added to the exterior, where it hits your tongue first.
ground red pepper	¼ teaspoon	Spicy works here.
olive oil	2 tablespoons	To coat and to flavor. Choose a bold olive oil.
red wine vinegar	2 teaspoons	For fun. Add only if you're serving them right away. Try lemon as an alternative.

Follow These Steps:

≫ Preheat your oven to 375°.

≫ Place the chickpeas on a baking sheet and bake in the oven for 10 minutes to dry them well.

≫ Combine the sumac, the salt, the red pepper, and the olive oil in a medium bowl. Transfer the chickpeas to the bowl and toss.

≫ Return the chickpeas to the baking sheet.

≫ Bake at 375° for 55 minutes or until crisp and browned, stirring occasionally.

≫ Transfer the chickpeas to a serving bowl and sprinkle with red wine vinegar. Serve immediately. Or if you're making these ahead of time, omit the vinegar and store the chickpeas in an airtight container.

SERVES 12 (SERVING SIZE: 1½ TABLESPOONS)
CALORIES 79; **FAT** 2.7G (SAT 0.3G, MONO 1.6G, POLY 0.2G); **PROTEIN** 3G; **CARB** 11G; **FIBER** 2G; **CHOL** 0MG; **IRON** 1MG; **SODIUM** 105MG; **CALC** 23MG

SUMAC BERRIES

LIKE, ON SOME BLACKENED FISH.
THAT WOULD BE AWESOME.

ALL-PURPOSE PECANS

HANDS-ON: 10 MIN.   **TOTAL:** 40 MIN.

*Quick science lesson: Albumen is another way to say egg white. Albumins are proteins.
You find those in things like eggs—and people. Albumen consists of mostly albumins and water.
Read: glue. Waterproof adhesive. Edible. Waterproof. Adhesive. So, if you want sugar and salt and
spicy stuff to stick to your pecans, or walnuts, or almonds, toss them in a little edible waterproof
adhesive. After a roast and a subsequent air dry, you have one versatile bar snack, salad
garnish, or crunchy topping. Use halves or pieces here, depending on intended use. Clearly,
this can be tilted more sweet or savory once you get the albumen thing straight.*

Food	How Much	Why
fresh thyme	½ teaspoon	Thyme contains limonene, a compound deriving its name from lemon rind. It's a lovely addition to sweet-savory things. In fact, you could use lemon zest if you didn't want the herb flavor here.
large egg white	1, lightly beaten	For its adhesive magic.
pecan halves	1 pound	We call for halves, but you can chop them or use pieces.
superfine sugar	1 tablespoon	Superfine coats more evenly.
fine sea salt	½ teaspoon	To pull this in a savory direction.
freshly ground black pepper	½ teaspoon	Straightforward spice.
ground red pepper	¼ teaspoon	Endorphin stimulator. The tactile experience of eating is important, too. In addition to contributing a slight fruitiness to the snack, red pepper pinches the senses, making the snacking experience more exciting.

Follow These Steps:

≫ Preheat your oven to 325°.

≫ Line a baking pan or restaurant-style half sheet pan with parchment paper or a silicone mat.

≫ Combine the thyme and the egg white in a medium bowl, stirring with a whisk.

≫ Add the pecans. Toss until evenly moistened.

≫ Combine the sugar, the salt, the black pepper, and the red pepper in a separate small bowl.

≫ While folding the pecans with one hand, evenly sprinkle in the sugar mixture.

≫ Spread the pecans in an even layer on the baking pan.

≫ Bake for about 17 minutes, or until the pecans begin to darken around the edges and are evenly glazed.

≫ Remove the roasting pan from the oven and let cool at room temperature.

≫ When the pecans have cooled, loosen them from the roasting pan and store in an airtight container.

SERVES 16 (SERVING SIZE: ¼ CUP)
CALORIES 200; **FAT** 20.4G (SAT 1.8G, MONO 11.6G, POLY 6.1G); **PROTEIN** 3G;
CARB 5G; **FIBER** 3G; **CHOL** 0MG; **IRON** 1MG; **SODIUM** 74MG; **CALC** 21MG

BACON-ROASTED POTATOES AND SHALLOTS

HANDS-ON: 20 MIN. **TOTAL:** 60 MIN.

This is a hot riff on the German potato salad my mother used to make. Here, pre-cooking the shallots helps ensure they get deeply browned and jammy in the oven. The bacon fat goes really far here, too, enhancing the molasses-y, malty finish. The technique you're left with is this: Cut up whichever tuber or root vegetable you have, pre-cook garlic/shallot/onion-like thing, toss in liquid fat, high-heat roast, "dress" with something glaze-y late in the process, and finish with fresh herbs.

Food	How Much	Why
shallots	1 pound, peeled and quartered	They're slightly higher in sugars than your standard yellow onion and are the perfect-size bulb to toss with the diced potatoes. Looks matter.
bacon	2 ounces, thinly sliced	For its fat and its cracklin' quality in the finished dish.
grapeseed oil	1 tablespoon	To hold the bacon fat's hand. All bacon fat, and it might be a little heavy. This adds some elegance.
russet potatoes	1 pound, cut into 1-inch dice	The interior of a russet is gloriously "fluffy." In contrast to the Maillard magic (browning—see page 72) that takes place on the exterior, that fluffiness is pure culinary harmony.
malt vinegar	2 tablespoons	It's delightfully mellow, and just works with potatoes. Think "fish and chips." Use the real stuff.
brown sugar	2 teaspoons	To conjure up a quickie glaze.
kosher salt	1/2 teaspoon	Potatoes. Must. Have. Salt.
fresh flat-leaf parsley	2 tablespoons chopped	Always finish fresh.

Follow These Steps:

>> Preheat the oven to 475°.

>> Put the shallots in a microwave-safe bowl. Microwave at HIGH for 1 minute.

>> Heat a small skillet over medium-low heat, add the bacon and **cook gently, with the intent to preserve some nearly clear bacon fat.** Separating the fat from the meat by melting the fat away is known as "rendering." **Cook until the bacon is crisp, but don't be so aggressive with the heat that you bring the fat to the smoking point.** Spoon out the bacon and save it for garnishing later. Leave the fat in the pan.

>> Turn off the heat. Add the grapeseed oil to the fat in the pan. Swirl and keep warm.

>> Put the potatoes and the shallots in a large bowl. Pour in the bacon fat and oil mixture and toss to coat.

>> Place the potatoes and shallots on a roasting pan, and roast at 475° for 36 minutes or until tender and evenly browned, turning them every 10 minutes or so. Remove them from the oven.

>> Combine the malt vinegar, the brown sugar, and the salt in a small bowl until the sugar dissolves. Pour the sugar mixture onto the potato mixture and toss using a flat metal spatula.

>> Roast the vegetables 4 minutes more, until the sugar-vinegar mixture creates a slight glisten on the potatoes.

>> Transfer the vegetables to a serving bowl and toss with the parsley. Garnish with the reserved bacon. Serve.

SERVES 5 (SERVING SIZE: 1/2 CUP)
CALORIES 216; **FAT** 8G (SAT 2G, MONO 2.7G, POLY 2.6G); **PROTEIN** 6G; **CARB** 33G; **FIBER** 2G; **CHOL** 8MG; **IRON** 2MG; **SODIUM** 304MG; **CALC** 48MG

SPICE-ROASTED EGGPLANT
WITH GARLIC YOGURT AND HARISSA

HANDS-ON: 20 MIN.   **TOTAL:** 45 MIN.

Many of the cuisines of North Africa have been an influence in the creation of this book. Here, we have harissa, mint, ras el hanout, and eggplant. This eggplant cooking technique, though, is straight outta high-volume kitchens where a lot of food needs to be cooked evenly and rapidly, without too much oversight. The flour lends the eggplant some additional structure, so it doesn't collapse. Make sure there's plenty of space between the cubes of eggplant, as we want water to evaporate into the oven, not get trapped as steam pockets (which would make the eggplant soggy).

Food	How Much	Why
plain 2% reduced-fat Greek yogurt	½ cup	It's one of your two condiments for the eggplant.
fresh garlic	1 tablespoon minced	Eggplant is pretty "round" tasting stuff, especially roasted. This will bite back.
kosher salt	⅜ teaspoon, divided	Some for the yogurt. Some to season the eggplant.
cooking spray		Without it, your pan would get more eggplant than whoever's eating.
Wondra flour	½ cup	Its starches are gelatinized, then it's turned back into a free-flowing fine flour. It coats evenly, and its resultant crunch is unparalleled.
ras el hanout	1 tablespoon	Rather than making one, use a premade blend. There's an art to the balance.
eggplant	6 cups, peeled and cut into 1-inch cubes	When you perfect this method, you'll want to cook other things this way. Like mushrooms. Or zucchini.
olive oil	2 tablespoons	North Africa. Olive oil.
fresh mint leaves	8, thinly sliced	There are a lot of roasted, toasted, spicy flavors going on here. Mint balances.
Mad Spicy Harissa *(page 60)*	¼ cup	We're playing with North African flavors. Harissa belongs.

Follow These Steps:

≫ Preheat the oven to 400°.

≫ In a small mixing bowl, combine the yogurt, the garlic, and ⅛ teaspoon salt. Stir and refrigerate.

≫ Spray a baking pan with cooking spray.

≫ Combine the Wondra flour and the ras el hanout in a large zip-top bag.

≫ Toss the eggplant with the flour mixture to evenly coat the eggplant. Shake out any excess through a colander into a large mixing bowl.

≫ Toss the floured eggplant with the olive oil and place in an even layer on the roasting pan.

≫ Roast at 400° until evenly browned and tender, 25 minutes. Turn once with a thin metal spatula during cooking.

≫ Sprinkle the eggplant with ¼ teaspoon salt. Scatter the mint on top and transfer the finished eggplant to a bowl.

≫ Serve on individual plates, with yogurt sauce and harissa.

SERVES 6 (SERVING SIZE: ½ CUP EGGPLANT, 4 TEASPOONS YOGURT, AND 2 TEASPOONS HARISSA)
CALORIES 157; **FAT** 9.1G (SAT 1.5G, MONO 6.2G, POLY 1G); **PROTEIN** 4G; **CARB** 16G; **FIBER** 4G; **CHOL** 0MG; **IRON** 1MG; **SODIUM** 215MG; **CALC** 30MG

MOROCCAN SPICE-RUBBED WHOLE ROASTED CAULIFLOWER

HANDS-ON: 25 MIN. **TOTAL:** 1 HR. 45 MIN.

Dress up a head of cauliflower, throw it in the oven, and benefit from caramelization and the non-enzymatic browning (often referred to simply as "toasted" or "browned") known in the food nerd-o-sphere as the Maillard reaction—see page 72 for more information. Roasty. Toasty. Caramel-y. Sweet. It's really a thing of beauty when fully roasted—tender, meaty, and completely satisfying.

PURE CAPSAICIN	15,000,000
U.S. GRADE PEPPER SPRAY	2,000,000–5,300,000
HABANERO	200,000–350,000
CAYENNE	30,000–50,000
SERRANO	8,000–23,000
JALAPEÑO	3,500–8,000
PASILLA	1,000–2,500
ANAHEIM	500–2,000
RED CHILE	500–750
SWEET BELL	0

THE SCOVILLE SCALE MEASURES THE HEAT IN CHILE PEPPERS AND OTHER FOODS BASED ON THE AMOUNT OF CAPSAICIN THEY CONTAIN.

Food	How Much	Why
large oranges	2	While they add some sweetness, it's their unique acidity that makes this incredible.
red onion	1 cup thinly sliced	For color and pungency.
kosher salt	½ teaspoon, divided	There are so-called "sweet spices" in here, plus the raisins and sugar. It needs the salt.
sugar	2 teaspoons	To cheat a little. Guaranteed caramel-y spots.
ground cumin	½ teaspoon	Cumin is so important in Moroccan cuisine that it has a place at the table along with salt and pepper
ground cinnamon	¼ teaspoon	Often found in Moroccan spice blends, including the ever-varied ras el hanout.
ground coriander	¼ teaspoon	Glorious against oranges.
ground ginger	⅛ teaspoon	For bite. Fresh ginger contains gingerol, which is a "cousin" to capsaicin (the stuff that makes chiles spicy). When ginger is dried, there is a reaction that creates shogaols (basically dehydrated gingerols), which are so spicy, they're measured in Scoville Units.
extra-virgin olive oil	3 tablespoons, divided	To carry the spices. Morocco: olive oil.
water	¼ cup	To hydrate the raisins.
raisins	2 tablespoons	Adds depth to the cauliflower's spice paste.
cauliflower	1 large head (20 ounces), trimmed	A large head looks dramatic, and the roasting time stated is tooled to this. If you go smaller, cut back the roasting time.
cooking spray		
Mad Spicy Harissa *(page 60)*	¼ cup	It's complex, works in harmony with the spice blend, and is sensational against the sweetness of this dish.

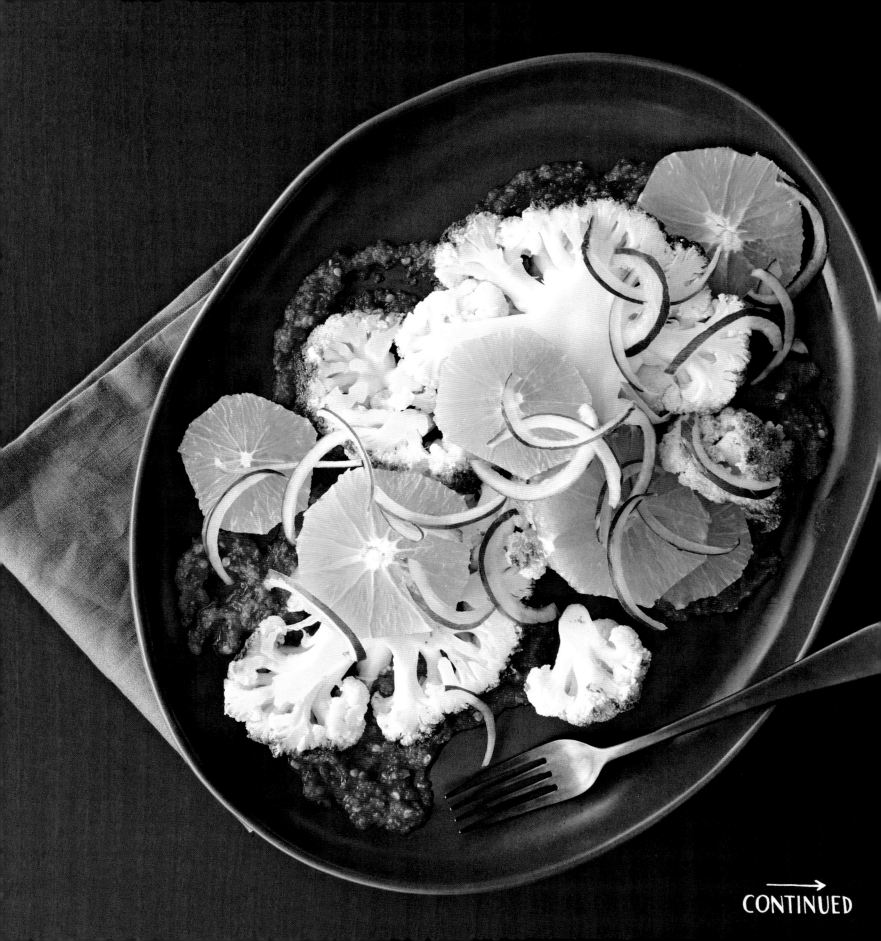

CONTINUED →

MOROCCAN SPICE-RUBBED WHOLE ROASTED CAULIFLOWER

2 large oranges

1 cup thinly sliced red onion

1/2 tsp. kosher salt, divided

2 tsp. sugar

1/2 tsp. ground cumin

1/4 tsp. ground cinnamon

1/4 tsp. ground coriander

1/8 tsp. ground ginger

3 Tbsp. extra-virgin olive oil, divided

1/4 cup water

2 Tbsp. raisins

1 large head cauliflower, trimmed

cooking spray

1/4 cup Mad Spicy Harissa

Follow These Steps:

>> Preheat your oven to 375°.

>> Ready a heavy-bottomed roasting pan or enameled Dutch oven.

MAKE A SALAD

>> Peel the oranges and cut each crosswise into 4 slices (per the photos).

>> In a small bowl, combine the sliced oranges and the onion, season with 1/8 teaspoon salt, toss, and set aside, covered, at room temperature.

CREATE A SEASONED OIL AND A PASTE

>> In a second small bowl, combine the sugar, the remaining 3/8 teaspoon salt, the cumin, the cinnamon, the coriander, the ginger, and 2 tablespoons oil. Stir to combine. Set aside.

>> In a third small, microwave-safe bowl, combine 1/4 cup water and the raisins.

>> Microwave at HIGH for 1 minute or until the raisins are tender (depending on the power of your microwave).

>> *Drain the raisins and mash to a paste with a fork so that it resembles (the thick kind of) barbecue sauce.*

SEASON THE CAULIFLOWER

>> Place the cauliflower on a large plate or cutting board.

>> Brush evenly with 1 tablespoon of the olive oil, then the raisin paste, and finally the spiced oil.

>> *Now, put the brush aside and get your hands in there. You know you want to.*

ROAST!

>> Spray your roasting pan evenly with cooking spray.

>> Place the cauliflower in your roasting vessel and roast for anywhere from 45 minutes to 1 hour and 15 minutes, or until tender. *(If a skewer can be inserted and removed without struggle, it's tender.)*

>> Baste periodically. Add a touch of water to the bottom of your pan if you find the edges of the cauliflower are caramelizing too rapidly.

>> Remove the cauliflower from the oven.

>> *Cover the cauliflower with the lid of your Dutch oven (if it's nowhere to be found, use foil)* and let rest for 15 minutes before carving.

CARVE AND SERVE

» As if to carve a roast, slice the cauliflower into 8 (½-inch to ¾-inch) slabs.

» To serve, smear the surface of each of 8 plates with about ½ tablespoon of harissa.

» Top each with a slab of cauliflower and then garnish with 1 slice of orange and some of the marinated onion.

» *Serve and revel in the meatless-ness.*

SERVES 8 (SERVING SIZE: 1 PLATE)
CALORIES 274; **FAT** 16.5G (SAT 2.3G, MONO 11.4G, POLY 1.8G); **PROTEIN** 6G; **CARB** 31G; **FIBER** 8G; **CHOL** 0MG; **IRON** 2MG; **SODIUM** 372MG; **CALC** 98MG

AN IDEA: SPRINKLE WITH SOME CHOPPED CRUNCHY CHICKPEAS (PG.263).

STEP BY STEP: Slicing Oranges

1) Slice the stem end and bottom off the oranges. Keep it straight, so you have a safe cutting experience.

2) Follow the contour of the orange, and cut just past the white pith. If you lose some flesh on the first cut, that's normal. Now, follow the "white line"—where the pith hits the orange. See? No flesh lost. (You or the orange.) Nice.

3) Slice the oranges. Relish in their beauty. Sneak a piece.

ROASTED APPLE-HONEY TOAST

HANDS-ON: 22 MIN.   **TOTAL:** 61 MIN.

Honey toast is not unfamiliar to folks from Tokyo-metro, Taipei, Singapore, or Bangkok. Really, it's genius. And simple. And able to be interpreted to your heart's content. As many ways as one can craft a sandwich, one can hook up some honey toast. Classically, it's a big fluffy slab of Pullman-type bread, with more than a little butter and a generous amount of honey. Here, the toast is dredged in a sugar to give it an irresistible crisp-meets-sticky exterior.

Food	How Much	Why
walnuts	¼ cup finely chopped	They're round in flavor and have some tannins to offset the sweetness of the dish.
Granny Smith apples	4, peeled and cut into 1-inch dice	With the sugar-forward nature of the toast, tart apples seemed to be the right choice.
brown sugar	¼ cup	Brown sugar provides some depth to the apple mixture.
cornstarch	2 teaspoons	To thicken the juices that release from the apples. Along with the brown sugar, you'll get a beautiful glaze.
kosher salt	dash	Acid. Sugar. Salt to balance.
lemon zest	1 tablespoon	For elegance.
fresh lemon juice	3 tablespoons (about 2 lemons)	It brightens the apple mixture, and provides some additional liquid so the cornstarch can do its thing.
butter	2 tablespoons, divided	Toast. Butter. No explanation needed.
honey	2 tablespoons	See title.
challah bread	8 (1.5-ounce) slices (thick)	You'll be able to find it. It's fluffy. It's rich.
superfine sugar	¼ cup	You'll see. Candied toast.
cooking spray		So the sugar and half the bread don't stick.
crème fraîche	½ cup	Makes sweets more luxurious. It's silken. It's slightly tangy. Ah.

Follow These Steps:

➤➤ Preheat your oven to 400°.

➤➤ Arrange the walnuts in a single layer on a baking sheet or a cast-iron skillet. Toast in the oven for about 6 minutes or until lightly toasted and fragrant, giving them a stir halfway through. Remove and set aside.

➤➤ Combine the diced apples, the brown sugar, and the cornstarch in a medium bowl. Toss to coat evenly. Now add the salt, the lemon zest, and the lemon juice. Toss again.

➤➤ Using a paper towel, rub an 11 x 7–inch baking dish with a tablespoon of butter. Pour in the apple mixture.

➤➤ Roast the apples at 400° for 30 minutes or until tender, folding every few minutes.

➤➤ Remove the apples from the oven and preheat the broiler.

➤➤ Combine 1 tablespoon of the butter and the honey in a small saucepan. Melt and stir until incorporated. (Or microwave on HIGH 1 minute until the butter melts and the mixture bubbles.)

➤➤ Brush the bread on all sides with the honey butter. Place the sugar in a shallow dish. Dredge the buttered bread in sugar.

➤➤ Place the bread slices on a baking sheet coated with cooking spray. Broil 3 minutes, turn, and broil 2 minutes more, until evenly toasted and glistening.

➤➤ To serve, smear a tablespoon of crème fraîche on each piece of toast. Top with roasted apples and walnuts. *Tell them it took you forever, and that it's too long a recipe to even discuss.*

SERVES 8 (SERVING SIZE: 1 SLICE BREAD, ½ CUP APPLES, ½ TABLESPOON WALNUTS, AND 1 TABLESPOON CRÈME FRAÎCHE)
CALORIES 330; **FAT** 12.5G (SAT 5.8G, MONO 2.9G, POLY 2.3G); **PROTEIN** 5G; **CARB** 51G; **FIBER** 2G; **CHOL** 28MG; **IRON** 2MG; **SODIUM** 265MG; **CALC** 89MG

AND MORE OFTEN THAN NOT,
THIS IS SERVED WITH ICE CREAM.

USING THIS TWO-STEP COOKING METHOD FOR THE CHICKEN, YOU CAN BE MORE AGGRESSIVE WITH OVEN TEMPERATURE, FOCUSING ON NOTHING BUT THE CRISPNESS OF THE SKIN.

FRANGO À PASSARINHO

HANDS-ON: 15 MIN. **TOTAL:** 60 MIN.

I worked at a wonderful boutique catering company in Manhattan called Table Tales. Alfredo was one of a couple of delivery drivers from Brazil. He had a shoeshine business on the side, which he'd built up by word of mouth, likely because he was one of the most congenial fellows you could ever meet. I rode with Alfredo one day, and he wondered aloud "why Americans work work work," and how, especially in New York, "people move so fast without appreciating the moments." And he went on to reflect about being poor in Brazil, but "feeling so happy" to enjoy soccer in the park and beer and Frango à Passarinho with friends. These crisp wings with garlic and plenty of fresh lime are certainly something to savor.

ALFREDO'S
FAVORITE
BEER

Food	How Much	Why
unsalted chicken stock	2 cups	This iteration of the dish is twice-cooked for a couple of reasons. First, cooking the chicken in hot liquid first is quicker than simply roasting in the oven. Secondly, it's a more even way to cook the chicken.
bay leaf	1 dried	A quick and efficient way to perfume the broth.
chicken wings	2 pounds	The frango.
cooking spray		Lightly coating the surface area of the wings with fat creates an even surface to efficiently and quickly tackle the 450° heat. This puts emphasis on getting things crisp. Fast.
kosher salt	½ teaspoon	It's bar food.
fresh cilantro	¼ cup coarsely chopped	Because Alfredo said so.
fresh lime juice	2 tablespoons	Think buffalo wings. There's a lot of acid on those, too.
garlic cloves	6, sliced	For its raw, beer-loving pungency.

Follow These Steps:

>> Preheat the oven to 450°.

>> Heat a large, straight-sided skillet over high heat. Add the chicken stock and bay leaf and bring to a simmer.

>> Add the wings, reduce the heat, and simmer for 20 minutes, covered.

>> Transfer the wings to a mixing bowl, and reserve the chicken stock for another use.

>> Line a jelly-roll pan with foil. Place the wings on top in a single layer.

>> Coat the wings with cooking spray and sprinkle with the salt.

>> Bake the wings at 450° for 24 minutes, turning occasionally, until crisp.

>> Transfer the wings to a large bowl. Toss with the cilantro, the lime juice, and the raw garlic. Serve with limes cut "seviche-style" (see page 27).

SERVES 6 (SERVING SIZE: 2 WINGS)
CALORIES 198; **FAT** 13.5G (SAT 3.7G, MONO 5.2G, POLY 2.8G); **PROTEIN** 17G; **CARB** 2G; **FIBER** 0G; **CHOL** 63MG; **IRON** 1MG; **SODIUM** 271MG; **CALC** 16MG

PORK LOIN PIQUE

HANDS-ON: 24 MIN.   **TOTAL:** 1 HR. 22 MIN.

With more and more natural foods retailers on the scene, heritage-breed pork is becoming easier to find. Both Berkshire and Red Wattle yield lovely loins, but ask your local butchers what they recommend—more and more, they're developing relationships with the folks who raise the animals. This pork loin recipe is inspired by the Puerto Rican condiment known as pique, varieties of which are made with pineapple and habanero chiles.

Food

Food	How Much	Why
fresh pineapple	2 cups diced	Inspired by pique. It pairs well with the citrusy aroma of habanero.
mango	1 cup diced	For its pectin content. Helps make the jam jammy.
fresh cilantro	½ cup coarsely chopped	Typically used in pique.
white vinegar	3 tablespoons	To add tartness while allowing the flavors of the fruit to dominate.
sugar	1 tablespoon	To encourage some caramelization.
dried oregano	½ teaspoon	It's used in pique.
freshly ground black pepper	½ teaspoon	Black pepper and tropical fruit. It just works.
habanero chile	½, slivered	It's just a touch, but you'll feel it. It makes white vinegar seem less like something you clean your windows with, too. It brings it upmarket.
kosher salt	¾ teaspoon, divided	We've been very purposeful with our use of salt. Some goes in the jam, some is rubbed on the pork, and some is used to finish.
boneless pork loin	1½ pounds	A reasonable size for six.
cooking spray		Prevents the pork, and any falling fruit, from sticking.

Follow These Steps:

» Preheat your oven to 325°.

» Combine the first 8 ingredients (through the habanero) in a bowl. Stir in ¼ teaspoon of the salt.

» Dry the pork loin well. Sprinkle evenly with ¼ teaspoon salt.

» Heat a large, straight-sided skillet over medium-high heat. Spray with cooking spray. Add the pork and cook 5 minutes, browning on all sides. Remove the pork and keep it warm.

» Add the pineapple mixture to the pan and cook down to a jam, stirring frequently to avoid scorching, about 10 minutes.

» Turn off the heat. *Grab a potato masher. Do the mash. Break up the pineapple.*

» Reserve half of the jam. Set aside at room temperature until service.

» Spray a small roasting pan with cooking spray.

» Place the pork loin in the roasting pan and spread the remaining half of the jam over the pork.

» Roast the pork at 325° for 40 minutes, basting and redistributing the jam onto the pork loin periodically. The pork loin is ready for finishing heat when the internal temperature reaches 125°.

» Raise the oven temperature to 450° and roast the pork 8 minutes. The internal temperature should reach 135°. *The exterior should be nicely caramelized from the fruit and sugar.*

» Remove from oven, season evenly with ¼ teaspoon of the salt, and let the meat rest for 10 minutes.

» Slice and serve with the reserved jam.

SERVES 6 (SERVING SIZE: 3 OUNCES PORK AND ¼ CUP JAM)
CALORIES 198; **FAT** 6G (SAT 1.7G, MONO 2.1G, POLY 0.7G); **PROTEIN** 22G; **CARB** 14G; **FIBER** 1G; **CHOL** 66MG; **IRON** 1MG; **SODIUM** 285MG; **CALC** 31MG

FARRO AND MUSHROOM
MEAT LOAF

HANDS-ON: 30 MIN. **TOTAL:** 1 HR. 50 MIN.

While writing this book, I had a sudden craving for farro and mushrooms. I had just experienced success with the Chicken-Pecan Meatballs (page 243) recipe, so I wanted to create another texturally similar dish. And that "NeutralQue" (page 57) needed another use, and—oh, cool—a mostarda-like direction would work perfectly with a Farro and Mushroom Meat Loaf. And that's how a food craving became a recipe.

Food	How Much	Why
"NeutralQue" (page 57)	1 cup	It makes for a great glaze when reduced.
mustard seeds	2 teaspoons	This is the first layer of mustard flavor.
orange marmalade	1 tablespoon	For the bitter notes.
fresh pear	1, peeled and diced	For its body and perfume.
black pepper	½ teaspoon	For punch.
whole-grain mustard	1 tablespoon	For its acid and more mature mustard flavor.
olive oil	1 tablespoon	For sautéing the aromatics including...
yellow onion	½ cup grated	...this for body and savory-sweetness...
oyster mushrooms	6 ounces, minced	...and these. (You can use any mellow-tasting mushroom. Don't use shiitake or dry.)
pancetta	1 ounce, minced	For some salt and its signature funkiness.
garlic cloves	4, minced	It's minced to draw out some toastiness.
ground turkey	1 pound	To soften the texture.
ground sirloin	1 pound	For just enough beefiness.
bread	2 cups diced	A contributor to a soft, delicate mouthfeel.
cooked farro	1 cup	It's delightfully chewy and nutty.
low-sodium white beans	½ cup, mashed to a paste	To contribute more silkiness to the meat loaf's final texture.
unsalted beef stock	½ cup	It's round and robust. Great with mushrooms.
fresh flat-leaf parsley	¼ cup coarsely chopped	It's a conditioned response to meatballs and meat loaves. It works.
Parmigiano-Reggiano cheese	2 tablespoons	Nuttiness with mushrooms. Reggiano is the choice.
kosher salt	¾ teaspoon	It's a carefully calibrated amount.
black pepper	½ teaspoon	Supports the flavor of the mustard glaze.
lemon zest	1 lemon	To brighten and bridge to the glaze.
egg white	1	To bind.
cooking spray		

MOSTARDA IS A SWEET AND PUNGENT
CONDIMENT— ESSENTIALLY FRUIT IN
A MUSTARDY SYRUP.

CONTINUED

FARRO AND MUSHROOM MEAT LOAF

1 cup "NeutralQue"

2 tsp. mustard seeds

1 Tbsp. orange marmalade

1 fresh pear, peeled and diced

1/2 tsp. black pepper

1 Tbsp. whole-grain mustard

1 Tbsp. olive oil

1/2 cup grated yellow onion

6 oz. oyster mushrooms, minced

1 oz. pancetta, minced

4 garlic cloves, minced

1 lb. ground turkey

1 lb. ground sirloin

2 cups diced bread

1 cup cooked farro

1/2 cup low-sodium white beans, mashed to a paste

1/2 cup unsalted beef stock

1/4 cup coarsely chopped fresh flat-leaf parsley

2 Tbsp. Parmigiano-Reggiano cheese

3/4 tsp. kosher salt

1/2 tsp. black pepper

zest from 1 lemon

1 egg white

cooking spray

Follow These Steps:

>> Preheat the oven to 425°.

MAKE THE SAUCE

>> Combine the first 6 ingredients (through mustard) in a small saucepan.

>> Bring to a simmer over medium-high heat; reduce the heat to low and simmer 20 minutes.

>> Now increase the heat to medium and boil 18 minutes, or until the mixture thickens into a glaze.

>> Remove from the heat and set aside.

MAKE THE MEAT LOAF MIXTURE

>> Heat a skillet over medium heat. Add the olive oil and swirl to coat.

>> Add the onions, the mushrooms, the pancetta, and the garlic. Sauté for 5 minutes, stirring frequently.

>> Remove from heat and cool to room temperature.

>> Combine the remaining ingredients for the meat loaf (except the cooking spray) in a large mixing bowl.

>> Fold evenly, but gently, until just combined.

>> Add the cool mushroom mixture.

BAKE!

>> Coat a roasting pan with cooking spray. Form a meat loaf about 3 inches tall by 4 inches wide on the pan.

>> Bake the meat loaf at 425° for 25 minutes, or until the internal temperature reaches 140°.

>> During the final minutes of roasting, baste the meat loaf with about 1/4 cup of the sauce. Reserve the remaining sauce for service. Pour the glaze over the meat loaf.

>> Bake an additional 7 minutes or until the internal temperature reaches 155°.

>> *Remove the lacquered meat loaf from the oven, and let it rest for 10 minutes.*

>> Slice and serve.

SERVES 8 (SERVING SIZE: 1 SLICE)
CALORIES 396; FAT 13.9G (SAT 4.2G, MONO 5.7G, POLY 2G); PROTEIN 27G; CARB 44G; FIBER 4G; CHOL 78MG; IRON 3MG; SODIUM 476MG; CALC 89MG

HOW TO COOK FARRO

DON'T ALWAYS TRUST THE RATIOS OF GRAIN TO LIQUID GIVEN ON THE PACKAGE OR YOU MIGHT FIND THE GRAINS SWELLING TO A GUMMY PUFF.

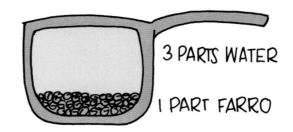

3 PARTS WATER

1 PART FARRO

FOR FARRO, USE ABOUT 1 PART FARRO TO 3 PARTS LIQUID. TO GET ONE CUP OF COOKED FARRO. YOU'LL NEED TO START WITH 1/3 CUP OF DRY.

BRING TO A BOIL, REDUCE HEAT, AND SIMMER 25 MINUTES OR UNTIL TENDER. AS IT COOKS, THE FARRO WILL FOAM, SO BE SURE TO USE A BIG SAUCEPAN.

DRAIN THE FARRO AND FLUFF WITH A FORK.

"SUPER-FRESH" FISH IS NOT SO MUCH ABOUT "JUST BEEN CAUGHT;" IT'S ABOUT THE HANDLING. IT SHOULD BE HUMANELY KILLED, RAPIDLY CHILLED, AND DELICATELY HANDLED.

FIRE ISLAND–STYLE
ROASTED BLUEFISH

HANDS-ON: 10 MIN. **TOTAL:** 33 MIN.

Bluefish is the pork shoulder of the sea. I think I'm the first to suggest that, because I Googled it, and no one else has said so. It's a ridiculous statement in that you'll likely not slow-smoke bluefish overnight and pull it apart with two forks. Still, bluefish is fatty stuff and takes to more assertive preparations—like the garlic, onion, bell pepper barrage it gets in this recipe. When super-fresh, bluefish is intoxicatingly rich in texture and among the most satisfying of seafoods. Blues are found along the Atlantic coast, with a lot of folks from Jersey and New York fishing them for recreation. Ask your fishmonger for something similar if you can't get your hands on just-caught bluefish.

Food	How Much	Why
red bell pepper	1, cut into fine julienne (about 1 cup)	Bluefish is pretty common on Long Island, where I grew up, and often served with "peppas and onions."
yellow onion	1, cut into fine julienne (about 1½ cups)	See above.
garlic cloves	4, sliced	The flavor of bluefish can stand up to a good bit of garlic. Slice it inconsistently. It'll provide some contrast.
olive oil	2 tablespoons	The fat from the fish against a good, strong olive oil... wow. Go for super-green and peppery here. Get the good stuff.
cooking spray		To keep things from sticking and to ration your good oil.
bluefish fillets	2 (1-pound) sides, skin on, bones out	If you can't get bluefish, choose something oily/fatty—*but not salmon.*
salt	¾ teaspoon	It's a more robust fish, so we've pushed for the salt maximum here.
fresh basil leaves	12, torn	Trapped in a packet, the perfume of basil will envelop every last bite.
lemon	1, thinly sliced	Certainly for some acid, but the real gift is the balance of bitter from the rind.

Follow These Steps:

➤➤ Preheat your oven to 475°.

➤➤ Toss the bell peppers, the onion, and the garlic with the olive oil.

➤➤ Lay two sheets of foil, each large enough to wrap a fillet with some room for steam space, on a clean counter.

➤➤ Spray the sheets with cooking spray.

➤➤ Lay down the bluefish fillets. Season with salt. Rub it in. Gently. With your fingers.

➤➤ *Lay an even blanket of the bell pepper mixture on each fish fillet. Use a rubber spatula to scrape every last drop of olive oil onto the fillets.*

➤➤ Lay down some basil over the peppers.

➤➤ Decoratively layer the lemons on the fillet.

➤➤ Wrap the foil packets as shown on page 141.

➤➤ Place the packets on a roasting pan and bake for 18 minutes or until the fish flakes easily with a fork, depending upon the thickness of the fish. A safe bet is to simply allow the fish to rest after taking it out of the oven for an additional 5 minutes or so, both to allow the steam to subside a bit and to ensure that the fish and vegetables are cooked through.

SERVES 4 (SERVING SIZE: 6 OUNCES FISH AND ½ CUP VEGGIES)
CALORIES 346; **FAT** 16.3G (SAT 2.8G, MONO 8.6G, POLY 2.9G); **PROTEIN** 42G;
CARB 5G; **FIBER** 1G; **CHOL** 122MG; **IRON** 1MG; **SODIUM** 570MG; **CALC** 31MG

FISH STICKS!

HANDS-ON: 30 MIN. **TOTAL:** 45 MIN.

Fish sticks. They're fun. The commercial fish stick certainly predates the chicken finger, though interestingly the commercial version of this geometric culinary wonder was introduced as a fish finger in the UK in the '50s. (As an aside, America takes credit for the chicken finger, with evidence of it on a Kowloon restaurant menu in Saugus, Massachusetts, sometime in the 1960s.) Don't tell your kids that story. They're hungry. This kid-friendly recipe keeps it mild and straightforward—with a sweet-tart-creamy dipping sauce.

Food	How Much	Why
cooking spray		For its ability to mist. If you have one of those oil-sprayer gadgets, use that.
skinless halibut fillets	2 pounds, cut into 1-inch-wide sticks	Halibut is mellow. It also holds-up as a "stick." Stuff like cod, not so much.
plain 2% reduced-fat Greek yogurt	½ cup	Greek yogurt is tight in texture. Standard plain yogurt would be too soupy.
sweet pickle relish	¼ cup	For our unadventurous tartar sauce interpretation. Remember, your kid's friend eats chicken fingers all the time.
fresh lemon juice	2 tablespoons	To brighten up the sauce.
2% reduced-fat milk	1 tablespoon	To thin out the sauce. You might not need it.
kosher salt	⅝ teaspoon, divided	It needs it.
whole-wheat bread	4 ounces, crusts removed	For a more healthful crumb. It also starts with some depth of color.
buttermilk	1 cup	It's adhesive and has flavor. I typically shun egg wash in favor of buttermilk.
all-purpose flour	1 cup	To dust the fish, allowing the buttermilk to adhere.
finely ground black pepper	½ teaspoon	Because smart little children eat their peppered food, don't they? (Insert sinister laugh here.)

Follow These Steps:

➤➤ Preheat your oven to 425°. Spray a baking sheet with cooking spray. Set aside.

➤➤ Pop the fish into the freezer for 10 minutes while you prepare the other ingredients. *You want the fish very very cold, but not fully frozen.*

➤➤ Combine the yogurt, the sweet pickle relish, the lemon juice, the milk, and ⅛ teaspoon salt. *Your kids will love you.* Cover the sauce and refrigerate until ready to serve.

➤➤ Pulse the bread in a food processor until it is a fine crumb.

➤➤ Heat a large skillet over medium heat. Place the crumbs in the skillet and toast 3 minutes, stirring frequently.

➤➤ Ready a standard breading setup with three shallow dishes: Flour. Buttermilk. Crumb.

➤➤ Remove the fish from the freezer and sprinkle with ½ teaspoon salt and pepper. *Coat the fish sticks in flour, then buttermilk (no remaining dry spots, please), and finally the crumb.*

➤➤ Arrange the fish sticks on the coated baking sheet, evenly spaced, and mist them evenly with cooking spray.

➤➤ Bake for 15 minutes, or until the breadcrumbs are crisp and the fish flakes easily when tested with a fork.

➤➤ Serve with the sweet pickle yogurt for dipping.

SERVES 6 (SERVING SIZE: 4 OUNCES FISH AND ABOUT 2 TABLESPOONS YOGURT DIPPING SAUCE)
CALORIES 260; **FAT** 4.5G (SAT 1.5G, MONO 1.3G, POLY 0.7G); **PROTEIN** 34G; **CARB** 20G; **FIBER** 2G; **CHOL** 79MG; **IRON** 1MG; **SODIUM** 508MG; **CALC** 83MG

SINGING THE SONG "THE DOWNEASTER
ALEXA" BY BILLY JOEL MAKES
THIS DISH MORE DELICIOUS.

OVEN-ROASTED GARLIC CLAMS
WITH CHARRED ENGLISH MUFFINS

HANDS-ON: 30 MIN. **TOTAL:** 50 MIN.

This one might strike you as odd. But if I told you a story behind this recipe—"This little seafood joint is owned by a guy who owns a pizza parlor in town. He makes a great chowder. One night he ran out of oyster crackers, so he buttered up some English muffins to serve with the soup."—and then I showed you this recipe, you might think we've conjured up the next interpretive culinary legend. Really, the dish is just a great conversation starter. And it's delicious.

FICTION.

Food	How Much	Why
littleneck clams	about 40	Littlenecks are quite tender, and cook quickly.
butter	2 tablespoons	Butter. Garlic. Clams. Simple.
garlic cloves	4, grated	See above.
cooking spray		To keep the garlic bits from sticking to the pan.
English muffins	4, split	Because English muffins are delicious and should be used more often (and not just at breakfast).
fresh Parmesan cheese	1 tablespoon grated	To boldly rebel against ideologues who think that things from the sea can't pair with cheese.
fresh flat-leaf parsley	2 tablespoons chopped	Without it, this dish might seem like it's missing something. Flat.
white wine	1 tablespoon	For a hint of acidity. There's so little, it doesn't need to see cook time.
crushed red pepper	2 teaspoons	It's a fair bit. It's a snack. Go for big flavor.

Follow These Steps:

>> Preheat the oven to 475°.

>> Scrub the clams under cold running water. Discard any questionable ones: live clams with the shells open or those that don't close when tapped, those with broken shells, or those that you can jiggle the two shell halves from side to side.

>> Combine the butter and the garlic in a small microwave-safe bowl; microwave at HIGH 30 seconds or until the butter melts.

>> Place the clams in a bowl and toss with the melted butter.

>> Coat a large deep roasting pan with cooking spray. Lay the clams in the roasting pan. *Roast at 475° for 15 minutes or until the shells pop, and not a moment more.* Remove the pan from the oven, cover with foil, and let them rest 5 minutes.

>> Now, set your oven to broil on high. Place the English muffins on a baking sheet, split sides up. Sprinkle the Parmesan cheese evenly on the split sides of the English muffins.

>> Broil 2 minutes or until slightly charred. You can leave the oven door slightly ajar while you're broiling the muffins. Just be careful. The top should be gloriously toasty/charred, and the bottom will be almost soft and steamy.

>> *Go back to the clams and pop them out of the shells.* Discard the shells. Keep the liquid. Combine the clam meat and juices with the parsley, wine, and crushed red pepper.

>> Lay 2 toasted muffin halves on each of 4 plates and evenly spoon the clam mixture on top. Serve immediately.

SERVES 4 (SERVING SIZE: 1 ENGLISH MUFFIN AND ¼ OF CLAM MIXTURE) **CALORIES** 276; **FAT** 8.2G (SAT 4.2G, MONO 1.9G, POLY 1G); **PROTEIN** 19G; **CARB** 31G; **FIBER** 0G; **CHOL** 43MG; **IRON** 3MG; **SODIUM** 759MG; **CALC** 163MG

CHILI AND COFFEE-RUBBED
EYE ROUND FOR SANDWICHES

HANDS-ON: 15 MIN. **TOTAL:** 1 HR. 35 MIN., PLUS OVERNIGHT

Deli-counter roast beef, even the top-shelf stuff, is often loaded with quite a bit of salt, and the flavor of beef is lost in briny translation. Here, we add some bold-flavored ingredients to the exterior of a very lean but flavorful cut—the eye round. You'll get an almost charred, spice-rubbed flavor that will delight fans of an old-school roast beef on rye. Make sure to use a probe thermometer, though, rather than relying just on time references in the recipe. The flatter the roast, the quicker it will cook. Try to find one with a consistent diameter throughout for the most even result.

Food	How Much	Why
beef eye round	2 pounds	It's an affordable cut that benefits from an assertive rub.
instant coffee	2 tablespoons	It takes to moisture like, well, something instant.
chili powder	1½ tablespoons	It also typically includes dried garlic and oregano, and that's lovely with oven-cooked beef.
kosher salt	2 teaspoons	Helps draw moisture out of the meat, which blends with the instant coffee and the chili powder. The oven dries the coffee-chili mixture into a near perfect crust.
yellow onion	¼ cup grated	Provides a little right-now moisture for the "rub" and adds texture to the exterior of the roast.
garlic cloves	4, grated	Grating exposes greater surface area, promoting rapid evaporation in the oven and making your own dried garlic. Right on the meat. Mmm.
orange zest	2 teaspoons grated	A classic complement to coffee-touched things.
fresh orange juice	2 tablespoons	Adds some welcome brightness to this otherwise earthy formula.

Follow These Steps:

>> Preheat your oven to 475°. *Be patient.* Let it fully preheat.

>> In a mixing bowl, *add all the ingredients and tumble the eye round, massaging deeply and evenly.*

>> Lay the eye round on a roasting pan and roast for about 20 minutes at 475°, turning at the halfway point.

>> Lower the heat to 300° and cook for another 30 minutes, or until the internal temperature reads about 120° for rare. Let rest at room temperature for 30 minutes.

>> Wrap in parchment, then in plastic, and refrigerate overnight if you can hold out. *Slice it as thinly as possible for building sandwiches.*

SERVES 9 (SERVING SIZE: ABOUT 3 OUNCES)
CALORIES 136; **FAT** 3.2G (SAT 1.1G, MONO 1.3G, POLY 0.3G); **PROTEIN** 23G; **CARB** 2G; **FIBER** 1G; **CHOL** 59MG; **IRON** 2MG; **SODIUM** 510MG; **CALC** 30MG

VARIATION: Get fancy with this method by splurging on a thick beef tenderloin roast. Replace the coffee with an equal amount of dry mustard, and the chili powder with an equal amount of brown sugar. When the beef comes out of the oven, still glistening from the sugar, roll it in a ¼ cup of chopped fresh tarragon. Slice thinly and serve on toasted baguettes brushed lightly with butter.

SLOW-ROASTED, PASTRAMI-RUBBED TURKEY

HANDS-ON: 10 MIN.   **TOTAL:** 2 HR. 30 MIN., PLUS OVERNIGHT

The word pastrami evolved from the Romanian pastramă, which likely originated from the Romanian phrase a pastră, meaning to keep or to preserve. Then why do Americans know pastrami as a brined, spice-crusted, smoked, and finally steamed deli meat? Because that kind of pastrami is worthy of joyful expletive-spouting. And joyful expletive-spouting is memorable. And it's the smoky spice crust that's the truly memorable part, because it has found its way onto bacon, salmon, tuna, and turkey, thus rendering the origins of the word pastrami...history. Mulţumesc, Romania.

TRANSLATION: THANK YOU.

HUNGARY
SZEGED
ROMANIA

Food	How Much	Why
dark brown sugar	1 tablespoon	Two reasons. One, the sugar melts and functions as a glaze. Second, black pepper and mustard, in particular, are elevated in the presence of molasses-y sugar.
onion powder	1 tablespoon	Absorbs juices. Helps the rub stay adhered.
garlic powder	1 tablespoon	See above.
black pepper	1 tablespoon	You say pastrami, I say black pepper...
ground coriander	1 tablespoon	...and coriander. Everything else is up to interpretation.
paprika	1 tablespoon	One could envision paprika from Szeged, Hungary, making its way into Romania. I did. So I included it in the rub.
ground mustard	2 teaspoons	Pungent works with sweet and spicy.
ground red pepper	2 teaspoons	Because you probably don't have hot and sweet paprika lying around. If you do, use hot paprika here.
kosher salt	1 teaspoon	A must, or this would be one bland breast.
allspice	½ teaspoon	Allspice appeared in many of the historic Romanian pastramă recipes drummed up while crafting this recipe. We tried it. We liked it.
butter	2 tablespoons, softened	Auto-baste.
warm water	¼ cup	Without it, you'd have spice-chunk, not a spreadable rub/paste.
whole skin-on turkey breast	1 (4¾-pound) breast	Keeping the skin on prevents the turkey from drying out while roasting.

CONTINUED →

SLOW-ROASTED, PASTRAMI-RUBBED TURKEY

1 Tbsp. dark brown sugar

1 Tbsp. onion powder

1 Tbsp. garlic powder

1 Tbsp. black pepper

1 Tbsp. ground coriander

1 Tbsp. paprika

2 tsp. ground mustard

2 tsp. ground red pepper

1 tsp. kosher salt

1/2 tsp. allspice

2 Tbsp. butter, softened

1/4 cup warm water

1 (4³/₄-lb.) whole skin-on turkey breast

Follow These Steps:

>> Preheat your oven to 275°.

MAKE THE SPICE PASTE
>> Combine the sugar and spices—the first 10 ingredients—in a bowl.

>> Blend the softened butter into the spices with a wooden spoon, and follow with the warm water to make a paste.

PREPARE THE TURKEY
>> Lay the turkey breast on a cutting board, and gently slide your hands under the skin, separating the skin from the flesh, but not tearing or removing. We'll use the skin to trap the butter-spice blend, and then we'll remove it after resting.

>> Now, rub the spice paste evenly under the skin.

>> Place the turkey breast on a roasting pan and cover with aluminum foil.

NOW, BAKE
>> Bake the turkey at 275° for 1 hour, covered.

>> Remove the foil and cook for another hour, or until the internal temperature is 155°.

>> Remove from the oven and let the bird stand at room temperature 20 minutes. *It will carry over perfectly.*

CARVE THE TURKEY
>> Remove the skin from the turkey breast and carve the lobes off the bone.

>> Wrap the lobes in parchment, then in plastic. Refrigerate overnight.

>> Use to make a killer turkey sandwich. Or, *skip the whole parchment-and-put-away thing and serve warm with pickles, some coarse salt, cracked pepper, a loaf of rye bread, and a little grain-mustard/mayo blend.*

SERVES 16 (SERVING SIZE: ABOUT 3 OUNCES)
CALORIES 131; FAT 2.2G (SAT 1.1G, MONO 0.5G, POLY 0.3G); PROTEIN 24G; CARB 2G; FIBER 1G; CHOL 69MG; IRON 1MG; SODIUM 193MG; CALC 19MG

STEP BY STEP:
Carving
a Turkey

1) Trace the knife along the breastbone.

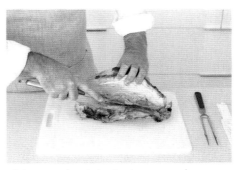

2) In steady ¼-inch-deep strokes, pull the breast meat away from the bone.

3) Drawing the knife against the breastbone with each stroke, finally trim the breast lobe away from the bone. Save the bone for soup.

4) Square yourself to the board and get ready to slice.

5) Place the breast lobe at an angle that supports the natural placement of your cutting hand. Slice thinly, using broad and even knife strokes. Don't saw. Please.

SLOW-BAKED CHICKEN THIGHS
WITH TOMATO, FENNEL, AND LEMON

HANDS-ON: 20 MIN. **TOTAL:** 2 HR. 10 MIN.

It's safe to say that chicken thighs are "cooked" when the internal temperature reaches 165°. If you want them to be fabulous, though, you have to zoom in a little closer. These are well-worked muscles—meaning more collagen and connective tissue. For that, you need the internal temperature to hold at 180° or higher for at least an hour, depending on the source and size of your (chicken) thighs.

Food	How Much	Why
butter	2 tablespoons, divided	To tilt this in a rounder, richer direction.
whole-wheat bread	1 (1-ounce) slice	For some color and more depth of flavor than white.
Parmesan cheese	2 teaspoons grated	Tomatoes. Parmesan. Delicious.
fennel bulb	2 cups shaved (about 2 bulbs)	The fennel will nearly melt into the dish. That's elegant.
kosher salt	½ teaspoon	To season.
boneless, skinless chicken thighs	2 pounds	They're so easy, rich-tasting, and affordable.
whole plum tomatoes	1 (28-ounce) can, drained	It makes up most of the moisture in the dish, making the dish essentially an oven-simmer.
garlic cloves	12, sliced ¼ inch thick	Sliced thick so they hold up, and you can experience the gloriousness of a sweet chunk of garlic on your fork.
lemons	3, sectioned	We section the lemon so it collapses fully into the sauce. That's why you remove all the white flesh.
fresh thyme leaves	1 tablespoon	It likely seems like a lot, but with the long cook time, the flavor softens and becomes more foundational, less "punchy."
fresh flat-leaf parsley	3 tablespoons chopped	To finish fresh.

Follow These Steps:

➤➤ Preheat the oven to 325°.

➤➤ Melt 1 tablespoon of the butter in the microwave and pour it in the bottom of a 13 x 9–inch glass or ceramic baking dish. Brush the butter to coat the bottom of the dish.

➤➤ In a food processor, combine the bread and the Parmesan cheese. *Pulse for a few seconds until you have a coarse, rustic crumb.*

➤➤ Lay the fennel down in the baking dish.

➤➤ Rub the salt into the chicken thighs and then lay the chicken thighs over the fennel.

➤➤ Hand-crush the tomatoes and tuck them into the spaces between the chicken.

➤➤ Scatter the garlic. And the lemons. Sprinkle the thyme over the chicken.

➤➤ Pinch the other tablespoon of butter into little bits and scatter them about your soon-to-be-baked masterpiece.

➤➤ Bake covered for 1 hour or until the thermometer reads 180°.

➤➤ Uncover and bake for another 45 minutes or so, basting every 5 minutes or so. *Belabor the basting process. Zoom in with your soul.*

➤➤ For the last 10 minutes of the baking, sprinkle the bread-crumbs on top and lightly drizzle with the basting juices.

➤➤ Remove from the oven, sprinkle evenly with the parsley, and let the chicken rest for 5 minutes before serving hot.

SERVES 6 (SERVING SIZE: 4 OUNCES MEAT AND ABOUT ½ CUP VEGETABLES)
CALORIES 267; **FAT** 10.3G (SAT 4.1G, MONO 2.9G, POLY 1.7G); **PROTEIN** 32G;
CARB 11G; **FIBER** 3G; **CHOL** 136MG; **IRON** 3MG; **SODIUM** 540MG; **CALC** 111MG

27-HOUR CHICKEN LEGS

HANDS-ON: 15 MIN. **TOTAL:** 3 HR. 15 MIN., PLUS OVERNIGHT

This recipe is an homage to duck confit—a technique in which the duck is cooked slowly in its own fat. It accomplishes many of the culinary aims of confit while sparing calories, expense, and the need to hunt for a bucket of duck fat. While this is really just a long, slow oven simmer, the three-hour cook time does a great job of dissolving the collagen in the chicken legs, giving you glistening meat and wonderful mouthfeel. Make a double-batch of this, and use it for salads, quesadillas, pastas, chicken-salad sandwiches, and snacking. Or serve these legs right from the oven with Pan-Charred Green Beans with Tarragon (page 196).

Food	How Much	Why
sugar	1 teaspoon	It's part of a super-light "cure" for the chicken legs. It will flavor, but will also play a role in drawing out some moisture from the chicken.
kosher salt	½ teaspoon	The salt is part two of the cure. It will dissolve along with the sugar, also drawing out moisture. The result will be a small pool of brine for the chicken.
skinless chicken leg quarters	6	The object of our affection.
unsalted chicken stock	4 cups	In lieu of a quart of fat.
shallots	¼ cup sliced (about 1 shallot)	They melt down beautifully, contributing to the mouth-feel. If you decide to pull the meat off the bone, fold it well with the sliced shallot and some reserved broth.
fresh thyme	2 teaspoons minced	Chemically speaking, it's quite complex, with notes of pine, lemon, and, well, thyme. It's no wonder it made its way into bouquet garni.
garlic cloves	3, sliced	They're sliced for visual appeal and added texture.
lemon zest	1-inch strips cut from 1 lemon	Use a peeler to remove only the yellow. If you remove any white, don't stress.

Follow These Steps:

≫ Combine the sugar and salt.

≫ Place the chicken legs in a roasting pan, sprinkle with salt and sugar mixture, and cure, covered, overnight in the refrigerator.

≫ Preheat the oven to 300°.

≫ In a Dutch oven, combine the stock, the shallots, the thyme, the garlic, and the lemon zest.

≫ Layer in the cured chicken legs.

≫ Cover the Dutch oven and place it in the oven.

≫ Cook for 3 hours, until the chicken legs are very tender.

≫ *If storing, pull the meat from the bones, return the meat to the "confit" liquid in the Dutch oven, and toss to combine.* Otherwise, serve and enjoy hot.

SERVES 9 (SERVING SIZE: ABOUT 4½ OUNCES)
CALORIES 121; **FAT** 3.3G (SAT 0.9G, MONO 1G, POLY 0.8G); **PROTEIN** 20G; **CARB** 2G; **FIBER** 0G; **CHOL** 69MG; **IRON** 1MG; **SODIUM** 249MG; **CALC** 16MG

IT'S A ONE-SIZE-FITS-MANY HERB BUNDLE THAT'S BEEN USED IN KITCHENS (AT MINIMUM) SINCE THE 1600S.

ROASTED LEMON LAMB RACK
WITH PEACHES AND FETA

HANDS-ON: 20 MIN. **TOTAL:** 1 HR. 12 MIN.

This recipe was originally written with apricots in mind. The problem is, a truly wonderful fresh apricot is hard to find in most places in America, and apricots don't travel well. If you can get your hands on Individually Quick Frozen (IQF) halves, or you happen to live where apricots thrive locally, get them. Treasure them. A discussion about alternatives raised issues of geography, inspiration, and adaptation. This recipe, while inspired by my half-Greek roots, was developed in Georgia. Georgia = Peaches.

Food	How Much	Why
fresh peaches	4, split and pitted	For acidity. For their texture when cooked. And for contrast against the feta.
shallots	4, peeled and quartered	To tilt the peaches savory.
olive oil	1 tablespoon	Inspiration: Mediterranean.
kosher salt	½ teaspoon, divided	Some for the peaches. Some for the lamb.
all-purpose flour	2½ tablespoons	To adhere lemon and oregano to the lamb racks.
fresh lemon juice	2½ tablespoons	Greece.
fresh oregano	1 tablespoon minced	Fresh oregano can handle more aggressive roasting. Dry would scorch and taste off at 475°.
sugar	2 teaspoons	To encourage some caramelization on the exterior of the lamb.
cooking spray		To keep the lamb racks from sticking to the pan.
lamb racks (preferably American)	2, trimmed and split (4 bones each)	Racks are lean, succulent, and nearly fork-tender. Cooking them medium-rare to medium is recommended.
feta cheese	2 tablespoons finely crumbled	See above.

CONTINUED

ROASTED LEMON LAMB RACK

4 fresh peaches, split and pitted

4 shallots, peeled and quartered

1 Tbsp. olive oil

½ tsp. kosher salt, divided

2½ Tbsp. all-purpose flour

2½ Tbsp. fresh lemon juice

1 Tbsp. minced fresh oregano

2 tsp. sugar

cooking spray

2 lamb racks, trimmed and split

2 Tbsp. finely crumbled feta cheese

Follow These Steps:

>> Preheat your oven to 475°.

MAKE A SAUCE

>> Toss the peaches and shallots in a bowl with the olive oil and ⅛ teaspoon of the salt.

>> Lay the peaches and shallots on a roasting pan, cut sides down, in a single layer.

>> Roast the peaches and shallots long enough for the peels of the peaches to separate from the flesh, about 7 to 10 minutes, depending on the ripeness and variety of peach. The shallots are now par-cooked. Put them in a small bowl while you peel the peaches.

>> Peel the peaches. *Then use the side of a large serving spoon and lightly crush the peaches as to create a stable bed on which to roast the lamb. But not just yet. Hold off on the roasting, please.*

BROWN THE LAMB

>> Now, in a small bowl, combine the flour, the lemon juice, the oregano, and the sugar, and make a uniform mixture. It should look a bit like cream.

>> Heat a large skillet over high heat. Spray with cooking spray.

>> Pat the lamb racks dry.

>> Place the lamb racks in the skillet. Briefly brown the lamb racks evenly on all sides. You're simply browning the exterior; you're not looking to cook them through. Turn off the heat. Place the lamb racks on a plate.

>> Dry the lamb racks again with paper towels. Brush on all sides with the flour mixture. Place in the refrigerator for 20 minutes or so for the mixture to dry a bit.

ROAST!

>> Place the lamb racks on top of the semi-crushed peaches. Place the shallots on the roasting pan, too. Roast for about 15 minutes, or until the internal temperature of the lamb is 135°.

>> Remove from the oven, place the lamb racks on a cutting board, and let them rest for 10 minutes at room temperature before carving.

FINISH, CARVE, AND SERVE

>> With a fork, further crush the peaches and loosely combine them with the shallots.

>> Carve the lamb rack using a flexible boning knife, tracing right down the bone.

>> To serve, spoon the shallots and peaches on plates. Place the lamb chops on the plate naturally. *Don't be too fussy about the placement.* Spoon some of the lemony juices on top and garnish with the crumbled feta and fresh oregano leaves.

SERVES 4 (SERVING SIZE: 2 LAMB CHOPS AND ½ TABLESPOON SAUCE)
CALORIES 310; FAT 12.3G (SAT 4.1G, MONO 5.3G, POLY 0.8G); PROTEIN 27G; CARB 24G; FIBER 2G; CHOL 97MG; IRON 3MG; SODIUM 339MG; CALC 53MG

NATURALLY OCCURRING ACIDS IN FOODS

ACID	DESCRIPTION	EXAMPLE SOURCES
ACETIC	EVENLY SOUR, PUNGENT	VINEGARS
CITRIC	CITRUSY TANGY, BRIGHT-CLEAN AROMA	CITRUS FRUITS, MANGO, RASPBERRY, STRAWBERRY, PINEAPPLE
FUMARIC	SUPER-SOUR, GRAM FOR GRAM, FAIRLY COMMON AS AN ADDITIVE	CÈPES/PORCINI MUSHROOMS, BEANS, CARROTS, TOMATOES
LACTIC	MILDLY ACIDIC, YOGURT-LIKE, LONG-LINGERING FLAVOR	CULTURED DAIRY PRODUCTS (BUTTERMILK, CRÈME FRAÎCHE, SOUR CREAM), LACTO-FERMENTED VEGETABLES (SAUERKRAUT, PICKLES, KIMCHI), SALUMI
MALIC	LINGERING, GRANNY SMITH APPLE-Y TARTNESS	APPLES, APRICOTS, CHERRIES, PEACHES, WATERMELON, WINE
TARTARIC	STRAIGHTFORWARD TARTNESS, QUITE ASTRINGENT	TAMARIND, GRAPES, CRANBERRIES, WINE

ROASTED ROOT VEGETABLES

HANDS-ON: 20 MIN. **TOTAL:** 1 HR. 20 MIN.

A number of root vegetables, namely carrots and parsnips, respond to cold temperatures by converting their starches to sugars. It's a fascinating feat of nature—vegetables producing their own delicately sweet antifreeze. That's why you should cook them often in the cold weather months. They're good. Also, empirically speaking, the chosen array of vegetables in this recipe have a similar feel, a similar body, and behave in an aligned-enough fashion in the oven that it's possible to cut them mindfully (see the whys), toss them together, and pop out (top) restaurant-quality results.

Food	How Much	Why
parsnips	½ pound, peeled and cut oblique style	The oblique cut, once you get it down, is your quickie-elegant cut to get maximum yield.
celery root	½ pound, ¾-inch dice	The celery root is cut fairly large, because it's spongier and will generally cook up quicker than the other vegetables...
shallots	½ pound, peeled and halved	...except for the shallots, which are lovely cooked "soft."
carrots	½ pound, peeled and cut oblique style	If you cut them note-for-note in size with the parsnips, they'll look gorgeous.
turnips	½ pound, peeled and cut into wedges	They're a bit funky and add a gentle pungency to the mix of delicate and sweet vegetables. Choose small ones—they're more pleasant to the tooth.
garlic cloves	16 large, peeled and tipped	Because garlic can and should be eaten in clove form. Roasted, it's umami bliss.
olive oil	2 tablespoons	Because of the garlic-rosemary treatment.
salt	½ teaspoon	This is sweet stuff. You need salt.
sugar	½ teaspoon	Really, I promise, it's not for additional sweetness. It's to help form a shiny exterior glaze that nearly chars against the pan.
rosemary leaves	1 tablespoon	To perfume the dish.
cooking spray		Helps you turn the vegetables without tearing them to shreds.

Follow These Steps:

>> Crank your oven to 500°.

>> In a mixing bowl, toss all the ingredients except the cooking spray together with your hands. *This is tactile stimulation at its finest if you love to cook. (You do, right?)*

>> Lay a large, dramatic sheet of heavy-duty foil across your work surface. Now, do that again.

>> See page 141 to learn how to ready the packet. Do that.

>> Seal up the packet as instructed. Lay it into a 13 x 9–inch baking dish and roast for about 15 minutes, until the veggies are starting to get tender.

>> Remove the pan from the oven and let the vegetables sit on there, sealed, for another 10 minutes, while you reduce the oven temperature to 425°. 500° is too hot for the next step. *Leave your oven door open for a minute or two to let some heat escape. Warm your hands.*

>> Now, give the packet a little shake before opening it. Spray the roasting pan with cooking spray. Dump the veggies into a single layer on the roasting pan. Throw out the empty packet. It's done.

>> Return the pan to the oven, occasionally monitoring and redistributing the vegetables to and away from the hot spots in the pan. *Nurture this dish.*

>> When the veggies are nicely browned, after 25 minutes or so, remove the vegetables from the oven and serve, perhaps with 27-Hour Chicken Legs (page 298) or Farro and Mushroom Meat Loaf (page 280) or Lower East Side Brisket (page 226).

SERVES 8 (SERVING SIZE: ABOUT ½ CUP)
CALORIES 114; **FAT** 4G (SAT 0.5G, MONO 2.5G, POLY 0.5G); **PROTEIN** 2G; **CARB** 19G; **FIBER** 3G; **CHOL** 0MG; **IRON** 1MG; **SODIUM** 207MG; **CALC** 63MG

COUNTRY RIBS &
SHOULDER SIDE RIBS

PEANUT AND PEPPERCORN
PORK BACK RIBS

HANDS-ON: 15 MIN. **TOTAL:** 1 HR. 50 MIN.

These ribs are simple but gorgeous. Otherwise ordinary sweet heat is rendered more interesting by layering on fresh, bulby green onions and cracked, nearly charred peanuts. We've balanced notes of sweetness, heat, and saltiness and kept the portion size modest. The ribs are first steamed in a foil packet. Seal the packet tightly to benefit from some of the gentle steam pressure that forms in the packet. The broiler does the work of browning and caramelizing. Monitor closely.

Food	How Much	Why
bone-in pork country ribs	8 bones (about 2½ pounds)	Country ribs are meatier, coming typically from the sirloin end of the pork loin.
kosher salt	½ teaspoon	You'll be par-cooking the meat in a foil packet with nothing but salt. The salt will mix with the juices, and the ribs will steam in this gentle brine.
turbinado sugar	2 tablespoons	It retains some of the cane flavor, resulting in a richer, more complex contribution to the glaze.
freshly ground black pepper	1 tablespoon	It's a lot. There's a good bit of fat in these pork ribs— enough to stand up to a good spicing.
Fresno or red jalapeño chiles	2, sliced	Some heat, but more for the texture they'll contribute to the exterior of the rib.
peanuts	2 tablespoons finely chopped	They're plentiful. They're inexpensive. And they're amazing with some char and chile.
green onions	¼ cup thinly sliced	The dish might be a little muddy without something bright. You could go with cilantro here if you like.
Key limes	4, cut "seviche-style" *(see page 27)*	Fat. Sugar. Salt. Spice. This dish needs acid for balance. Lime's perfume pairs well with chile.

Follow These Steps:

>> Preheat your oven to 325°.

>> Rub the ribs evenly with salt. Wrap in foil (see page 141 for instructions) and bake for 1 hour and 20 minutes.

>> Meanwhile, combine the sugar, the black pepper, and the chiles in a mortar and pestle, and grind into a paste.

>> Remove the ribs from the oven and switch the setting to broil on high.

>> Coat the top side of the ribs with the chile paste. Evenly.

>> Return the ribs to the oven and broil until the sugar starts to create a lacquer, about 5 minutes.

>> Pull the oven rack out far enough so you can then scatter the peanuts in an even layer on the ribs. *Use the back of a spoon to help secure the nuts into the sticky sugar lacquer.*

>> Broil for 1½ minutes, allowing the peanuts to toast in some places, nearly char in others.

>> Remove from the oven and let the ribs rest until reasonable to touch.

>> Garnish with plenty of green onions, fresh lime, and any cooking juices from the pan.

SERVES 8 (SERVING SIZE: 1 RIB)
CALORIES 231; **FAT** 9.2G (SAT 3G, MONO 4.1G, POLY 1.3G); **PROTEIN** 30G; **CARB** 5G; **FIBER** 1G; **CHOL** 105MG; **IRON** 2MG; **SODIUM** 245MG; **CALC** 39MG

CLAM SHACK-STYLE BROILED FISH

HANDS-ON: 10 MIN. **TOTAL:** 20 MIN.

Long before the word "local" had any cachet, a Long Island bayside hideaway called The Cull House procured everything from mussels and clams to flounder and weakfish mere steps away from its kitchen doors. It's been both successful and semi-secret for more than 30 years. The "Broiled Platter" is a mainstay of neighborhood coastal clam shacks like The Cull House. You'll be asked: Broiled or fried? Broiling is the gloriously effortless absence of technique. You can't hide your ingredient quality, though, so make sure to select the super-fresh. To let the broiler do the work, you need fast-cooking foods (lean fish, thinly sliced vegetables), a touch of fat (too much, and you'll have a fire on your hands), and a good bit of moisture (wine, stock, water, similar). Your technique is this: Pay attention and don't burn the food.

Food	How Much	Why
olive oil	1 tablespoon	The fish is mild. This adds a little flavor.
flounder or other super-fresh, lean saltwater fish	4 (6-ounce) fillets	It's dinner.
paprika	½ teaspoon	Honestly, for color. It's a nostalgia thing.
shallots	2, thinly sliced	Shallots and garlic provide the bulby, savory contrast to the white wine in the dish.
garlic cloves	2, minced	See above. Also provides texture.
white wine	½ cup	See shallots.
butter	1 tablespoon	Butter: The universal carrier for broiled fish.
kosher salt	½ teaspoon	We're adding salt to finish here. Seasoning the fish ahead of time would start drawing out moisture.
freshly ground black pepper	¼ teaspoon	Add it with the salt. You're used to that.
fresh flat-leaf parsley	1 tablespoon coarsely chopped	Finish fresh.
lemons	2, cut into quarters (8 wedges total)	Wedges are a classic finish.

Follow These Steps:

➤➤ Set your oven to broil. Allow the broiler to preheat for about 10 minutes.

➤➤ Brush the inside of a roasting pan with the olive oil.

➤➤ Dry the fish fillets well with paper towels and lay them into the roasting pan, flat side down. Sprinkle the tops with paprika.

➤➤ Add the shallots, the garlic, the white wine, and the butter to the pan.

➤➤ Broil 10 minutes (depending upon the thickness of the fillets), basting frequently. **The tops of the fillets should be browned, and the fish still barely translucent at its thickest point.**

➤➤ Remove the fish from the oven, and season evenly with salt and pepper.

➤➤ Transfer the fish fillets to a platter.

➤➤ Stir the parsley into the pan sauce and spoon over the fish fillets.

➤➤ Serve with lemon wedges.

SERVES 4 (SERVING SIZE: 1 FILLET)
CALORIES 176; **FAT** 9.1G (SAT 2.9G, MONO 4G, POLY 1G); **PROTEIN** 18G; **CARB** 2G; **FIBER** 0G; **CHOL** 73MG; **IRON** 1MG; **SODIUM** 396MG; **CALC** 39MG

SORGHUM-ROASTED SALMON

HANDS-ON: 16 MIN.   **TOTAL:** 25 MIN.

Sorghum is essentially a grass, raised primarily as a feed grain in the heartland of the U.S. In the southeastern U.S., though, if you say sorghum, someone might exclaim "biscuit!" Sorghum syrup, made from a variety known as sweet sorghum, has a light, molasses-y, toasty, minerally flavor that takes well to savory-sweet applications. This simply glazed salmon was a hit with the Cooking Light Test Kitchen team in recipe trials.

Food	How Much	Why
sorghum	3 tablespoons	It's an easy-to-work-with syrup, and its warm-toasty flavors go well with all things roasted or grilled.
hot water	1 tablespoon	To dilute the mustard.
dry mustard	1 teaspoon	For pungency and character.
freshly ground black pepper	¼ teaspoon	Sorghum and black pepper. Sweet and piquant. Works. With. Everything.
lemon zest	2 tablespoons grated (about 2 lemons)	Perfume. The dish might be a little one-dimensional without it.
salmon	4 (6-ounce) fillets	A richer fish such as salmon takes to the oven better than a lean fish, and can stand up to the sorghum-mustard treatment.
cooking spray		To make your life easier.
fresh lemon juice	3 tablespoons (about 2 lemons)	It's essentially the sauce.
salt	½ teaspoon	It's added to finish so it sticks to the hot glaze, and so that none of the rationed sodium ends up in unusable browned bits in the pan.

Follow These Steps:

>> Preheat the oven to 450°.

>> Combine the sorghum, 1 tablespoon of hot water, the mustard, the black pepper, and the lemon zest in a small bowl.

>> Brush the top sides of the salmon fillets evenly with the sorghum mixture.

>> Spray a baking pan evenly with cooking spray.

>> Lay the salmon fillets evenly spaced on the baking pan.

>> Roast for 9 minutes, basting halfway through with lemon juice, until the internal temperature reaches 110°. Remove the fillets from the oven.

>> Preheat the broiler. Broil the fillets for 1 minute.

>> Sprinkle the fillets evenly with salt.

>> Serve hot.

SERVES 4 (SERVING SIZE: 1 FILLET)
CALORIES 330; **FAT** 13.9G (SAT 3.1G, MONO 5.8G, POLY 3.2G); **PROTEIN** 36G; **CARB** 13G; **FIBER** 1G; **CHOL** 87MG; **IRON** 1MG; **SODIUM** 377MG; **CALC** 51MG

SYRUPS FROM ALABAMA, GEORGIA, OR TENNESSEE SHOULD BE EASY TO GET BY MAIL IF SORGHUM IS NEW TO YOU. A VERY CONSISTENT, HIGH-QUALITY SORGHUM IS MADE BY THE GUENTHER FAMILY AT MUDDY POND SORGHUM MILL IN THE HILLS OF TENNESSEE.

OTHER RISOTTO-FRIENDLY RICES: VIALONE NANO, CARNAROLI & CALROSE (SUSHI RICE-YEP, IT WORKS TOO).

DUTCH OVEN SAFFRON RISOTTO

HANDS-ON: 10 MIN. **TOTAL:** 60 MIN.

Rice has two kinds of starches—amylose and amylopectin. Amylose is more prominent in long-grain rices and is the reason they cook up fluffy, distinct, and separate. Amylopectin, on the other hand, gelatinizes when cooked, and the short- and medium-grain rices used for risotto have an ideal quantity of amylopectin. Interestingly, the pricier Carnaroli and Vialone Nano rices have relatively high amylose levels, and so will cook up more distinct and separate while still lending enough amylopectin to thicken the cooking liquid. We toast only half of the rice here, so that we can immediately "wash off" some starch from the not-toasted batch of rice when the broth is added. Constant stirring? Not really necessary. You'll see.

Food	How Much	Why
lemon zest	1 tablespoon grated	The flavor compounds in zest are largely fat-soluble, so we tumble it with the buttery rice before the stock is added.
fresh lemon juice	2 tablespoons	This is a rich dish. Some acidity is welcome.
saffron	⅛ teaspoon	Rice is a spectacular vehicle for the incomparable flavor and lovely hue of saffron.
lower-sodium chicken broth	4½ cups	The cooking liquid.
butter	1 tablespoon	To toast the rice. The solids from the butter toast, too.
yellow onion	1 cup minced	For body and flavor, but it also serves as a barrier between grains of rice, lending some contrasting texture.
Arborio or other risotto-friendly rice	1½ cups	Keep in mind that Arborio has the lowest amylose levels of the recommended rices and is more sensitive to being overcooked.
salt	½ teaspoon	To season.
white pepper	¼ teaspoon	It has a particular funkiness that marries well with creamy things. Think mushroom.
fresh pecorino Romano cheese	2 tablespoons grated	Sharper. Brighter. Saltier.

Follow These Steps:

» Preheat your oven to 375°.

» Place the lemon zest in a small bowl. Combine the lemon juice and the saffron in a separate small bowl.

» Heat the broth in a small saucepan over medium heat until just simmering. Do not boil.

» Heat a large Dutch oven over medium-high heat.

» Add the butter. Sauté and swirl until the foaming point.

» *Add the onion and stir 4 minutes, until glassy and soft.*

» Add half of the rice and stir to combine. Toast the rice gently, about 2 minutes. Now, add the lemon zest and the rest of the rice. Stir to combine.

» Add all of the broth to the rice.

» Add the saffron-lemon juice mixture.

» Add the salt and the white pepper.

» Cover and transfer to the oven. Bake for 40 minutes, until the moisture is almost fully absorbed by the rice.

» Carefully pull the oven rack out a bit. *Remove the lid, and stir and fold with a wooden spoon until the risotto is creamy, yet the rice grains are still distinguishable.*

» Sprinkle the cheese over the top of the risotto and bake, uncovered, an additional 8 minutes. Serve immediately.

SERVES 6 (SERVING SIZE: ABOUT ¾ CUP)
CALORIES 215; **FAT** 3G (SAT 1.9G, MONO 0.5G, POLY 0.1G); **PROTEIN** 7G; **CARB** 40G; **FIBER** 2G; **CHOL** 11MG; **IRON** 0MG; **SODIUM** 350MG; **CALC** 22MG

STUFFING À LA CASSOULET

HANDS-ON: 25 MIN.   **TOTAL:** 1 HR. 35 MIN.

This main dish is wholly inspired by cassoulet, a slow-braised/baked French casserole made with a mix of meats and white beans that's often topped with coarse, fresh breadcrumbs. Whether you call this dish stuffing or dressing, the flavors of cassoulet lend themselves perfectly to such a creation. Blend the ingredients together and you get a quite credible cassoulet—just inverted.

Food	How Much	Why
boneless, skinless chicken thighs	1 pound	They're not quite duck legs in richness, but they're readily available and work both texturally and flavor-wise.
unsalted chicken stock	2 cups	To moisten the stuffing/dressing.
yellow onion	1 cup diced	Inspired by France, we're going with mirepoix for our aromatics, and that's two parts onion...
carrots	½ cup diced	...one part carrot...
celery	½ cup diced	...and one part celery.
garlic cloves	3, sliced	A crucial part of cassoulet, particularly in Toulouse.
vegetable oil	2 tablespoons	For browning the sausage.
Italian turkey sausage	8 ounces, casings removed	It's readily available and keeps this light.
baguette	8 ounces, cut into ½-inch cubes and toasted	Nothing's being stuffed or dressed. Regardless, this is your stuffing.
fresh flat-leaf parsley	3 tablespoons coarsely chopped	To refresh.
fresh thyme	2 teaspoons minced	When in France...
kosher salt	¾ teaspoon	The perfect amount.
low-sodium white beans	1 (14-ounce) can, drained	Some kind of white bean is needed. These are easy.
diced tomatoes	1 (14-ounce) can, drained	You find a bit of tomato in most cassoulet recipes.
cooking spray		So you can get out every last bit.

Follow These Steps:

>> Preheat your oven to 400°.

>> Place the chicken thighs, the chicken stock, the onion, the carrots, the celery, and the garlic in a saucepan. Bring to a boil.

>> Reduce the heat and cook 30 minutes at a slight simmer, until the thighs are tender and the stock has reduced to about 1½ cups.

>> Remove the chicken thighs from the stock, set aside, and when cool enough to touch, pull the meat into shreds. Reserve.

>> Heat a large skillet over medium-high heat. Add the oil and swirl. Cook the turkey sausage 10 minutes, until browned and fully cooked, yet still slightly moist.

>> In a large mixing bowl, combine the reduced stock mixture, the chicken, the sausage, the baguette, and the next 5 ingredients (through tomatoes). Toss.

>> Coat an 11 x 7-inch glass or ceramic baking dish with cooking spray. Transfer the chicken mixture to the sprayed baking dish and bake, uncovered, for 30 minutes, until the liquid is well absorbed, and the top is evenly browned.

SERVES 8 (SERVING SIZE: ABOUT ⅔ CUP)
CALORIES 304; **FAT** 11.1G (SAT 2.4G, MONO 5.1G, POLY 2.3G); **PROTEIN** 23G; **CARB** 27G; **FIBER** 4G; **CHOL** 58MG; **IRON** 3MG; **SODIUM** 689MG; **CALC** 57MG

FRANCE
•TOULOUSE

ARTICHOKE AND MELTED FENNEL LASAGNA

HANDS-ON: 45 MIN.   **TOTAL:** 2 HR. 30 MIN.

Food	How Much	Why
Buttermilk Ricotta (*page 114*)	2 cups	Could you buy ricotta? Sure, but the buttermilk ricotta in this book is slightly zingy, and is less weepy than the store-bought stuff.
fresh flat-leaf parsley	¼ cup coarsely chopped	Its grassy qualities work beautifully against tangy/acidic things. Think: crisp white wine.
fresh pecorino Romano cheese	1 tablespoon grated	In trying to keep things sharp here, pecorino wins over Parmigiano.
fresh thyme	2 teaspoons minced	Thymol, the predominant compound in thyme, is fat-soluble, so a butterfat-rich cream sauce is a wonderful vehicle for this herb.
egg	1, lightly beaten	To help bind the cheese mixture.
butter	1 tablespoon	For the roux. And for richness.
olive oil	2 tablespoons, divided	For the roux. And for character.
all-purpose flour	3 tablespoons	For the roux. To thicken.
half-and-half	¼ cup	To enrich the sauce. The roux thickens.
chicken broth	1 cup	For a savory foundation.
lemon zest	from 1 lemon	Plays a supporting aromatic role.
fresh lemon juice	from 1 lemon	To contrast the roundness of the cream sauce.
yellow onion	3 cups julienne	With the fennel, creates the bulk of the dish.
fennel bulb	2½ cups fine julienne	Slow-cooked, fennel loses its licorice-like bite, becoming subtle and deeply savory.
garlic cloves	8, thinly sliced	Adds more savory flavor.
salt	¾ teaspoon	To season.
black pepper	½ teaspoon	Enough to provide a little bite.
dry white wine	¼ cup	To brighten and play off the lemon.
frozen artichoke hearts	18 ounces, thawed and coarsely chopped	You can't beat them for convenience.
cooking spray		So those corner pieces cooperate.
no-boil lasagna noodles	12	There's something crepe-like about the no-boil sheets that provides an elegance to the dish.

You've heard that people eat with their eyes. Well, it's not true. That's impossible. People do, however, respond to color in ways both physiological and psychological. Lasagna, of course, is a classic comfort food. And monochromatic color schemes are recognized as soothing. This, then, is an exercise in making lasagna both soothing and comforting. The result is rich, subtle, and luxurious, highlighting the flavors of artichoke and fennel with the bright touch of lemon. Add a glass of crisp white wine and a frisée salad with a drizzle of olive oil and a pinch of salt, and all your stresses will melt away.

CONTINUED

2 cups Buttermilk Ricotta

¼ cup coarsely chopped fresh flat-leaf parsley

1 Tbsp. grated fresh pecorino Romano cheese

2 tsp. minced fresh thyme

1 egg, lightly beaten

1 Tbsp. butter

2 Tbsp. olive oil, divided

3 Tbsp. all-purpose flour

¼ cup half-and-half

1 cup chicken broth

zest from 1 lemon

juice from 1 lemon

3 cups julienne-cut yellow onion

2½ cups fine julienne-cut fennel bulb

8 garlic cloves, thinly sliced

¾ tsp. salt

½ tsp. black pepper

¼ cup dry white wine

18 oz. frozen artichoke hearts, thawed and coarsely chopped

cooking spray

12 no-boil lasagna noodles

Follow These Steps:

≫ Preheat your oven to 350°.

MAKE TWO FILLINGS

≫ Combine the ricotta, the parsley, the pecorino, the thyme, and the egg in a medium bowl. Set aside until it's time to layer the lasagna.

≫ Make a blonde roux: Heat a small saucepan over low heat. Add the butter and 1 tablespoon of the olive oil, and stir until the butter melts. Whisk in the flour until the mixture is well combined.

MAKE A ROUX BLONDE BY COOKING GENTLY ENOUGH TO AVOID BROWNING EITHER THE BUTTER OR THE SOLIDS. WHEN THE GENTLE "TOASTY" AROMA SURFACES, YOU'RE THERE.

≫ Whisk in the half-and-half, stirring constantly.

≫ Whisk in the chicken broth, the lemon zest, and the lemon juice. Stir constantly and simmer gently for 5 minutes or until thickened. Turn off the heat.

≫ Heat a large, straight-sided skillet over low heat. Add 1 tablespoon olive oil and swirl. Now, add the onions, the fennel, the garlic, the salt, and the pepper.

≫ Cover and cook the vegetables over low heat 30 minutes or until they are soft and translucent, stirring occasionally.

≫ Uncover and raise the heat to medium. Stirring constantly, cook off excess liquid. Add the wine and cook until the wine evaporates, about 30 minutes, stirring constantly to make the onion mixture almost "melted" and jammy.

≫ Remove the onion mixture from the heat. Add the broth mixture and the artichokes to the onions, and warm through.

BUILD LAYERS

≫ Liberally spray a 13 x 9-inch glass or ceramic baking dish with cooking spray.

≫ Spread ¾ cup of the warm onion mixture in the dish, followed by a single layer of 4 lasagna noodles, followed by 1 cup of the ricotta mixture.

≫ Repeat. Use all of the remaining ricotta mixture. Preferably, the top layer will be the onion mixture.

≫ Place the 4 remaining lasagna noodles on top, followed by the last of the onion mixture. **You were snacking on it, weren't you?**

BAKE, BROIL, AND SERVE

» Cover tightly and bake at 350° for 40 minutes. Preheat broiler.

» Uncover and broil 5 minutes, or until the top layer is a photo-friendly golden brown.

» Rest for at least 15 minutes before slicing and serving.

SERVES 8
CALORIES 301; **FAT** 10.8G (SAT 3.8G, MONO 4.2G, POLY 1G); **PROTEIN** 11G; **CARB** 42G; **FIBER** 7G; **CHOL** 39MG; **IRON** 2MG; **SODIUM** 441MG; **CALC** 172MG

HOW TO LAYER THIS LASAGNA

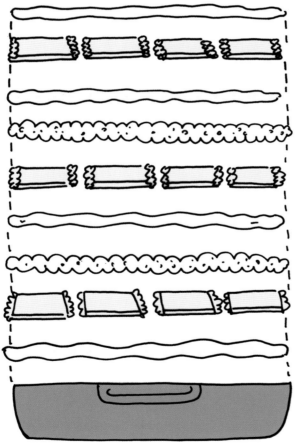

REMAINING ONION MIXTURE

4 LASAGNA NOODLES

3/4 CUP WARM ONION MIXTURE

1 CUP RICOTTA MIXTURE

4 LASAGNA NOODLES

3/4 CUP WARM ONION MIXTURE

1 CUP RICOTTA MIXTURE

4 LASAGNA NOODLES

3/4 CUP WARM ONION MIXTURE

PLAYING WITH FIRE

Grilling, pit cooking, and smoking

Archaeologists, anthropologists, and other science-minded folks are still debating when humans began cooking with fire and whether command and control of fire was what sparked the transition from *homo erectus* to *homo sapiens*. Fascinating stuff, indeed, but those discussions don't usually involve recipes. That's where this chapter comes in. Most of us enjoy a fire-cooked meal, and what follows is some guidance on how to manage the relationship between ingredient and fire source.

I WOULD ARGUE THAT KAMADOS ARE AMAZING TOOLS FOR LOW-SLOW, INDIRECT COOKING, BUT THEY CAN BE TOUGH TO MANAGE (REQUIRING QUITE A BIT OF PREP TIME) IF YOU WANT TO GRILL DIRECTLY—AND QUICKLY.

The Great Grill Debate: Gas vs. Charcoal

First, let's address the gas grill versus charcoal grill choice. It doesn't matter. Big ceramic kamado, like the Big Green Egg? They're fine, too. What matters is your comfort level with your fire-cooking device of choice. And note, quality grill grates are as important as the source of heat. Invest wisely. If you're going with a charcoal device, make sure there's enough room to create an indirect heat setup (see page 325). Use enough good-quality charcoal for your heat source, and you won't have any problems getting a searing heat. If using a gas grill, make sure you spend a little extra to ensure that your grill can a) get super-hot for direct grilling, and b) has enough burners to manage indirect, low-slow grilling.

CHARCOAL VS. GAS

Now, the grilled flavor that turns us on does not come from the heat source. There is no gas flavor. There is no charcoal flavor. Charcoal burns a little dryer than propane or natural gas, but "grilled flavor" comes from the moisture and fat from what's being grilled dripping onto the heat source, steaming, and flaring back up at your food. Where some flavor can be imparted is via the use of wood or wood chips, where the lignin, an aromatic polymer present in wood, converts to a substance called guaiacol, which is responsible for the spiced-smoke flavor that's particularly pronounced in bacon. A substance called syringol is responsible for some of the aroma from wood smoke.

As in every other cooking method outlined in this book, learning to master the application of heat is one of two skill sets needed to succeed at the grill. The other is flavor composition, which you've been exposed to in myriad tips and tricks throughout the book. With fire, you can go bold on flavor, as char invites intensity.

AVOID HAVING EXCESSIVE OIL OR FAT ON THE SURFACE OF WHAT YOU'RE GRILLING. YOUR FOOD CAN CATCH FIRE, AND THAT KIND OF MUDDY SMOKINESS ISN'T WELCOME ON ANYTHING.

Direct Heat

In direct grilling, heat control is key. Super-high heat is generally only welcome with steaks and chops that are intended to be cooked from rare to medium since an intense fire will char the exterior before the heat has much time to penetrate to the interior. Generally, a controlled medium to medium-high heat is ideal for grilling on direct heat. Burgers and kebabs are better over controlled heat. Items that cook quickly (ones you'd sauté or pan roast), that are tender and juicy without low-slow cook times, are good candidates for direct grilling.

For exceptional presentation results, make sure your grill grates are well seasoned, and don't tinker with what's being grilled too quickly. The surface of what's being cooked will char against the grill grates, and will release easily if you're patient. When it comes to direct grilling, there are two presentation schools of thought: You can monitor closely and go for photo-friendly diamond-shaped grill marks, or flip more frequently for a more even, "manual rotisserie" effect—the surface will be more raggedly charred. Both are acceptable methods.

DIRECT

FOOD IS PLACED DIRECTLY OVER THE FIRE.

COOKS FOOD QUICKLY.

INDIRECT

THE FIRE IS BUILT ON ONE OR BOTH SIDES OF THE FOOD, BUT NOT DIRECTLY UNDER IT.

GRILL IS COVERED, ALLOWING THE HOT AIR TO CIRCULATE AROUND THE FOOD.

Indirect Heat

When food needs to endure a long stay on the grill, indirect heat is your only choice. It's ideal for large cuts of meat and tougher cuts that have more connective tissue. The Greek-Style Slow-Grilled Leg of Lamb on page 362 leaves the meat on the low, slow (indirect) heat long enough to break down the collagen in the meat, yielding tender results (think pulled pork), and the Immigrant-Edition Pollo a la Brasa (page 358) takes advantage of what happens to chicken legs when they're subjected to long, controlled cooking—crackling-crisp skin and moist, fork-tender meat.

With indirect heat, the foods are cooked long enough to benefit from some wood smoke. However, we've left wood-smoking techniques out of this book, instead focusing on controlling the application of heat so we can focus on perfecting your method first.

ADANA-INSPIRED
TURKEY-LAMB KEBABS

THE COUNTRY

HANDS-ON: 26 MIN. **TOTAL:** 1 HR. 26 MIN.

*Start grating onions. Now. They do it in Greece. Morocco, too. And in Turkey.
Anytime you had a fantastic ground meat kebab, grated onion was likely involved.
Onions are chemically complex wonders, and according to Eric Block, author of Garlic and
Other Alliums, tinkering with onions' structure, as in cutting or crushing—or even bruising—causes
a "cascade of reactions." Most of those reactions bode well for ground meats when you move
swiftly with your onions. (You don't want to leave the grated onions around too long, as
off flavors can develop.) Grate, mix, and grill. Serve with Mint and Sumac "Salsa" on page 76.*

Food	How Much	Why
ground lamb	½ pound	As done in Adana, Turkey.
ground turkey	½ pound	To lighten this up a bit. Plus, straight ground lamb can be intense.
onion	¼ cup grated	See the headnote above.
garlic	2 tablespoons finely minced	It works in concert with onion to flavor the dish.
Turkish red pepper paste	2 tablespoons	For depth of flavor and some caramel notes, plus some heat if you choose a hot variety. (I do.) Search in Middle Eastern markets or online for *biber salçasi*.
ground sumac	2 teaspoons	For acid balance. Sumac is tangy.
Marash pepper	1 teaspoon	It's deep, almost round in flavor, and a little spicy. Substitute Espelette or Aleppo.
ground coriander	½ teaspoon	For its citrus notes.
kosher salt	¼ teaspoon	This dish needs it.
plain 2% reduced-fat Greek yogurt	½ cup	For a quickie "sauce" of sorts.
water	1 tablespoon	To dilute the yogurt a bit.

Follow These Steps:

➤ Ritually fire up your grill of choice.

➤ In a chilled bowl, combine the lamb, turkey, and next 7 ingredients (through salt). Mix by hand, but don't mush. If you can, refrigerate for at least an hour.

➤ Using long, flat skewers, mold the meat around the skewers to make long, flat paddles, about 1¼-inch wide, and thick enough to hold together. You'll feel when it does.

➤ Distribute the meat among 4 skewers. *Contemplate why you didn't double the recipe and invite more guests.*

➤ *Grill the kebabs for about 3 minutes on each side, turning only when you feel confident that the meat is sufficiently cooked and certain to Not. End. Up. Down. There. Ugh.*

➤ Remove to a platter. Either leave the kebabs on the skewer, or not.

➤ In a small bowl, thin out the yogurt with 1 tablespoon of water.

➤ Serve with the yogurt and Mint and Sumac "Salsa" (page 76).

SERVES 4 (SERVING SIZE: 1 KEBAB AND 2 TABLESPOONS YOGURT SAUCE)
CALORIES 250; **FAT** 12.6G (SAT 4.9G, MONO 3.6G, POLY 0.7G); **PROTEIN** 25G;
CARB 9G; **FIBER** 1G; **CHOL** 76MG; **IRON** 2MG; **SODIUM** 433MG; **CALC** 42MG

BUFFALO CHICKEN BURGERS

HANDS-ON: 35 MIN. **TOTAL:** 35 MIN.

Born of a craving while writing this chapter, I jumped on the idea of a lean, Buffalo sauce–spiked chicken burger experience—somewhere between a wing and a burger. Just for fun. The result has all the twang of a well-balanced Buffalo wing, but is a much better way to enjoy carrot, celery, and blue cheese. No buns necessary.

Food	How Much	Why
ground chicken	1½ pounds	It's a chicken burger.
diced whole-grain bread	4 ounces	The panade addiction continues, resulting in a really good meatloaf-y mouthfeel.
2% reduced-fat milk	5 tablespoons, divided	To moisten the panade.
onion	½ cup minced	To get some flavor into the interior of the burger and add some additional moisture.
freshly ground black pepper	½ teaspoon	Simply seasoned.
kosher salt	¼ teaspoon	See above.
hot sauce	5 tablespoons, divided	Buffalo. Use a cayenne version.
butter	1 tablespoon, melted	To soften the hot sauce.
blue cheese	1 ounce (about ¼ cup), crumbled	Use the cheese instead of a gloopy dressing.
low-fat buttermilk	2 tablespoons	As part of a dressing.
canola mayonnaise	2 tablespoons	To enrich the dressing. Mayo "rounds off" flavor.
carrot	1 cup very thinly sliced	No one really likes sticks.
celery	1 cup very thinly sliced	See above.
green onions	¼ cup very thinly sliced	Bright and pungent, all at once. A great finish.

Follow These Steps:

➤➤ Fire up the grill or a grill pan over medium heat.

➤➤ In a medium bowl, combine the chicken, bread, ¼ cup of milk, onion, pepper, and salt.

➤➤ Fold together, allowing the bread to absorb all of the liquid. *Do not mash. Keep the mixture loose and irregular.*

➤➤ Divide the chicken mixture into 6 equal portions. Form 6 (½-inch-thick) burgers, bringing them together just tightly enough to hold their shape.

➤➤ Combine ¼ cup hot sauce and butter in a shallow dish. Working with 1 patty at time, roll patties in butter mixture.

➤➤ In a medium bowl, combine 1 tablespoon of the milk, 1 tablespoon hot sauce, the blue cheese, the buttermilk, and the mayonnaise. Add the carrots and celery, and fold to combine. Let wilt slightly at room temperature while the burgers are grilling.

➤➤ Grill the burgers 5 minutes per side, or until the internal temperature reaches 155°. They'll carry over.

➤➤ Platter the burgers, brushing each with ⅓ cup celery salad. Sprinkle burgers evenly with green onions.

SERVES 6 (SERVING SIZE: 1 PATTY AND ⅓ CUP CELERY SALAD)
CALORIES 315; **FAT** 17.8G (SAT 5.6G, MONO 7.5G, POLY 3.3G); **PROTEIN** 25G; **CARB** 17G; **FIBER** 3G; **CHOL** 109MG; **IRON** 2MG; **SODIUM** 660MG; **CALC** 95MG

THE AUTHOR
HAS A CRUSH
ON THAILAND.

THAI STREET CHICKEN

HANDS-ON: 20 MIN. **TOTAL:** 1 HR. 30 MIN.

All over Thailand, especially in urban areas, street-food stalls are everywhere, their sights and smells delightfully overwhelming. Chicken offerings are abundant, varied, and almost universally Mad Delicious. Four condiments are showcased at restaurants and makeshift street-side dining areas: white sugar (sweet), Thai chiles in vinegar (sour-piquant), fish sauce (salty-savory), and intensely flavorful crushed dry chile (depth-heat). In this recipe, the dipping sauce that accompanies honors the Thai condiment caddy. And the marinade on this chicken is deeply savory, welcoming generous amounts of the sauce. Eat your veggies, too, with your fingers. We left them raw.

Food	How Much	Why
cilantro roots	3 pieces	A staple ingredient in Thai cuisine. Substitute ½ cup cilantro stems and ½ cup parsley stems.
palm sugar or brown sugar	1 tablespoon	For depth of flavor and caramel-molasses notes.
white pepper	2 teaspoons	White pepper is an essential ingredient in Thai kitchens and food stalls.
fish sauce	2 tablespoons	Fermented, salty, and glutamate-rich, it seasons and heightens the meatiness of the dish.
oyster sauce	1 tablespoon	...so does this, but it adds some sweetness, too.
garlic cloves	4, grated	You're making a paste.
skinless, boneless chicken thighs	1½ pounds (6 thighs)	For grilling.
cooking spray		To season the grill grates.
carrots	1 cup, fine julienne	For enjoying some lively raw vegetables at will along with your chicken. The flavor is so robust, you can break it up with these veggies.
cucumbers	2, peeled, scored, and sliced	Again, for the solitary enjoyment of eating raw vegetables and grilled chicken.
fresh cilantro	12 whole sprigs	To eat. Whole.
limes	2, cut into wedges	There's a lot of umami in this dish. You need acid balance.
Dipping Sauce (page 333)		For the sweet-sour-salty-spicy-ness that makes this Mad Delicious.

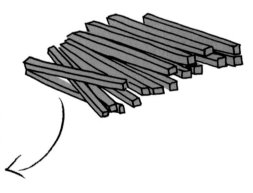

CONTINUED

THAI STREET CHICKEN

3 pieces cilantro roots

1 Tbsp. palm sugar

2 tsp. white pepper

2 Tbsp. fish sauce

1 Tbsp. oyster sauce

4 garlic cloves, grated

1½ pounds skinless, boneless chicken thighs

cooking spray

1 cup fine julienne-cut carrots

2 cucumbers, peeled, scored, and sliced

12 whole cilantro sprigs

2 limes, cut into wedges

Dipping Sauce

Follow These Steps:

>> Fire up a charcoal grill to low heat, creating a slow, even bed of coals.

MAKE THE MARINADE

>> Place the cilantro roots (or cilantro and parsley stems) in a large zip-top plastic bag. Seal the bag. Use the side of a rolling pin to bruise.

>> Add the sugar, the white pepper, the fish sauce, the oyster sauce, and the garlic to the bag and combine. *Add the chicken thighs. Massage until well incorporated.*

>> Seal and refrigerate for 30 minutes.

>> Remove chicken from bag; discard marinade.

SKEWER THE CHICKEN

>> *Using flat and long stainless steel skewers, thread the chicken thighs so that they resemble a flat, Middle Eastern–style kebab.*

>> Using cooking spray, spray a clean grill rag and wipe down the grates of the grill very well. Use long tongs if proximity to fire makes you uncomfortable.

LET'S GRILL!

>> Place the chicken skewers on the hot grill.

>> Grill for 15 minutes, assuming the heat is between 275° and 300° and controlled; otherwise, you'll find yourself turning more frequently.

>> Flip and grill for another 15 minutes, or until you can easily pull off a piece of cooked chicken as if it has been slow-cooked.

>> Remove the chicken to a platter, and let rest 10 minutes.

>> Slide the thighs off of the skewers and onto the platter, arranging them to one side of the platter.

>> On the other side of the platter, in rows, line up the carrots, cucumbers, cilantro, and lime wedges. Serve with the Dipping Sauce.

SERVES 6 (SERVING SIZE: 1 CHICKEN THIGH, ⅔ CUP VEGETABLES, AND ABOUT 2½ TABLESPOONS SAUCE)
CALORIES 169; FAT 4.9G (SAT 1.2G, MONO 1.6G, POLY 1.2G); PROTEIN 23G; CARB 7G; FIBER 1G; CHOL 94MG; IRON 2MG; SODIUM 356MG; CALC 38MG

DIPPING SAUCE FOR THAI STREET CHICKEN

HANDS-ON: 10 MIN. **TOTAL:** 10 MIN.

*Here's another chance to layer onto your "NeutralQue."
You're hitting the sweet, sour, salty, spicy flavors in perfect
harmony, albeit at fortissimo. Embrace the bird chile!*

Food	How Much	Why
"NeutralQue" (*page 57*)	¾ cup	It's neutral, yet provides the needed sweet and sour.
fresh lime juice	4 tablespoons	Thais use a lot of lime juice. This is a preferred acidic ingredient.
fish sauce	1 teaspoon	For "meatiness" and some salt.
Thai bird chiles	2, minced	Floral and crazy-intense.
garlic clove	1, crushed	Harmonizes acid and umami.
white pepper	½ teaspoon	Layers perfectly into the fish sauce. Fermented on fermented.

Follow These Steps:

» Combine all ingredients in a small bowl. Refrigerate until chilled.

» Serve with Thai Street Chicken or other grilled meats.

SERVES 6 (SERVING SIZE: ABOUT 2½ TABLESPOONS)
CALORIES 92; **FAT** 0.1G (SAT 0G, MONO 0G, POLY 0G); **PROTEIN** 1G;
CARB 24G; **FIBER** 1G; **CHOL** 0MG; **IRON** 0MG; **SODIUM** 194MG; **CALC** 25MG

THIS SAUCE IS PART OF THE
THAI CONDIMENT CADDY.

KOREAN-INSPIRED PORK CHOPS

HANDS-ON: 15 MIN. **TOTAL:** 2 HR. 15 MIN.

Korean flavors have fully arrived in America, showing up in everything from street-chic kimchi and short rib tacos to elegant traditional small plates at places such as Hanjan in the Flatiron District of New York. This recipe introduces gochujang, a spicy-sweet-fermented chile paste made with rice, soybean, and chile. It's worth keeping a substantial container on hand, as it can be stirred into broths, enjoyed as a condiment, or used in a pork chop marinade. This recipe rolls food truck–style, with a bold and punchy dose of kimchi in the marinade. It's zingy and satisfying, worthy of an ice-buried Korean beer and a playlist of the latest K-pop hits.

Food	How Much	Why
spicy kimchi	½ cup	It's effervescent, tangy, funky, spicy, and complex.
water	½ cup	To carry the ingredients.
gochujang (Korean fermented red pepper paste)	2 tablespoons	The fermented soy spikes the meatiness. The sugar lacquers. The chile tints and warms.
fresh gingerroot	2 tablespoons grated	Some fresh against the funk.
sugar	1 tablespoon	To ensure a good caramel-y finish.
garlic cloves	4, grated	There's likely garlic in your gochujang. In this recipe, more is better.
bone-in pork loin chops	4 (6-ounce) chops	They're pretty.
green onions	8 whole onions, roots trimmed	Your side dish.

Follow These Steps:

» Combine the first 6 ingredients (through garlic) in a mini food processor. Process until smooth.

» Place the pork chops in a large, sturdy zip-top plastic bag. Pour the marinade over the top.

» *Massage the marinade into the chops,* and then seal and refrigerate for 2 hours.

» Fire up your grill for direct heat or grill pan to medium-high heat.

» Remove the pork chops from the marinade and discard the marinade.

» Grill the pork chops for about 2½ minutes on each side, or until a thermometer reads 140° internally. Move them to a platter to rest for 5 minutes before serving.

» Grill the green onions for about 1 minute on each side. Serve with the chops.

SERVES 4 (SERVING SIZE: 1 PORK CHOP AND 2 GREEN ONIONS) **CALORIES** 291; **FAT** 10G (SAT 3.4G, MONO 4G, POLY 1.4G); **PROTEIN** 37G; **CARB** 11G; **FIBER** 1G; **CHOL** 100MG; **IRON** 2MG; **SODIUM** 547MG; **CALC** 99MG

ANCHO-RUBBED BEEF FLAP

HANDS-ON: 25 MIN. **TOTAL:** 25 MIN.

You're likely familiar with skirt and flank steaks. This is better. Flap, from the bottom sirloin, makes butchers and cooks smile because its tenderness-to-flavor ratio is ideal. Almost-high heat will facilitate the crust you need while allowing the steak to develop a more end-to-end "eye." The sugar-salt-chile rub becomes an irresistible crust on this now on-the-radar cut. Serve this with First-Cut Salsa Fresca (page 29) and Maria's Cilantro Cebollas (page 79).

Food

Food	How Much	Why
dried ancho chile	2 chiles	Ancho has a deep raisin-y flavor that works nicely in smoky-sweet preparations.
sugar	2 teaspoons	See ancho. This is for the sweet in smoky-sweet.
kosher salt	½ teaspoon	It's steak. Salt.
garlic cloves	2, peeled	A perfect bridge between salt and sugar. Plus, when crushed, garlic's enzymes are doing their thing, and it becomes almost adhesive-like, a great thing for holding spices on steak.
beef sirloin flap	1 pound	Flavor-to-tenderness ratio, as described in the headnote.
cooking spray		To make your life easier.
lime	1, halved	A little juice from charred limes is your "sauce."

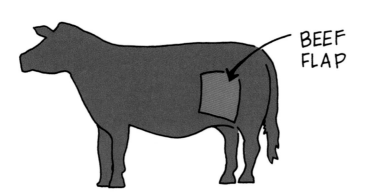

BEEF FLAP

Follow These Steps:

≫ Fire up a grill or grill pan over medium-high heat. You should be able to hover your hand a few inches above the grill surface for 5 seconds or so, but not more, before you'll need to pull away. *That's hot enough.*

≫ Toast the chiles on the fire for about 1 minute, turning once. *A little char is good; burned is not.*

≫ Pull the stem end off of the chiles, shake out most of the seeds, and grind the chiles in a food processor.

≫ Add the sugar, salt, and garlic to the ground chiles in the processor bowl. Pulse until well combined.

≫ Massage the steak deeply with the ancho rub. *Flap meat is quite cavernous, so use your thumbs and fingers to press the rub into all the cracks and crevasses.*

≫ Spray a clean grill rag with cooking spray. Rub into the grill grates until they glisten.

≫ Place the lime on the grill, cut sides down, and char for about 2 to 3 minutes before removing from the grill. Set aside in a small bowl.

≫ Grill the steak, about 4 minutes on each side for medium-rare. *Don't tinker with it. Allow for some uneven charring.*

≫ Transfer the steak to a cutting board to rest for 5 minutes.

≫ *Cut on a sharp bias, with your knife nearly parallel to the board, in very thin slices.*

≫ Squeeze the grilled lime halves over the sliced beef. Serve.

SERVES 4 (SERVING SIZE: 3½ OUNCES)
CALORIES 215; **FAT** 9.3G (SAT 2.5G, MONO 3.5G, POLY 0.7G); **PROTEIN** 25G;
CARB 7G; **FIBER** 2G; **CHOL** 73MG; **IRON** 3MG; **SODIUM** 305MG; **CALC** 39MG

BAJA-STYLE GRILLED FISH TACOS
WITH CABBAGE AND CREMA

HANDS-ON: 25 MIN. **TOTAL:** 25 MIN.

Travel to San Diego, and you'll find fish tacos everywhere, from gastropubs to quick-service joints to celebrated restaurants. Hop the border into Mexico, hitting up Tijuana, Puerto Nuevo, and Ensenada, and you'll experience myriad opportunities to explore tortillas and Pacific Ocean fare. For this Baja-inspired recipe, it's especially important to regulate heat, erring on the gentler side, as the mahimahi needs sufficient time to firm up without charring too deeply. Be mindful about seasoning the grill grates and super-careful when turning. If you botch it the first time around, make sure to build the tacos strategically by blanketing your first-run grilled fish with perfectly shredded cabbage.

Food	How Much	Why
plain 2% reduced-fat Greek yogurt	¼ cup	This is the base of our homemade version of crema. A little acid works with the rub here.
light sour cream	¼ cup	Enriches the crema a bit.
1% low-fat milk	2 tablespoons	Thins the crema.
dried pasilla chile	1	Adds a rich, almost meaty chile flavor to the rub.
brown sugar	2 teaspoons	The molasses flavor works with the chile and chars up beautifully (and quickly—be mindful of the heat).
canola oil	2 teaspoons	This is a shout-out to my mom. She always combined salt, sugar, and dry spices with oil as a pretreatment to roasted and grilled things. It works.
kosher salt	½ teaspoon	To contrast the sugar in the rub.
garlic clove	1, grated	Grating garlic helps ensure it sticks to the fish.
jalapeño pepper	1, grated	To evenly spike the flavor of the fillets.
mahimahi	2 (¾-pound) fillets, deboned and skinned	It's mellow-flavored and durable, a great choice for grilling.
cooking spray		To keep the fish from sticking to the grill.
corn tortillas	8 (6-inch) tortillas	The scent (and flavor) of masa, the corn dough that becomes a tortilla, is quintessentially Mexican.
water	3 tablespoons	Keeps the tortillas from getting brittle on the grill.
white cabbage	2 cups finely shredded	As seen in Baja, California.
Mexican limes	4, cut "seviche-style" (see page 27)	See above.
yellow onion	1 cup fine julienne	The bite of raw onion is a welcome contrast against all of the robust flavors.
First-Cut Salsa Fresca (page 29)	1 cup	One of myriad salsas you could employ. This one, well, because there's a recipe for it in this book.
fresh cilantro leaves	1 tablespoon	Fresh to finish.

MAHIMAHI IS A GOOD CHOICE FOR GRILLING, AS IT'S MORE DURABLE THAN YOUR AVERAGE FINFISH.

CONTINUED →

BAJA-STYLE GRILLED FISH TACOS

1/4 cup plain 2% reduced-fat Greek yogurt

1/4 cup light sour cream

2 Tbsp. 1% low-fat milk

1 dried pasilla chile

2 tsp. brown sugar

2 tsp. canola oil

1/2 tsp. kosher salt

1 garlic clove, grated

1 jalapeño pepper, grated

2 (3/4-lb.) mahimahi fillets, deboned and skinned

cooking spray

8 (6-inch) corn tortillas

3 Tbsp. water

2 cups finely shredded white cabbage

4 Mexican limes, cut "seviche-style"

1 cup fine julienne yellow onion

1 cup First-Cut Salsa Fresca

1 tablespoon fresh cilantro leaves

Follow These Steps:

PREPARE THE CREMA

>> In a small bowl, combine the yogurt, the sour cream, and the milk in a small bowl. Whisk to blend evenly. Cover and refrigerate.

MAKE A SPICE RUB

>> Heat a grill or grill pan to medium-high.

>> Grind the pasilla chile in a food processor (or a coffee-type grinder designated for your spices and other non-coffee items). You should have 1 tablespoon of ground chile.

>> In a medium bowl, combine the pasilla, the brown sugar, the canola oil, the salt, the garlic, and the jalapeño.

>> Lay the fish fillets on a large plate or platter and massage on all sides with the pasilla mixture. Refrigerate while you season the grill.

GET READY… AND GRILL

>> Spray a clean grill rag with cooking spray and rub the grill grates liberally. Repeat until the grill is well seasoned and ready to be kind to fish.

>> Grill the fish fillets for about 4 minutes on each side, leaving it untouched and unturned during the first 4 minutes.

>> *Turn the fillets once and only once, or you'll have fish bits everywhere. People will feel cheated when you try to hide massacred fillets in their tacos.*

>> Using a thin fish spatula, lift the fish gently from the grill and place on a platter.

>> *Now, brush the tortillas lightly with 3 tablespoons water and grill until marked and softened. This happens fast—30 seconds.*

>> Bundle them up in a clean tea towel and lay the bundle in a bowl or basket.

>> Serve the fish on a platter with a large serving spoon. Present the fish alongside the tortillas, the cabbage, the cut limes, the onions, the First-Cut Salsa Fresca, the crema, and the fresh cilantro.

SERVES 4 (SERVING SIZE: 2 TACOS)
CALORIES 362; FAT 7.9G (SAT 2G, MONO 2.6G, POLY 1.8G); PROTEIN 38G; CARB 36G; FIBER 6G; CHOL 131MG; IRON 3MG; SODIUM 590MG; CALC 162MG

WARMER-WATER SWORDFISH CAN
BE, UM, WORMY, SO SHY AWAY
FROM COOKING THOSE ON THE
RARE SIDE. IF YOU GET COLD-WATER
SWORDFISH, YOU'LL LIKELY BE OKAY
TO EAT THOSE MEDIUM-RARE.

SWORDFISH STEAK AU POIVRE

HANDS-ON: 25 MIN. **TOTAL:** 25 MIN.

Swordfish is mellow yet rich, evocative of a well-marbled heritage pork loin chop. Here, thick swordfish steaks are treated like steaks. The only hint of this being a sea-inspired preparation is a hit of lemon juice and zest, which brightens the dish just enough to honor the mildness of the fish. (You can also cook mahimahi, albacore tuna, and marlin this way.) The Monterey Bay Aquarium Seafood Watch recommends harpoon- or handline-caught swordfish, which are sustainable choices.

Food	How Much	Why
dry red wine	½ cup	Part of our "steak" sauce.
lower-sodium beef broth	¼ cup	For fun.
brandy	2 tablespoons	To honor the au poivre tradition.
red wine vinegar	2 tablespoons	Acetic acid harmonizes with the citric lemon. Citrus alone would make the sauce taste unfinished—weird, even.
fresh thyme leaves	1 teaspoon minced	For depth.
lemon zest	1 teaspoon grated	To activate the olfactory side of the flavor experience.
fresh lemon juice	2 tablespoons	Hinting at a seafood dish.
black peppercorns, coarsely cracked	2 tablespoons	The poivre part.
sugar	2 teaspoons	Sugar softens some of the acids in the dish.
kosher salt	¾ teaspoon	It's steak.
large egg white	1, lightly beaten	To bind the spices.
swordfish steaks	4 (6-ounce) steaks, about 1½ inches thick	The steak of the sea.
cooking spray		To season the grill.
butter	1 tablespoon, softened	Cooked swordfish is interestingly absorbent—why not soak in a touch of butter?

Follow These Steps:

>> Place a small saucepan over medium heat.

>> Combine the red wine, the beef broth, the brandy, the red wine vinegar, the thyme leaves, the lemon zest, and the lemon juice in the pan. Bring to a boil, reduce the heat, and keep at a rolling simmer until reduced to ¼ cup, about 12 minutes.

>> Hold the sauce warm until you're ready to serve.

>> Combine the peppercorns, sugar, and salt on a small plate or shallow dish. Set aside.

>> In another mixing bowl, whip the egg white to a stable froth, but not quite to stiff peaks.

>> Pat the swordfish steaks dry with paper towels. Now, brush on all sides with the egg white. *Set the steaks on a wire rack (or a plate) for a few moments to allow the egg white to get slightly tacky.*

>> Heat a grill or grill pan to medium-high heat.

>> *Spray a clean grill rag with cooking spray and evenly wipe the grill grates until clean and evenly glistening.*

>> Press the fish into the peppercorn mixture on one side of each fillet.

>> Place the steaks peppercorn-side down onto the grill. Cook for 5 minutes without moving.

>> Using a fish spatula, turn the fish and finish cooking through, about 3 minutes. Transfer to a plate to rest.

>> Using a spoon, swirl the softened butter into the sauce.

>> Serve, spooning the sauce over the fish fillets.

SERVES 4 (SERVING SIZE: 1 FILLET AND ABOUT 1 TABLESPOON SAUCE)
CALORIES 324; **FAT** 15.1G (SAT 4.6G, MONO 5.9G, POLY 2.1G); **PROTEIN** 35G; **CARB** 6G; **FIBER** 1G; **CHOL** 120MG; **IRON** 1MG; **SODIUM** 543MG; **CALC** 32MG

MUCH OF THE FISH IN SUSHI & SASHIMI
YOU'VE EATEN IN THE U.S. HAS BEEN
FROZEN, AND EVEN THE BEST SUSHI
CHEFS EMPLOY FREEZING IN
KEEPING THINGS, ER , FRESH.

MISO-GRILLED TUNA
AND WATERMELON SALAD WITH WASABI SHALLOTS

HANDS ON: 30 MIN. **TOTAL:** 30 MIN.

Let's talk fish. It can be frozen. Rather than focus on so-called freshness, it's more important to understand how the fish was handled. Was it caught, handled gingerly, and buried straight as an arrow in crushed ice? Then you might want to buy that fish fresh. If it was caught, filleted, and blast-frozen on the ship, then you might want to buy that fish frozen. This recipe gets all restaurant-y, with a playful combination of barely cooked tuna and fresh watermelon. Add more wasabi if you like.

Food	How Much	Why
cooking spray		
white miso paste	1 tablespoon	Funky and salty, it's the foil to the watermelon. It chars up nicely, too.
water	2 tablespoons, divided	To thin the miso and to make a loose wasabi paste.
grapeseed oil	2 teaspoons	It's neutral. Miso should predominate in this dish.
fresh tuna	4 (4-ounce) steaks (about 1 inch thick)	Actually, it might be better to say "raw" tuna here.
shallots	1 cup shaved	They wilt fast against the wasabi treatment.
sugar	1 teaspoon	To temper the wasabi.
wasabi paste	2 teaspoons	For the shallots.
lime juice	2 tablespoons	This is your acid.
soy sauce	1 tablespoon	Some fermented saltiness pushes back against the sweetness of the melon.
freshly ground black pepper	2 teaspoons	You're seeing a pattern of the use of pepper with sweet things. You'll likely grind pepper on your watermelon from now on.
watermelon	2 cups cut into 1-inch cubes	Its sweetness is a complement to tuna.
fresh chives	2 tablespoons minced	To finish. To push it to great.

Follow These Steps:

>> Fire up your grill to high. Away from the heat, coat the grill grate evenly with cooking spray.

>> In a small bowl, combine the miso, 1 tablespoon of water, and the grapeseed oil.

>> Rub the tuna steaks evenly with the miso paste mixture.

>> Refrigerate, uncovered, for 15 minutes.

>> Combine 1 tablespoon of water, the shallots, the sugar, and the wasabi. Toss well and let marinate at room temperature, folding occasionally as the juices release from the shallots.

>> Combine the lime juice, the soy sauce, and the black pepper in a large bowl.

>> Add the watermelon to the lime-soy mixture and toss. Let rest at room temperature until ready to serve.

>> Grill the steaks, until only marked, about 45 seconds. *The tuna for this dish is best served ultra-rare.*

>> On a cutting board, with your sharpest knife, cut the tuna into ¾-inch-thick pieces against the grain.

>> Gently fold the tuna into the watermelon salad.

>> To serve, lay a bed of the tuna and watermelon salad on each of 4 plates. Scatter the wasabi shallots on top, and sprinkle evenly with the chives.

SERVES 4 (SERVING SIZE: 1 CUP TUNA SALAD AND 3 TABLESPOONS SHALLOT MIXTURE)
CALORIES 265; **FAT** 8.9G (SAT 1.7G, MONO 2.3G, POLY 3.4G); **PROTEIN** 29G; **CARB** 17G; **FIBER** 1G; **CHOL** 43MG; **IRON** 2MG; **SODIUM** 539MG; **CALC** 40MG

FIRE-ROASTED MUSHROOMS
WITH RICOTTA SALATA

HANDS-ON: 15 MIN. **TOTAL:** 45 MIN.

*Mushrooms are particularly well suited to grilling—see page 349 for a guide to the myriad
types and their flavors. Most are at least 80% water by weight, allowing for aggressive
heat treatment. Gun for a mix of cultivated and foraged, if possible, for both visual and
flavor complexity. Take a look at the surface area of the mushrooms, and make your best
guess at tearing and cutting the various mushrooms into pieces that will allow for uniform
cooking time. Don't be afraid to use plenty of white mushrooms. They are perfectly lovely,
and do not warrant the "plain" reputation they often carry. Mushrooms are glorious carriers
of all things bulby and herby, but they need to be mindfully seasoned—using ingredients
both sweet and salty—or they run the risk of being one-dimensional. And, hey, wash your
mushrooms before you use them. They absorb an insignificant amount of water.*

THE FAIRLY COMMON
BELIEF THAT MUSHROOMS
SHOULDN'T BE WASHED
DOESN'T HOLD WATER.
WELL, JUST A FEW
MEANINGLESS DROPS.

Food	How Much	Why
mushrooms (a combination of chanterelle, portobello, cremini, and/or white mushrooms)	2 pounds	Buy an assortment of whatever you can find fresh.
olive oil	3 tablespoons	To highlight the flavors of the mushrooms. Butter works, too, but "buttery" instead of "mushroomy" would come to mind first.
fresh thyme	1 tablespoon minced	Woodsy. Its pine-like flavors are welcome here, particularly against fire.
sugar	1½ teaspoons	Mushrooms benefit from balanced seasoning. Repeat after me: Sugar is a seasoning, too.
kosher salt	½ teaspoon	Friends with sugar. And mushrooms.
garlic cloves	3, grated	Grated to activate maximum enzymatic pleasure. Plus, you won't get burned bits.
shallot	1, grated	Same as above. Slightly different flavor compounds.
lemon zest	1 lemon	Cool trick: perfume of lemon...
red wine vinegar	1½ tablespoons	...combined with earthier acidity.
ricotta salata	1 ounce (about ¼ cup), shaved	This cheese has a rounding effect on the dish. It will feel exponentially richer, even with a few shavings.

CONTINUED →

FIRE-ROASTED MUSHROOMS

2 lb. assorted mushrooms

3 Tbsp. olive oil

1 Tbsp. minced fresh thyme

1½ tsp. sugar

½ tsp. kosher salt

3 garlic cloves, grated

1 shallot, grated

zest from 1 lemon

1½ Tbsp. red wine vinegar

1 oz. ricotta salata, shaved

Follow These Steps:

» Fire up a grill to medium-high. We'll use direct heat for this dish.

PREP THE MUSHROOMS

» Wash and dry the mushrooms.

ALMOST EVERY U.S. STATE HAS A MUSHROOM CLUB WHERE YOU CAN LEARN ABOUT EVERYTHING FROM FORAGING TO COOKING TO CULTIVATION.

» *Cut the mushrooms into uniform, just-beyond-bite-sized pieces. They'll shrink when you cook them.*

» In a bowl, combine the olive oil, the thyme, the sugar, the salt, the garlic, and the shallot.

MARINATE!

» Add the mushrooms and toss to coat. Allow the mushrooms to soak up the marinade for 5 minutes.

» Place a grill basket for vegetables on the grill, and preheat it for 10 minutes before adding the mushrooms.

AND THEN GRILL

» Put the mushrooms in the grill basket and grill them, stirring every 3 minutes or so, for about 20 minutes total or until they're tender and cooked throughout. Add the lemon zest at the last moment. Stir.

» Transfer the mushrooms to a platter and sprinkle with the red wine vinegar. Top with the shaved ricotta salata.

SERVES 8 (SERVING SIZE: ½ CUP)
CALORIES 87; **FAT** 6.2G (SAT 1.3G, MONO 3.8G, POLY 0.7G); **PROTEIN** 3G; **CARB** 6G; **FIBER** 1G; **CHOL** 3MG; **IRON** 1MG; **SODIUM** 190MG; **CALC** 18MG

GRILLED RADICCHIO
WITH TOMATO AND RICOTTA

HANDS-ON: 40 MIN. **TOTAL:** 40 MIN.

This is one hearty salad. It's also a symphony of flavors and textures, where mellow, crunchy romaine meets beautifully bitter radicchio. Garlic flavors are layered in—both raw and grilled—as are acids: buttermilk, lemon, vinegar. A simple tomato-basil experience is tucked right in there, too. Serve with the simplest of grilled meats or chicken.

Food	How Much	Why
romaine hearts	2, split, core intact	Romaine hearts stand up to a quick visit to the grill and soften the intensity of the radicchio.
radicchio	1 head, quartered	Well suited to grilling, as char is a lovely contrast to bitter. Think beer and steak.
red onion	1, sliced ¼ inch thick	Thick-sliced for this hearty dish.
fresh lemon juice	5 tablespoons, divided	You have a pre- and post-treatment of lemon.
kosher salt	½ teaspoon, divided	Bitter benefits from salt.
extra-virgin olive oil	3 tablespoons, divided	Choose a "fruity" olive oil, as you'll get plenty of vegetal, peppery flavors from the other ingredients.
garlic cloves	4, 2 halved and 2 minced	Some to scent the grilled bread, which will bring out the deep flavors of the garlic. The other "layer" is in the dressing, where the garlic is raw and pungent.
crusty artisan bread, your preference	4 (½-inch-thick) slices, cut in half	Makes this a meal.
Buttermilk Ricotta (page 114), or part-skim ricotta cheese	1 cup	Contrasting rich and round cheese against the bitter radicchio, and the sharp and acidic lemon and vinegar makes for a very complete culinary experience.
fresh basil leaves	12, fine chiffonade	To perfume the ricotta mixture.
freshly ground black pepper	½ teaspoon	Works with bitter things.
red wine vinegar	2 tablespoons	The habit of blending acids continues.
beefsteak tomatoes	2, cut into wedges	A hearty salad needs a hearty tomato.

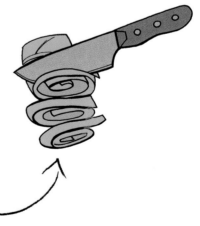

CONTINUED

GRILLED RADICCHIO WITH TOMATO AND RICOTTA

2 romaine hearts, split, core intact

1 head radicchio, quartered

1 red onion, sliced ¼ inch thick

5 Tbsp. lemon juice, divided

½ tsp. kosher salt, divided

3 Tbsp. extra-virgin olive oil, divided

4 garlic cloves, 2 halved and 2 minced

4 (½-inch-thick) slices crusty artisan bread, cut in half

1 cup Buttermilk Ricotta

12 fresh basil leaves, fine chiffonade

½ tsp. freshly ground black pepper

2 Tbsp. red wine vinegar

2 beefsteak tomatoes, cut into wedges

Follow These Steps:

>> Fire up your grill. Medium-high flame/heat.

>> Ready a large bowl.

PREP THE VEGETABLES, DRESSING, AND SIDES

>> Combine the romaine hearts, the raddichio, and the onion in the large bowl.

>> Add 2½ tablespoons lemon juice, ⅜ teaspoon salt, and 2 tablespoons of the olive oil.

>> Toss to coat the vegetables. Let sit for 10 minutes before grilling.

>> Take the 2 halved garlic cloves and rub by hand into the slices of bread.

>> Combine ⅛ teaspoon salt, the ricotta, the basil, and the pepper in a small bowl. Refrigerate.

>> Combine 2½ tablespoons of lemon juice, 1 tablespoon of olive oil, the red wine vinegar, and the 2 minced garlic cloves in a small bowl. Stir with a teaspoon. Keep this vinaigrette loose and easy.

GRILL!

>> Grill the onions first for 5 minutes or until nicely marked and wilted.

>> *Follow up with the romaine and the radicchio, finding the hottest spots on your grill. Grill until well marked, about 2 minutes, not a moment more.* Remove to a plate.

>> Grill the bread, cooking 2 minutes on each side to slightly char. Remove to the plate.

ONION: TAKES LONGER.

LEAFY GREENS: JUST A COUPLE OF MINUTES.

BREAD: JUST UNTIL SLIGHTLY CHARRED.

USE YOUR BEST PLATING SKILLS

» Create an arrangement of the radicchio, the romaine, and the tomatoes on a large platter.

» Scatter the grilled onions on top.

» Spoon the vinaigrette over the salad and sprinkle with the remaining salt and the pepper.

» *Spoon the ricotta mixture onto the grilled bread, being conscious to leave some grilled bits showing.*

» Serve the bread and salad with forks and steak knives.

SERVES 8 (SERVING SIZE: ½ BREAD SLICE AND ⅛ OF SALAD MIXTURE)
CALORIES 203; FAT 14G (SAT 6G, MONO 5.3G, POLY 1.2G); PROTEIN 10G; CARB 10G; FIBER 2G;
CHOL 35MG; IRON 1MG; SODIUM 205MG; CALC 263MG

STEP BY STEP: Getting to the Perfect Level of Char

1) Not charred enough.

2) Charred for those with a preference for all things delicate.

3) Perfectly charred.

GRILLED SWEET CORN, CRAB, AND ASPARAGUS SALAD

HANDS-ON: 30 MIN. **TOTAL:** 40 MIN.

Asparagus and sweet corn are perfect complements. Asparagus has some onion-like qualities and offers gently bitter notes. Corn is straight-ahead sweet. Here, they are rendered luxurious with a generous amount of sweet lump crabmeat and a cream-based vinaigrette. It may sound counterintuitive, but cream actually lightens up a vinaigrette, as it's somewhere between 36% and 40% fat, whereas oils are 100% fat. Tender herbs, such as tarragon, shine in cream, too.

Food	How Much	Why
corn	4 ears	It's corn season. No? Turn the page.
asparagus	1 pound, trimmed and peeled	For a gently bitter contrast to corn.
sweet onion	½ cup diced	You're not cooking the onion, so let's keep it subtle with this small amount.
jalapeño pepper	¼ cup diced	Spicy and sweet works.
fresh chives	1 tablespoon finely chopped	Chives add an onion-y quality while offering grassy notes. Welcome.
heavy cream	3 tablespoons	For your vinaigrette.
fresh tarragon	1 teaspoon chopped	Once you taste corn with tarragon, you'll be a believer.
white wine vinegar	1 teaspoon	To mimic a béarnaise-like flavor profile. Indeed, this would be a great salad on top of a beef tenderloin medallion.
freshly ground black pepper	½ teaspoon	Black pepper shines in cream.
kosher salt	¼ teaspoon	There's a lot of sweet going on. This balances it.
garlic cloves	2, minced	It softens against cream, and provides a singular raw "punch" to the dish.
lump crabmeat	8 ounces	You're worth it.

Follow These Steps:

» Fire up a grill or grill pan over medium-high heat.

» *Grill the corn evenly for 20 minutes, allowing here-and-there charring, but not deep charring.*

» When the corn is evenly grilled and is very hot, transfer to a stainless steel mixing bowl, and cover with foil. Leave in a warm location to carry-over cook for 10 minutes.

» Grill the asparagus evenly, about 3 minutes, or until almost tender, leaving a little crunch.

» *Shave the corn kernels off of the cob, encouraging clusters to stay intact if possible.* Set aside.

» Cut the grilled asparagus into ³⁄₄-inch pieces.

» Combine the onion, jalapeño, chives, cream, tarragon, vinegar, black pepper, salt, and garlic in a large bowl.

» Add the asparagus and corn to the bowl; toss to coat.

» Finally, gently fold in the crabmeat. Serve warm.

SERVES 6 (SERVING SIZE: ³⁄₄ CUP)
CALORIES 131; **FAT** 4G (SAT 1.9G, MONO 1.1G, POLY 0.6G); **PROTEIN** 10G; **CARB** 16G; **FIBER** 3G; **CHOL** 33MG; **IRON** 2MG; **SODIUM** 224MG; **CALC** 46MG

GRILLED BLACK PEPPER BANANAS
ON SUGARED RUM TOAST

HANDS-ON: 25 MIN. **TOTAL:** 25 MIN.

If you're from the U.S., your everyday banana is the Cavendish. Visit any food market with international flair, though, and you'll likely find a broad array, from reds and manzano bananas to plantains to the Hua Moa banana, a unique chubby plantain-like banana that, when ripened fully, can be eaten raw (unlike plantains). The riper the bananas, the quicker they will soften during cooking, so be mindful when handling. Venture away from the familiar with this sweet and spiced quickie dessert, which earned rave reviews during testing.

Food	How Much	Why
butter	2½ tablespoons, divided	Some for the toast. Some for a sauce.
brioche or challah bread	4 (¾-ounce) "blocks," crusts removed	You'll be sugar-dredging this. Then you'll grill. You may never bake again.
granulated sugar	2 tablespoons	This will bind with the butter and create something between a glaze and a candy on the bread.
brown sugar	3 tablespoons	The molasses gives depth and is welcome with charred things.
rum	¼ cup	Bananas. Rum.
freshly ground black pepper	1 teaspoon	Methinks sugar and black pepper are more natural partners than salt and pepper.
kosher salt	⅛ teaspoon	Salt heightens flavors and helps combat cloying sweetness.
bananas	4, peeled and cut in half lengthwise	If you can find them, use minis or the manzanos. Any perfectly ripe banana will work, though.
cooking spray		To keep things moving.

Follow These Steps:

≫ Ready a grill or grill pan on medium-high heat.

≫ *Melt 1½ tablespoons of the butter, and evenly brush on the sides of the bread "blocks."*

≫ Sprinkle the granulated sugar evenly on a small plate. Dredge the bread blocks evenly in the sugar. Set aside on a plate.

≫ Combine 1 tablespoon of the butter, the brown sugar, the rum, the pepper, and the salt in a small saucepan. *Bring to a simmer over medium-high heat. (Be careful; the rum will flame up when it comes to a boil.) When flames subside, stir with a whisk until it is a uniform, syrupy sauce.*

≫ Spray the bananas lightly with cooking spray.

≫ Grill the bananas, depending on level of ripeness, for 2 to 4 minutes on each side or until well marked, brushing evenly with the rum sauce all the while.

≫ Carefully remove the bananas from the grill. Set aside on a platter.

≫ Grill the bread blocks on all sides for about 20 seconds, or just long enough to mark them.

≫ To serve, spoon some of the rum sauce on 4 plates, top each with a piece of grilled brioche, and spoon the bananas over the bread.

SERVES 4 (SERVING SIZE: 1 BANANA, 1 PIECE OF BREAD, AND ¾ TABLESPOON SAUCE)
CALORIES 304; **FAT** 10G (SAT 4.9G, MONO 2.8G, POLY 0.9G); **PROTEIN** 3G; **CARB** 50G; **FIBER** 3G; **CHOL** 38MG; **IRON** 1MG; **SODIUM** 236MG; **CALC** 18MG

IMMIGRANT-EDITION
POLLO A LA BRASA

HANDS-ON: 25 MIN. **TOTAL:** 7 HR. 10 MIN.

This is some deeply seasoned chicken, and apparently it's not authentic or representative of real-deal Pollo a la Brasa from Peru. That's okay. People move. They muddle cuisines, tinkering with their own, influencing others. This is immigrant cuisine, boldly altered and delicious. Chicken quarters, cooked gently on a covered grill, achieve textural perfection—crisp skin and a meltingly tender confit-like interior.

Food	How Much	Why
fresh lime juice	¼ cup (about 3 limes)	Peru knows limes.
red wine vinegar	¼ cup	To provide some contrast to the lime.
aji amarillo paste	3 tablespoons	Find this anywhere Peruvian ingredients are sold. While there is no similar substitute, a habanero pepper sauce would jive with the ingredients in this recipe.
sugar	2 tablespoons	To soften the acids.
dried oregano	2 teaspoons	Oregano is cultivated widely in Peru. It likes chicken.
freshly ground black pepper	2 teaspoons	To layer in some pungency against the piquancy of chile.
ground cumin	½ teaspoon	For depth and smokiness.
garlic cloves	6, grated	Grated, the garlic permeates the entire chicken grilling experience.
bone-in chicken leg-thigh quarters	6	They can handle a couple of hours on the grill.
kosher salt	½ teaspoon	Added at the end for maximum salt presence.

Follow These Steps:

>> Combine the lime juice and the next 7 ingredients (through garlic) in a large bowl. Stir well.

>> *Marinate the chicken in the above mixture. Cover and refrigerate 4 hours to overnight. Longer is better.*

>> Ready a charcoal grill for cooking over low-slow indirect heat, maintaining a temperature of 250°.

>> Sprinkle the chicken with salt.

>> Place the chicken legs on the unheated side of the grill (away from the source of the heat) and cover the grill.

>> Turning every 15 minutes or so, cook for 2 hours 45 minutes, or until the chicken pulls away from the bone with little effort.

SERVES 6 (SERVING SIZE: 1 LEG QUARTER)
CALORIES 210; **FAT** 8.1G (SAT 2.2G, MONO 2.9G, POLY 1.9G); **PROTEIN** 26G; **CARB** 7G; **FIBER** 1G; **CHOL** 89MG; **IRON** 2MG; **SODIUM** 425MG; **CALC** 29MG

TANDOORI-SPICED CHICKEN

HANDS-ON: 15 MIN. **TOTAL:** 5 HR.

Tandoors are ovens—cylindrical and deep—typically with slightly curved walls. They have tradition-ally been used for cooking naan. Tandoori chicken is a brilliantly marinated chicken cooked in said tandoor. It's BBQ chicken, folks, Punjabi-style. The great lesson here is the use of yogurt, both for its acidity and as a near-ideal base for a spice paste. The coagulated proteins in yogurt help the paste adhere to the chicken (and anything else) quite well. I opted to skip the oft-used red food coloring.

Food

Food	How Much	Why
plain 2% reduced-fat Greek yogurt	³/₄ cup	Its acidity. Its ability to "glue" the spices to the chicken.
lemon zest	1 teaspoon grated	Perfume.
fresh lemon juice	2 tablespoons	To boost acidity against the richer dark meat.
fresh gingerroot	1 tablespoon grated	We're going with a lot of dry spices. This freshens.
paprika	1 tablespoon	Brings some color and takes on smokiness brilliantly.
canola oil	1 tablespoon	Fat helps carry the flavor of some of the spices.
ground coriander	2 teaspoons	For its citrus notes.
ground red pepper	2 teaspoons	For its straightforward spiciness.
turmeric	1 teaspoon	Some bitter backbone.
kosher salt	¹/₂ teaspoon	Helps create a mild quickie brine for the chicken.
ground cumin	¹/₂ teaspoon	For depth.
dry mustard	¹/₂ teaspoon	For pungency.
ground cinnamon	¹/₄ teaspoon	For aroma and the illusion that sugar is present.
ground cardamom	¹/₄ teaspoon	For its pine-meets-citrus-meets-cut flowers aroma.
garlic cloves	4, minced	Garlic acts as a harmonizer.
bone-in chicken leg-thigh quarters	4	Dark meat is more tolerant of long marinating times and fire.
cooking spray		To season the grill.

Follow These Steps:

» In a large zip-top bag, combine all the ingredients, except for the chicken and cooking spray.

» Run a boning knife straight down each chicken thigh and drumstick, as if to begin deboning. *These pockets will allow some of the marinade to get into the meat, and will permit more even cooking later on.*

» Add the chicken to the yogurt mixture. Massage and turn the chicken legs to ensure that they're liberally coated with yogurt and spice. *Get some marinade in those thigh and leg bone pockets.*

» Refrigerate for 4 hours to overnight. Longer is better.

» Fire up a grill to medium-high heat. Indirect heat is best for this dish.

» Coat a grill rack with cooking spray and place it over the unheated side of the grill, away from the flames.

» Grill the chicken legs for 20 minutes on each side, with the grill covered, brushing with remaining marinade every 5 to 7 minutes.

» Move the chicken to the heated side of the grill. Grill 2 minutes on each side or until lightly charred.

SERVES 4 (SERVING SIZE: 1 LEG QUARTER)
CALORIES 268; **FAT** 13.5G (SAT 5G, MONO 3.9G, POLY 2.4G); **PROTEIN** 30G; **CARB** 6G; **FIBER** 2G; **CHOL** 112MG; **IRON** 2MG; **SODIUM** 423MG; **CALC** 71MG

GREEK-STYLE
SLOW-GRILLED LEG OF LAMB

HANDS-ON: 50 MIN. **TOTAL:** 7 HR. 30 MIN.

Greeks prefer their lamb cooked through—as in well done. It's not a dry, unpleasant well done, mind you, but from a long, low and slow dry heat that results in a significant (often deeply seasoned and lemony) exterior crust, and an almost fork-tender interior. Things will shrink, but flavors will also concentrate. Turn the lamb fairly frequently. Meat juices will stay in motion, and you'll get an evenly moist interior.

SEE PAGE 303 FOR MORE
INFORMATION ABOUT ACIDS.

Food	How Much	Why
boneless leg of lamb	3 pounds, netted	They're readily available, already netted.
garlic cloves	4, sliced	You'll get pleasantly charred bits, and tender steamed pieces. Yum.
yellow onion	¾ cup grated	Onion, too. See above.
cucumber juice	1 cup (from 1 cucumber grated and squeezed or processed in a juicer)	The flavors that we associate with cucumbers occur when they are cut or bruised. There's a lot of enzymatic action taking place. Juicing or grating maximizes that.
flat-leaf parsley	½ cup coarsely chopped	You see parsley paired with lemon often. It's complementary—and parsley contains limonene, a flavor compound evocative of citrus zest.
lemon juice	¼ cup	It's Greek. Lemon...
olive oil	1 tablespoon	...and olive oil.
fresh oregano	1 tablespoon minced	Fresh oregano and grilled meats. Yes, please. Fresh holds up better against fire.
fresh thyme	2 teaspoons minced	Oregano alone would be too harsh.
kosher salt	1⅛ teaspoons, divided	Some to rub the lamb, some to season the sauce.
red onions	2, sliced ½ inch thick	They insulate the lamb during the second stage of cooking. Plus, you can eat them.
plain Greek yogurt	1 cup	The base for the sauce.
red wine vinegar	2 tablespoons	Harmonizing acids makes for a more interesting sauce experience. Here, we're using lactic, acetic, and citric.
black pepper	a few grindings	To season the sauce.
large heirloom tomatoes	6, each cut into 8 slices	Because ripe tomatoes, slow-cooked lamb, and charred onions make life worth living.

CONTINUED

GREEK-STYLE SLOW-GRILLED LEG OF LAMB

3 lb. boneless leg of lamb, netted

4 garlic cloves, sliced

³/₄ cup grated yellow onion

1 cup cucumber juice

¹/₂ cup coarsely chopped flat-leaf parsley

¹/₄ cup lemon juice

1 Tbsp. olive oil

1 Tbsp. minced fresh oregano

2 tsp. minced fresh thyme

1¹/₈ tsp. kosher salt, divided

2 red onions, sliced ¹/₂ inch thick

1 cup plain Greek yogurt

2 Tbsp. red wine vinegar

a few grindings of black pepper

6 large heirloom tomatoes, each cut into 8 slices

Follow These Steps:

>> Place the lamb leg in a large baking dish. *Pierce the lamb in about as many equally spaced slits as you have slices of garlic. (No need to count them. You're cooking.) Slide the garlic into the pockets.*

PREP THE MARINADE

>> Combine the grated onion, cucumber juice, parsley, lemon juice, oil, oregano, and thyme in a medium bowl.

>> Pour the onion mixture over the lamb leg and marinate in the refrigerator for at least 4 hours, preferably longer—as long as 24 hours.

GET READY TO GRILL...

>> If you have a rotisserie-type contraption for your grill, fantastic. If not, don't sweat it. Ready your grill for low-slow cooking over indirect heat. *Charcoal is ideal. Gas, in this instance, is perfectly acceptable.*

...AND GRILL

>> Remove the lamb from the marinade and discard the marinade. Rub with 1 teaspoon of the salt. Place the lamb leg on the grill over indirect, medium-low heat. Cover and cook 1¹/₂ hours, turning every 15 minutes or so.

>> Fan the onion slices on the unheated side of the grill over indirect heat. Place the lamb on top of the onions, allowing them to slowly cook—all the while being basted by the lamb.

>> Cook the lamb, covered, another hour, turning every 15 minutes. *Remember, spit-style Greek lamb is typically cooked well done and beyond, until the leg is nearly fork-tender.*

>> Remove the lamb and the onions from the grill, allowing the lamb to rest for 10 minutes before carving.

>> Remove the netting and carve the lamb into thin slices, reserving at least ¹/₄ cup of the juices for stirring into the yogurt sauce.

MAKE THE SAUCE AND SERVE

>> To prepare the sauce, combine the Greek yogurt, the red wine vinegar, ¹/₈ teaspoon salt, the pepper, and the reserved lamb juices in a small bowl.

>> Fan the tomatoes on a large serving platter followed by the onions, followed by the sliced lamb, followed by the yogurt sauce.

SERVES 12 (SERVING SIZE: ABOUT 3 OUNCES LAMB, 4 SLICES TOMATO, 1 SLICE ONION, AND ABOUT 1¹/₂ TABLESPOONS SAUCE)
CALORIES 222; FAT 8.6G (SAT 3.5G, MONO 2.9G, POLY 0.7G); PROTEIN 26G; CARB 10G; FIBER 3G; CHOL 76MG; IRON 3MG; SODIUM 296MG; CALC 54MG

COCHINITA PIBIL
WITH HABANERO, ORANGE, AND ONION

HANDS-ON: 35 MIN. **TOTAL:** 2 HR. 15 MIN.

You could, if you wanted to, dig a large pit in a yard, build a bed of coals, and bury some banana leaf-wrapped pork in the ground. But this recipe is quicker. Indirect heat helps to gently cook the pork tenderloin, a cut that's easy to overcook. Smoke from the coals seeps in while the foil packet traps the spices, chiles, and juices in this (steamed/smoked) interpretation of the Yucatán classic.

Food	How Much	Why
ground white pepper	2 teaspoons	It provides pungency and a pleasant fermented funkiness.
dried Mexican oregano	2 teaspoons	This is what's used. Following suit.
ground cumin	1 teaspoon	It's a component of the classic dish, but notice its restrained use.
fresh orange juice	1 cup, divided	A native sour orange juice is used in the Yucatán. Go with what's available to you.
fresh lime juice	2 tablespoons	...and spike with the juice of a Key/Mexican lime to sour things up.
white vinegar	2 tablespoons, divided	Some for the marinade. Some to pickle the onions. We're looking for straightforward acidity.
achiote paste	1 tablespoon	It's not just for color; its subtle flavor offers both floral and earthy notes. You'll likely find seasoned paste. That's okay.
garlic	1 tablespoon minced	For the marinade.
pork tenderloin	1 (1-pound), trimmed	It's lean and has a structure that allows for great-looking pulled pork.
red onion	2 cups thinly sliced	Pickled onion is a common accompaniment in the Yucatán.
habanero pepper	1 teaspoon minced	This is the chile of choice. The perfume is almost sweet, and the habanero has none of the vegetal qualities of other chiles.
sugar	1 teaspoon	To soften and harmonize.
kosher salt	½ teaspoon, divided	Meat. Salt.
fresh cilantro	½ bunch, trimmed and washed	It warrants classification as a salad green. It's an herb that should be enjoyed stem and all. Here's your chance.

THIS. IS. HOT. FRUIT.

CONTINUED

COCHINITA PIBIL WITH HABANERO, ORANGE, AND ONION

2 tsp. ground white pepper

2 tsp. dried Mexican oregano

1 tsp. ground cumin

1 cup fresh orange juice, divided

2 Tbsp. fresh lime juice

2 Tbsp. white vinegar, divided

1 Tbsp. achiote paste

1 Tbsp. minced garlic

1 (1-lb.) pork tenderloin, trimmed

2 cups thinly sliced red onion

1 tsp. minced habanero pepper

1 tsp. sugar

½ tsp. kosher salt, divided

½ bunch fresh cilantro, trimmed and washed

Follow These Steps:

>> Set up a charcoal grill to cook indirectly (see page 325). Build up a good medium-high heat coal bed on one side, and leave the other side with little to no coal bed. Try to maintain a temperature of about 300° to 325°.

MAKE A MARINADE. PICKLE SOME ONIONS

>> Combine the white pepper, the oregano, the cumin, ½ cup orange juice, the lime juice, 1 tablespoon vinegar, the achiote, and the garlic in a large zip-top plastic bag. *Blend well by squeezing the outside of the bag.*

>> Add the pork to the marinade. Seal the bag and refrigerate for an hour or so.

>> In a medium bowl, combine the red onion, the habanero, the sugar, ½ cup orange juice, and 1 tablespoon vinegar. Season with ⅛ teaspoon salt and toss to combine.

>> Leave the onions at room temperature, covered, to quick-pickle.

WRAP AND COOK THE TENDERLOIN

>> Remove the pork from the marinade, and discard the marinade.

>> Sprinkle the pork with ⅜ teaspoon salt. *Wrap the pork in a foil packet (or banana leaves if you're feeling adventurous) and seal well, with the seam on top.*

>> Poke 3 (1-inch) slits in the packet near the seam. Make them large enough for steam to sneak out and for smoke to invade.

>> Cook, covered, for 25 minutes, on the unheated side of the grill.

REST. PULL. AND SERVE

>> Remove the packet from the grill and allow to rest, about 10 minutes, before slicing or pulling. *It's your call to slice or pull. I pull.*

>> Place the pork and juices on a serving platter and drape with the quick-pickled onions.

>> Serve with hot sauce and cilantro. Tortillas optional.

SERVES 4 (SERVING SIZE: 3 OUNCES PORK AND ½ CUP ONION MIXTURE)
CALORIES 305; FAT 4.2G (SAT 1.1G, MONO 1.3G, POLY 1.1G); PROTEIN 28G; CARB 39G; FIBER 6G;
CHOL 74MG; IRON 2MG; SODIUM 397MG; CALC 95MG

STEP BY STEP: Wrapping the Pork

1) Lay the pork on the leaf and wrap to cover, as shown.

2) Wrap tightly over the top of the tenderloin. Leave relatively little air space.

3) Roll it up. You can tie it with twine, if desired. Otherwise, simply cook seam side down.

YOU CAN ALSO DO THIS SAME TECHNIQUE USING FOIL.

MAD DELICIOUS RESOURCES

The ingredients included on these pages are those that add unrivaled flavor to the recipes in which they're used. Seek them out. It's worth it.

Marash pepper
(for Adana-Inspired Turkey-Lamb Kebabs, page 327)
Kalustyan's, Formaggio Kitchen, Vanns Spices, Middle Eastern markets

citric acid powder
(for Buttermilk Ricotta, page 114)
available in supermarkets near the canning or cheesemaking supplies

Korean red pepper powder
(for Congee, page 133)
koaMart, Asian markets

Calabrian chiles
(for Toasted Penne with Chicken Sausage, page 208)
Alma Gourmet

Espelette pepper powder
(also known as piment d'Espelette, used in several recipes)
World Spice Merchants, Sur La Table

powdered peanut butter
(for Georgia Peanut–Fried Chicken, page 224)
large supermarkets, Target, Walmart, and health-food stores

ground sumac
*(for Crunchy Chickpeas, page 263,
and Adana-Inspired
Turkey-Lamb Kebabs, page 327)*
**Penzeys, Dean & Deluca,
Vanns Spices, Kalustyan's,
Williams-Sonoma,
Middle Eastern markets**

sorghum
(for Sorghum-Roasted Salmon, page 310)
MuddyPondSorghum.com

Thai water spinach
*(for Thai-Style Water
Spinach, page 200)*
Asian markets

Turkish red pepper paste
*(also known as biber salçasi,
for Adana-Inspired Turkey-
Lamb Kebabs, page 327)*
**Istanbul Food Bazaar,
Middle Eastern markets**

bottarga
*(for Whole-Wheat Spaghetti
alla Bottarga, page 129)*
Gustiamo.com, Alma Gourmet

MAD DELICIOUS BLOOPERS!

Even the pros make mistakes, and we made some good ones while testing recipes for this book. We hope what you've learned from Cooking Light Mad Delicious encourages you to experiment and create your own recipes. When you do, take this lesson from our mishaps: Sometimes you don't get the results you hoped for. Troubleshoot and try again. Be fearless. You can make it work.

1 The first batch of Sweet Garlic Slaw (page 44) tasted like... nothing. Endless tinkering of acids and seasonings helped us get it where it needed to be.

2 Don't use fruits and vegetables out of season (or when geography makes it impossible to get good quality). The results will be horrible, no matter the technical precision. We learned this when we tried to use out-of-season peaches (blech) and not-from-anywhere-near-here apricots.

THERE'S SNOW SUCH THING AS A WINTER PEACH.

3 What was supposed to be one of the simplest recipes in here, the Red Curry Boiled Peanuts (page 125), was a pain to get right. Getting enough curry in there required help and a batch at home, made by *Cooking Light* test kitchen staffer Robin Bashinsky. That's dedication.

4 The Chickpea Gnocchi (page 214) was leaden, until the a-ha! idea of adding self-rising flour to the gnocchi surfaced—extending the possible variations of gnocchi forevermore.

5

Making light of the Red Sauce Joint Peppers and Eggs Hero (page 181) was no easy task, as the question "Can we add sausage?" rescued what would have been a hospital-esque result.

MISSING SAUSAGE

6

Until *Cooking Light* test kitchen staffer Adam Hickman recommended pre-toasting crumbs for the Fish Sticks! (page 286), they were the blandest food I had ever created. Actually, the first result was embarrassing.

7

It was pretty easy to tell when a recipe fell flat at the tasting table. *Cooking Light* Executive Food Editor Ann Taylor Pittman's subtle "faces of flavor" told me what was missing without saying a word. Fascinating. Effective. Efficient.

FISH STICKS

ICE COLD!

THESE WERE *ACTUALLY* BETTER

8

The first round of Artichoke and Melted Fennel Lasagna (page 317), while sounding sexy, was as appealing as noodle kugel left on a counter for a week. Moisture is a good thing. There was none.

NUTRITIONAL INFORMATION

How to Use It and Why

Glance at the end of any *Cooking Light* recipe, and you'll see how committed we are to helping you make the best of today's light cooking. With chefs, registered dietitians, home economists, and a computer system that analyzes every ingredient we use, *Cooking Light* gives you authoritative dietary detail like no other magazine. We go to such lengths so you can see how our recipes fit into your healthful eating plan. If you're trying to lose weight, the calorie and fat figures will probably help most. But if you're keeping a close eye on the sodium, cholesterol, and saturated fat in your diet, we provide those numbers, too. And because many women don't get enough iron or calcium, we can help there, as well. Finally, there's a fiber analysis for those of us who don't get enough roughage.

Here's a helpful guide to put our nutritional analysis numbers into perspective. Remember, one size doesn't fit all, so take your lifestyle, age, and circumstances into consideration when determining your nutrition needs. For example, pregnant or breast-feeding women need more protein, calories, and calcium. And women older than 50 need 1,200mg of calcium daily, 200mg more than the amount recommended for younger women.

In Our Nutritional Analysis, We Use These Abbreviations

sat	saturated fat	CARB	carbohydrates	g	gram
mono	monounsaturated fat	CHOL	cholesterol	mg	milligram
poly	polyunsaturated fat	CALC	calcium		

DAILY NUTRITION GUIDE

	Women ages 25 to 50	Women over 50	Men ages 24 to 50	Men over 50
CALORIES	2,000	2,000 or less	2,700	2,500
PROTEIN	50g	50g or less	63g	60g
FAT	65g or less	65g or less	88g or less	83g or less
SATURATED FAT	20g or less	20g or less	27g or less	25g or less
CARBOHYDRATES	304g	304g	410g	375g
FIBER	25g to 35g	25g to 35g	25g to 35g	25g to 35g
CHOLESTEROL	300mg or less	300mg or less	300mg or less	300mg or less
IRON	18mg	8mg	8mg	8mg
SODIUM	2,300mg or less	1,500mg or less	2,300mg or less	1,500mg or less
CALCIUM	1,000mg	1,200mg	1,000mg	1,000mg

The nutritional values used in our calculations either come from
The Food Processor, Version 10.4 (ESHA Research),
or are provided by food manufacturers.

METRIC EQUIVALENTS

The information in the following charts is provided to help cooks outside the United States successfully use the recipes in this book. All equivalents are approximate.

Cooking/Oven Temperatures

	Fahrenheit	Celsius	Gas Mark
Freeze Water	32° F	0° C	
Room Temp.	68° F	20° C	
Boil Water	212° F	100° C	
Bake	325° F	160° C	3
	350° F	180° C	4
	375° F	190° C	5
	400° F	200° C	6
	425° F	220° C	7
	450° F	230° C	8
Broil			Grill

Liquid Ingredients by Volume

¼ tsp	=			1 ml	
½ tsp	=			2 ml	
1 tsp	=			5 ml	
3 tsp	= 1 Tbsp	= ½ fl oz	=	15 ml	
2 Tbsp	= ⅛ cup	= 1 fl oz	=	30 ml	
4 Tbsp	= ¼ cup	= 2 fl oz	=	60 ml	
5⅓ Tbsp	= ⅓ cup	= 3 fl oz	=	80 ml	
8 Tbsp	= ½ cup	= 4 fl oz	=	120 ml	
10⅔ Tbsp	= ⅔ cup	= 5 fl oz	=	160 ml	
12 Tbsp	= ¾ cup	= 6 fl oz	=	180 ml	
16 Tbsp	= 1 cup	= 8 fl oz	=	240 ml	
1 pt	= 2 cups	= 16 fl oz	=	480 ml	
1 qt	= 4 cups	= 32 fl oz	=	960 ml	
		33 fl oz	=	1000 ml	= 1 l

Dry Ingredients by Weight

(To convert ounces to grams, multiply the number of ounces by 30.)

1 oz	=	¹⁄₁₆ lb	=	30 g
4 oz	=	¼ lb	=	120 g
8 oz	=	½ lb	=	240 g
12 oz	=	¾ lb	=	360 g
16 oz	=	1 lb	=	480 g

Length

(To convert inches to centimeters, multiply the number of inches by 2.5.)

1 in	=			2.5 cm	
6 in	=	½ ft	=	15 cm	
12 in	=	1 ft	=	30 cm	
36 in	=	3 ft	= 1 yd	90 cm	
40 in	=			100 cm	= 1 m

Equivalents for Different Types of Ingredients

Standard Cup	Fine Powder (ex. flour)	Grain (ex. rice)	Granular (ex. sugar)	Liquid Solids (ex. butter)	Liquid (ex. milk)
1	140 g	150 g	190 g	200 g	240 ml
¾	105 g	113 g	143 g	150 g	180 ml
⅔	93 g	100 g	125 g	133 g	160 ml
½	70 g	75 g	95 g	100 g	120 ml
⅓	47 g	50 g	63 g	67 g	80 ml
¼	35 g	38 g	48 g	50 g	60 ml
⅛	18 g	19 g	24 g	25 g	30 ml

INDEX

ACKNOWLEDGMENTS

This all started at a food blogger conference. The funny thing though—I wasn't a blogger, or a writer. So I thought. You see, I own an ice cream company, and was drumming up support for our emerging brand, and I thought getting to know bloggers would be a good thing. They're authentic, enthusiastic, and passionate people. They write about food. "Maybe they'll write about my ice cream if they think it's any good," I thought. The experience ended up being a transformative life moment. So, first thanks go to my former sales director, Stacy Tunick, for having the chutzpah (at Food Blog South, by the way) to tell a food editor from Oxmoor House that "Keith is a great writer." I didn't hear Stacy say it. A few phone calls, concept iterations, and proposals later, I found myself in the midst of a book deal.

Honestly, I had little idea what that meant, as I was a busy start-up entrepreneur with less than zero extra time, and figured I'd get the gist of this writing thing in time. Food Editor Shaun Chavis nurtured me right into the publishing arena, starting, you know, with people from that little magazine called *Cooking Light*. That she championed me, a rookie writer, in securing this incredible project, is something that I'll be thankful for 'til death. Shaun allowed a latent dream of mine to become reality.

During my few trips to their beautiful campus in Birmingham, Alabama, I fell in love with everyone I met and had the pleasure of working with, particularly the absolutely brilliant and tireless *Cooking Light* test kitchen team. This is really their book. The comedic erudition of Tiffany Vickers Davis and Robin Bashinsky will be forever imprinted in my psyche. Deb Wise and Adam Hickman are among the most zen and engaged cooks I've ever met. Thank you for making me fall in love with cooking again. I learned a ton just observing and listening to Sidney Fry, nutrition editor, and Timothy Cebula, senior food editor. You're both elegant human beings. To Scott Mowbray and Ann Taylor Pittman, thank you for adopting me, the book concept, and for allowing me to rub grilled oily tarragon on corn in Ann's backyard. Building that fire in the rain was just what my soul needed.

I was carried to the finish line via the painstaking work of editor Rachel West and designers Claire Cormany and Maribeth Jones (I am in love with the typography and layout). The brilliant illustrator Heather Diane Hardison listened patiently to a clunky pile of ideas and gave them life.

To my incredible wife, Nicki Schroeder, for adorning a patient smile while listening to me read sections aloud ad infinitum, I love you. My children, Madison and Jackson, were not harmed in the making of this book. To the High Road Craft Ice Cream team, you're as smart, sexy, and serious as ever. I'm proud to be on this journey with you.

ABOUT THE AUTHOR

After nearly 20 years in professional kitchens, Keith Schroeder took his culinary prowess into the laboratory. In October 2010, Keith launched High Road Craft Ice Cream and Sorbet, where he crafts exquisite ice cream, gelato, and sorbet for luxury retailers and fine restaurants throughout the nation.

A graduate of the Art Institute of Atlanta, Keith always felt drawn toward the culinary arts and eventually ended up in the food industry. After gaining experience as a culinary instructor (at the New England Culinary Institute in Burlington, Vermont), caterer, and executive chef (at the Westin Atlanta, among others), he attended Coles College of Business at Kennesaw State University to get his executive MBA. While at Coles, Schroeder and partner Hunter Thornton won the 2010 International New Ventures Competition at the University of Nebraska, earning sufficient seed capital to open High Road Craft Ice Cream.

Keith lives in the woods, just north of Atlanta with his wife, and High Road's Chief Marketing Officer, Nicki (which makes for a good time), and has two wonderful children, Madison and Jackson.

ABOUT THE ILLUSTRATOR

Heather Hardison is an illustrator and sign painter living and working in Oakland, California. She is originally from North Carolina and studied at North Carolina State University. Her work can be found at www.heather-hardison.com.

©2014 by Time Home Entertainment Inc.
135 West 50th Street, New York, NY 10020

Cooking Light® is a registered trademark of Time Inc. Lifestyle Group. All rights reserved. No part of this book may be reproduced in any form or by any means without the prior written permission of the publisher, excepting brief quotations in connection with reviews written specifically for inclusion in magazines or newspapers, or limited excerpts strictly for personal use.

ISBN-13: 978-0-8487-0428-5
ISBN-10: 0-8487-0428-2

Library of Congress Control Number: 2014938999
Printed in the United States of America
First Printing 2014

Oxmoor House

Editorial Director: Leah McLaughlin
Creative Director: Felicity Keane
Art Director: Christopher Rhoads
Executive Photo Director: Iain Bagwell
Executive Food Director: Grace Parisi
Senior Editor: Betty Wong
Managing Editor: Elizabeth Tyler Austin
Assistant Managing Editor: Jeanne de Lathouder

Cooking Light Mad Delicious

Editor: Rachel Quinlivan West, RD
Project Editor: Emily Chappell Connolly
Designer: Maribeth Jones
Art Editor: April Smitherman
Assistant Test Kitchen Manager: Alyson Moreland Haynes
Recipe Developers and Testers: Tamara Goldis, RD; Stefanie Maloney; Callie Nash; Karen Rankin; Leah Van Deren
Food Stylists: Victoria E. Cox, Margaret Monroe Dickey, Catherine Crowell Steele
Senior Photographer: Hélène Dujardin
Senior Photo Stylists: Kay E. Clarke, Mindi Shapiro Levine
Senior Production Manager: Sue Chodakiewicz
Assistant Production Manager: Diane Rose Keener

Contributors

Author: Keith Schroeder
Illustrator: Heather Diane Hardison
Editor: Shaun Chavis
Brand Manager: Michelle Turner Aycock
Designers: Claire Cormany, Chip Kidd
Copy Editors: Chip Brantley, Dolores Hydock
Proofreaders: Julie Bosche, Jacqueline Giovanelli
Indexer: Mary Ann Laurens
Fellows: Ali Carruba, Kylie Dazzo, Elizabeth Laseter, Amy Pinney, Anna Ramia, Deanna Sakal, Megan Thompson, Tonya West
Recipe Developers and Testers: Wendy Treadwell, RD
Food Stylists: Tami Hardeman, Ana Price Kelly
Photographers: Jim Bathie, Beau Gustafson, Brian Woodcock
Photo Stylists: Mary Clayton Carl, Lydia Degaris-Purcell
Nutrition Analysis: Carolyn Land Williams, PhD, RD

Cooking Light®

Editor: Scott Mowbray
Creative Director: Dimity Jones
Executive Managing Editor: Phillip Rhodes
Executive Editor, Food: Ann Taylor Pittman
Executive Editor, Digital: Allison Long Lowery
Senior Food Editors: Timothy Q. Cebula, Cheryl Slocum
Senior Editor: Cindy Hatcher
Nutrition Editor: Sidney Fry, MS, RD
Associate Editor: Hannah Klinger
Assistant Editor: Kimberly Holland
Assistant Food Editor: Darcy Lenz
Test Kitchen Manager: Tiffany Vickers Davis
Recipe Testers and Developers: Robin Bashinsky, Adam Hickman, Deb Wise
Art Directors: Rachel Cardina Lasserre, Sheri Wilson
Designer: Hagen Stegall
Assistant Designer: Nicole Gerrity
Tablet Designer: Daniel Boone
Photo Editor: Amy Delaune
Senior Photographer: Randy Mayor
Chief Food Stylist: Kellie Gerber Kelley
Assistant Prop Stylists: Lindsey Lower, Claire Spollen
Food Styling Assistant: Blakeslee Wright Giles
Production Director: Liz Rhoades
Production Editor: Hazel R. Eddins
Production Coordinator: Christina Harrison
Copy Director: Susan Roberts McWilliams
Copy Editor: Kate Johnson
Office Manager: Alice Summerville
CookingLight.com Editor: Mallory Daugherty Brasseale
CookingLight.com Assistant Editor/Producer: Michelle Klug
Contributors: David Bonom; Katherine Brooking, RD; Maureen Callahan, RD; Melissa Haskin; Sarah Hudgins; Frances Largeman-Roth, RD; Marge Perry; Allison Fishman Task
Produce Guru: Robert Schueller
Garden Gurus: Mary Beth and David Shaddix

Time Home Entertainment Inc.

President and Publisher: Jim Childs
Vice President and Associate Publisher: Margot Schupf
Vice President, Finance: Vandana Patel
Executive Director, Marketing Services: Carol Pittard
Publishing Director: Megan Pearlman
Assistant General Counsel: Simone Procas